PUBLISH YOUR BOOK

PUBLISH YOUR BOOK

Proven Strategies and Resources for the Enterprising Author

PATRICIA FRY

ALLWORTH PRESS
NEW YORK

Allworth Press books may be purchased in bulk at special discounts for sales promotion, corporate gifts, fund-raising, or educational purposes. Special editions can also be created to specifications. For details, contact the Special Sales Department, Allworth Press, 307 West 36th Street, 11th Floor, New York, NY 10018 or info@skyhorsepublishing.com.

15 14 13 12 11   5 4 3 2 1

Published by Allworth Press, an imprint of Skyhorse Publishing, Inc.
307 West 36th Street, 11th Floor, New York, NY 10018.

Allworth Press® is a registered trademark of Skyhorse Publishing, Inc.®, a Delaware corporation.

www.allworth.com

Cover design by Grillo Group, Chicago

Library of Congress Cataloging-in-Publication Data is available on file.
ISBN: 978-1-58115-884-7

Printed in the United States of America.

Dedicated to
hopeful authors everywhere.

CONTENTS

ABOUT THE AUTHOR

Patricia Fry has been writing for publication since 1973 and earning a living as a freelance writer, author, publisher, and editorial consultant for nearly twenty-five years. Hundreds of her articles have appeared in about 300 different magazines including *Writer's Digest, Authorship, Canadian Author, Freelance Writer's Report, Spannet, SPAWNews, PMA (IBPA) Independent, Writer's Connection, Entrepreneur, Woman's Own, Country Journal, Catholic Digest, The Artist's Magazine, Pages, The World and I, The Toastmaster, Executive Update, Cat Fancy, Los Angeles Times, Kiwanis, Your Health* and many, many others.

She is the author of thirty-five published books and counting. She established her publishing company in 1983, before it was fashionable, affordable or even convenient to self-publish. Around two dozen books have been produced through Matilija Press to date. She has also worked with traditional royalty publishers and co-publishers. This author has contributed to several other published books including, *Confessions of Shameless Self Promoters* by Debbie Allen, *The Obvious Expert* by Elsom and Mark L. Eldridge, *Book Marketing from A-Z* by Francine Silverman, *Feminine Writes* produced by the National Association of Women Writers, and Entrepreneur Media's *Start Your Own Self-Publishing Business.*

Patricia is the executive director of SPAWN (Small Publishers, Artists and Writers Network) http://www.spawn.org.

In 1998, she was chosen as a local Living Treasure in the literary category. She fulfilled her obligation by developing a program to take into the schools called, "Write for Life." A few years later, she carried this theme into a highly successful workshop which she presented for a group of homeschooled children. By the end of their eight weeks together, the students had designed and published a book of their works.

Patricia writes the monthly *SPAWN Market Update* for the SPAWN website. She speaks at conferences and workshops throughout the U.S. and teaches publishing/book promotion-related classes both face-to-face and online. She also works with clients on their writing/publishing projects.

It is with pleasure that Patricia shares, through this book, her passion for writing and her knowledge of the publishing industry. For, in order to survive in this business, you must have a good measure of both.

Visit Patricia's informative blog often: http://www.matilijapress.com/publishingblog.

PREFACE

My driving force—my motivation—for writing this book is **you**: the hopeful author, the inexperienced author, and even the fairly savvy author. You email me through the SPAWN website or my own website. You contact me in response to some of my articles and books. You stop by my booths at book festivals. You come to my workshops at conferences. And many of you ask me one of three questions:

1. I'd like to become a writer. How do I get started?
2. I've written a book, how do I go about getting it published?
3. What's the best way to promote a book?

Or you come to me complaining:

1. Publishers keep rejecting my manuscript.
2. I can't get my books into major bookstores.
3. My publisher is doing nothing to promote my book.

Herein, I've responded to these questions/comments and hundreds more. While this book provides nearly a thousand information bites, resources, lessons, and examples, it is not designed to take the place of hard work. This is an educational guide for authors, but it is not going to get you published—not unless you USE what you learn here to move your career forward.

Throughout these pages, you will bathe in the wisdom of publishing experts. If you heed the warnings, study the instructions, apply the tools, and pursue the resources, you have a definite chance of reaching your professional publishing goals.

INTRODUCTION

More people today than ever before are becoming authors. Unfortunately, most of them fail in their quest for success.

Publishing—The Raw Truth

According to a Jenkins Group survey, seventy-six percent of books published in this country each year do not make a profit. Why?

- Uninformed authors approach the publishing process all wrong.
- Even excellent, worthy books go unnoticed when the author isn't industry-savvy.
- Inexperienced authors tend to quit promoting their books when the going gets tough.

It used to be that authors wrote books and publishers produced, promoted, and distributed them. After participating in a few book signings, the author was free to go back to his home office and write his next bestseller. In order to be a successful author today, however, you must have a significant understanding of the publishing industry and be willing to establish a sense of intimacy with your book even beyond the writing process. It's imperative that you become involved in the promotion of your book and, in some cases, the production.

Technology has fueled dramatic changes in the publishing industry—and the news isn't all bad. Hopeful authors are faced with greater challenges today, it's true; but there are also more options and opportunities.

According to self-publishing guru, Dan Poynter, in 1970, there were only about 3,000 publishing companies. Today, there are somewhere around 85,000—many of them small/independent publishers who have established companies through which to produce their own books. However, hundreds of them are traditional royalty publishers seeking worthwhile projects. Yes, there are a lot of publishers out there—more than just the big six. So why is it so difficult to land a publishing contract? In a word, *competition*.

Some years ago, I heard it said that eighty-one percent of the public believe they have a book in them. With expanded publishing options, more and more of these people are actually writing their books. And millions of them are currently seeking publishers. Is there room in this industry for all hopeful authors? Probably not. But, according to R. R. Bowker, a whopping 1,052,803 books were published in 2009—over 750,000 of them coming from pay-to-publish and independent publishers.

My aim is not to discourage you, but to illustrate that there's more to becoming a successful published author than simply writing a good book. Besides a measure of talent and skill, it takes a bit of industry savvy, the ability to engage your left brain (participate in the business aspects of publishing), and the willingness to take the necessary steps. While writers, if they wish, can luxuriate in a world of creativity, authorship is a business. Once you decide that you want to be published, you must don your businessperson's hat.

What happens if you don't heed this advice? You've probably already witnessed some of the consequences. You hear Elaine from your writers' group whining incessantly because she can't find a publisher for her magnificent manuscript. Yet she stubbornly refuses to follow publishers' submission guidelines. She hasn't written a book proposal. She is sending out an inferior, ineffective query letter or she has bypassed this step altogether and is submitting an unsolicited manuscript. By refusing to learn or acknowledge publishing protocol, she's setting herself up for failure.

What about Brian, the guy in your online discussion group who is furious because his publisher isn't selling more copies of his book? Either he doesn't understand that promotion is his responsibility or he is in denial.

Many inexperienced authors go into publishing with more ideals than information. They want their books to fly off of bookstore shelves by the hundreds. They dream of collecting big royalty bucks, but they aren't willing to lift a finger to make it happen.

In today's publishing climate, a traditional royalty publisher won't issue you a contract unless you have a marketing plan firmly in place. And the more credentials you flash, the better. A publisher isn't going to sink his money into your project unless he's at least ninety-eight percent certain that it's a risk worth taking. As the author, it's your job to convince him or her that you can and will do your part. Don't let people like Elaine and Brian discourage you from fulfilling your publishing dreams. Obviously, they've chosen to spend more time complaining about the process than to understand it.

A Few Encouraging Words

Even though you might not see it as such at first, this is a book of encouragement. And it is a reality check. Those of you who will ultimately succeed in meeting your writing/publishing goals are those who can step outside your comfort zone and embrace the information, guidelines, and resources within these pages.

Things were simpler when I had my first book published in the 1970s. Long-term standards kept the industry fairly steady. Competition was just tough enough that good literature was the rule instead of the exception. And then along came the digital revolution, and practically everything changed. In order to be successfully published, you must change as well. And this means do not sit down and write your book as a first step. There is much to be learned and much to do before you start writing.

I often hear from authors who have made some bad choices. Hundreds or thousands of dollars later, they wonder what to do. As I said, there are more publishing options than ever before. Many hopeful authors choose the quick and easy road to publishing. They hand over their manuscripts and large sums of money to the first company that agrees to publish their book. In most cases, this is one of the growing number of subsidy "self-publishing" "pay-to-publish" companies that readily appear during an Internet search for a publisher. This was the case with Jeff.

After receiving form rejection letters from several medium-size publishers and being ignored by a few mega-publishers, Jeff saw an ad for AuthorHouse and contacted them. He said, "They accepted my manuscript and boy did that make me feel good. So, of course, I signed a contract with them. It has been six months and the only books sold are those that I sold personally—about a dozen to relatives and co-workers. Even the local bookstore won't carry my book. I'm frustrated and I don't know what to do."

I helped Jeff develop a marketing plan for his book, which he reluctantly pursued. He told me later, "I really thought that when I finished writing the book, my part of this was over. And here I am marketing and distributing the thing."

Reality check for hopeful authors: **Book promotion is your responsibility.**

I meet hundreds of unpublished authors every year online and at book festivals and writers' conferences who are completely unaware of their publishing options, the possible ramifications of their choices, and their responsibilities as a published author. In this business, ignorance can be costly.

So what are our publishing options? There are the major publishing houses and subsidy or fee-based "self-publishing" (pay-to-publish) services. But there are also hundreds of small to medium-size royalty publishers who are eager for a bestseller, and niche publishers seeking fresh, new projects. You could produce an ebook or you can publish the book yourself. You might even solicit funds to help support your project. No kidding, I once had a publisher ask me if I could arrange for corporate funding to help them pay production costs for one of my manuscripts. And I've known self-published authors who solicited funds for the production of their books. Some do this by selling back-of-the-book advertising pages.

So, which publishing approach is best? It depends on your project and it depends on you. There are advantages and disadvantages to each of these publishing methods. What might be an advantage to one hopeful author could be a definite disadvantage to another. Before making a decision, I urge you to consider the following:

- How important is it that the book be published?
- Can you afford to take a financial risk?
- How quickly do you want/need the book published?
- What level of quality do you desire for the finished product?
- How much control do you want and how much are you willing to relinquish?
- How far and wide do you want your product to reach? Is this book of local, regional, national, or international interest?
- What is the size and scope of your target audience?

- Do you have a head for business?
- Are you able and willing to promote this book?
- What is your platform—your way of attracting readers and your connections?

Please respond to these questions. Your answers will assist you as you continue through the pages of this book. Don't worry about those questions you don't, yet, understand. You'll gain clarity as you read on.

Perhaps you're like a lot of other hopeful authors—you've already made some mistake in your preliminary publishing ventures. Don't despair. There is hope. There's hope for you and me and for the future of American literature. Hope comes in the form of knowledge and responsible publishing and promotion. This book will guide you to that end. So get ready for the journey. Relax, breathe deeply, engage your right and left brain, and open your mind, for successful authorship should be a whole body experience.

Stop! Don't Write That Book . . . Yet

This book is designed for authors at any stage of a book project. But I am most eager to address those of you who have yet not finalized your manuscripts. To you, I would like to say:

Step Away from the Keyboard, Now!

You probably didn't expect to read this statement in a book about how to become a published author. Of course, I want you to write the book that's rolling around in your head and your heart, but not quite yet. There's work to be done before you put pen to paper or fingers to keyboard. First, you need information so you can develop a strategy.

You wouldn't open a retail sporting goods store or start a telecommunications company unless you had at least a basic understanding of the industry. You'd become familiar with your customers, your competition, your suppliers and distributors. You'd develop a marketing plan and you'd probably make sure you had some financial backing. Like it or not, publishing is a business and your book is a product. While writing can be a marvelously delightful creative endeavor, the process of publishing involves a generous dose of marketing savvy and business sense. Launch blindly into the publishing field and use a scattershot method of producing and promoting a book and you'll likely fail. There are hundreds of thousands of disappointed authors out there who can back up this statement.

As I said in my Introduction (which you should read, by the way), it is estimated that over eighty percent of all adult Americans have the desire to write a book. More and more of these people are actually doing it.

Technology is certainly in the author's favor. Anyone who can construct a sentence can turn out a manuscript. If you have a computer and printer, you can even produce a book. Those who don't want to be the publisher can hire a publisher. Of course, if you're diligent (or lucky) and have a viable manuscript, you have a good chance of landing a traditional royalty publisher. The opportunities for hopeful authors are amazingly vast. Most new authors, however, short-circuit their chances of publishing success by going about the process of producing a book all wrong.

Okay, you've written a book and you want to have it published. What more is there to consider? Nothing, if you wrote the book to give as gifts to your immediate family members and a few friends. If you want your book to sell in large quantities, however, you will need buyers. You know, customers—folks who will purchase your book. It's only after publication—when sales are practically nonexistent—that many first-time authors realize they must have made a mistake.

One disheartened author told me, "I was so eager to get this book published, I'm afraid that I didn't take time to learn the ropes. Now I have forty-two boxes of books in my garage and no idea how to sell them. I guess I was naïve to think that I could distribute them through bookstores, because that is just not happening. I learned too late that bookstores are not there for the author—that is, unless your publisher is Simon and Schuster."

What? Bookstore managers aren't eager to carry newly published books? Why? Consider this: One reason is logistics. According to RR Bowker, the keeper of book publishing statistics, there are 7.5 million American book, audio and video titles listed in their database. Even the largest bookstore can accommodate only around 150,000 titles. That's less than two percent of all titles.

Additionally, there have probably always been poorly written, shoddily bound books produced, but never as many as since the most recent technological revolution. Along with some wonderful books, a proliferation of low quality books began appearing throughout the mid to late 1990s—most of them coming from pay-to-publish companies and lackadaisical independent publishers. What choice did credible bookstore managers, book reviewers, and distributors have? How would they avoid endorsing inferior products while embracing and recommending only those books of superior quality? Rather than taking the time to consider the merit of each individual book, many of them decided to accept only books published through traditional channels. They would exclude books produced by pay-to-publish (subsidy publishing) services and independent publishers (self-published authors).

Some bookstore managers, reviewers, and distributors even began to shun books produced by legitimate royalty publishers if they used digital printing technology. For several years, the doors to traditional marketing opportunities were closed for many digitally produced books. Fortunately, this stigma is lifting and, in 2011, key players within the bookselling realm are using more reasonable criteria for evaluating the worth of all books.

I met Frances at a writers' conference in St. Louis where I spoke on book promotion. She had published her novel through one of the many pay-to-publish companies two years earlier and was still struggling to recoup her investment. She paid extra for one of the promotion packages they offered, but said, "I've sold fewer than 100 books and that was without their help. They haven't actually sold any." According to Frances's calculations, she needed to sell 100 more books in order to break even. But she was at a loss as to how to do it. She bought lists of bookstores nationwide and mailed flyers to 1,000 of them with no success whatsoever. She visited every bookstore within a fifty-mile radius of her home and managed to place a few books on consignment. She also arranged for a few book signings which weren't all that successful.

Frances told me, "If it wasn't for the fact that I need to replace that money, I'd forget the whole thing and chalk it up to a bad decision. But I'm facing retirement and I need the money. If I had it to do over again, I would never have gotten involved in publishing."

Frances was a paraplegic and her novel featured a paraplegic couple, yet she hadn't even considered soliciting reviews in disability and senior magazines or giving readings at rehabilitation hospitals and nursing homes. I suggested that she write a provocative press release and send it to newspaper editors, radio talk show hosts, and website hosts nationwide. I asked her to do some research, and she discovered that there are approximately one million Americans using wheelchairs—or one in every 250 people. This should be a significant enough number to warrant national coverage for a book related to personal disabilities.

The last I heard, Frances had sent out review copies to several magazine editors and newspaper columnists. Her book was being featured on a couple of appropriate websites. She had done some radio interviews by phone and was scheduled to make a TV appearance locally. Her total sales to date were 350 and counting.

Few first-time authors think beyond the bookstore when considering book promotion. Even fewer consider book promotion at all until they're faced with a book that no one is buying.

> NEWS FLASH!!! It is up to the author to promote his/her book, and the time to start planning your promotional strategy, fellow writers, is BEFORE you write the book.

Before you invest your time, energy, and money into a project, you need to know whether there is a market for your book. Is your idea valid? Is there a need for this book? Is there room for another book on this topic? Exactly who is your target audience? Who do you want to educate, influence, affect, or entertain? What books would compete with yours? This is also the time to think about building promotional opportunities into your book. (Learn how to make your book more salable in Chapter Six.)

Dismiss Those Discouraging Words

You may feel as though I'm trying to dissuade you from pursuing your writing/publishing dreams. On the contrary, my purpose in writing this book is to guide you toward a successful publishing experience. In so doing, I must squelch some of your preconceived ideas and burst your bubbles—at least those bubbles that are blocking your success.

Some readers will decide not to follow the suggestions in this book and a few of them will stumble blindly into a sweet publishing deal that makes them a lot of money. I've seen it happen. I've also watched inexperienced authors blow their money and their chances for success by refusing to adhere to some measure of publishing protocol. Unfortunately, the latter is the more common scenario.

There are people out there who will try to discourage you from writing a book. Sour Sallys and Gloomy Glens in your writers' group will tell you that the manuscript market is saturated. They'll say that it is next to impossible to get your book published, let alone get it into bookstores or have it reviewed through the most prominent channels. Is this true?

It was true when I produced the first and second editions of this book (2006–2007), but things are changing in favor of the savvy author. And that's why I have decided to revise and update this book for you. However, while quality self-published and pay-to-publish books are more well-received in 2012, publishing is still a fiercely competitive business that requires a strong business head. The playing field has changed, there are new players entering the game, and the opportunities are greater. But it is still tough to succeed in this business. Should this stop you from bringing out your amazing book? Emphatically, No!

As you will discover while studying this book, there are abundant opportunities for authors outside of the antiquated publishing mold. There are numerous publishing options and countless avenues for book promotion and distribution. However, if you're still following the publishing model established in the 1960s and '70s, you are in for a culture shock. It's time that you learn some new concepts and strategies. My intent is not to offer encouragement where there is no hope, but to inspire you to become educated about the publishing industry and to do the research necessary on behalf of your project.

For those of you who are still questioning today's publishing climate and your chances of breaking in, I'd like to bust some popular myths for your benefit. Read on.

Myth Busters for Hopeful Authors

Myth #1: It's impossible for a first-time author to land a traditional royalty publishing contract.

Myth Buster: You'll hear people say this and you may even see it stated on writers' online forums. And then you'll read in a newsletter or in a book such as this one that there were 1,052,803 books published in 2009. Believe it or not (actually, I prefer that you believe it), over 288,000 of those books were published by traditional royalty publishers. Do your homework and produce a viable product and you, too, could land a traditional royalty publisher.

A student in my online book proposal class had her first book published by Houghton Mifflin. One of my clients landed a contract with Scholastic Books for her first young adult fantasy. A thirty-something author I met recently had his first book—a memoir—picked up by HarperCollins. Yes,

Virginia, there is a royalty publisher for your excellent book—that is, if it is timely enough, has a wide enough audience, and there's a strong marketing plan in place.

Myth #2: Most publishers accept manuscripts only through agents.

Myth Buster: Wrong. There are oodles of publishers who prefer to deal directly with the author. My student—the one who landed a book deal through Houghton Mifflin—did so without the assistance of an agent. The 2012 edition of the *Writer's Market* (a directory of publishers and magazine editors) lists over 500 traditional publishing companies. Approximately ninety percent of them do not require that you engage an agent.

Myth #3: If I have an agent, I will definitely get published.

Myth Buster: Not necessarily. Unfortunately, while there are some very good agents, there are also some who are ineffective and unscrupulous. Even a good agent can't always second-guess publishers. (Read more about locating and successfully working with an agent in Chapter Eight.)

Myth #4: I don't have to worry about fine-tuning my manuscript. If the publisher is interested, he will have it edited.

Myth Buster: Don't EVEN go there! It may surprise you to know how many hopeful authors believe this. Of course, publishers hire editors and, if accepted, your manuscript will probably go through a stringent editing process. But it is your responsibility to present to the publisher the very best possible manuscript. You need to hire a good editor before you submit your work to any publisher. Adopt this motto: *Make a good impression the first time and every time*. This goes for every email, letter, and manuscript you send to publishers, book reviewers, and even fellow authors. You are a writer—let it show.

Myth #5: Bookstores won't carry self-published or pay-to-publish books.

Myth Buster: Have you contacted any of your local, independent bookstores about your self-published or subsidy published book? Have you approached specialty bookstores related to the topic of your book? Do you stop by independent bookstores to introduce yourself and your book when you're traveling? Stop focusing on the mega-bookstores and see if you can entice their smaller counterparts to carry your book. In fact, I recommend that you do business with independent bookstores the next time you want to purchase a book. They are your friends. Support them and they will be able to support you.

Myth #6: No one will review self-published or pay-to-publish books.

Myth Buster: Most new authors tend to focus on one segment of book reviewers—prepublication reviewers through prestigious library journals. These reviews are difficult to get even when you've gone through the right channels. Some of these reviewers are opening avenues for self-published and pay-to-publish books for a fee. From what I hear, however, authors/publishers are not getting their money's worth for these paid services.

In the meantime, there are tens of thousands of editors for legitimate magazines, newspapers, newsletters, and websites hungry for good books to review. You're probably already aware of magazines that relate to your book topic or genre. Contact the editors of these publications and offer to send them a review copy. Visit online directories to locate other possibilities. This is another case of thinking outside the box.

Myth #7: Writing the book is the hardest part of the process.

Myth Buster: How many of you thought this to be true while you were involved in researching and writing your book? Those of you with published books feel differently now, don't you? To avoid author shock, always, I mean ALWAYS write a book proposal first. Once you've properly and thoughtfully completed a book proposal, you will be, at least, somewhat prepared for the work and the stress that lies ahead.

You Want to Write a Book Because?

Have you ever asked yourself why you write? I often interview writers who thank me for asking this question because it causes them to reflect and helps them to set more meaningful goals. We don't always consider the reasons why we write (or paint or sculpt). We just do it. Likely, you're in touch with what inspires you to write—your muse. But what motivates you to write for publication: Money, prestige, fame, a yearning to share your joy or grief, the desire to help people or to facilitate change, or a need to establish credibility in a particular field?

I write for publication in order to justify my passion for writing. I tell people that *I can't not write*. Since I have to earn a living, I've established a business around my love of writing.

Most writers have this innate (or is it insane?) desire to be read/heard—maybe even understood. Elizabeth K. Burton is the author of *Dreams of Darkness, Shadow of the Scorpion,* and *The Ugly Princess*. She writes to be read. She says, "I love telling stories; if I make money at it, all the better. It's getting it out to the readers that compels me."

Some writers are eager to fill a void. Sandra J. Cropsey wrote her children's book because she perceived a need. She was already writing plays and short stories when, one December several years ago, while watching Christmas specials with her children, she realized that none of the popular Christmas stories involved trains. "What is Christmas without trains?" she reasoned. And she created *Tinker's Christmas*, a children's storybook featuring a train.

Many authors today write books designed to help others. They've endured something or learned something they feel is of value to a segment of the population. Sharing, for most of them, serves two purposes. In the process of helping others, they are helping themselves. Writing can be healing—therapeutic. It's is a way of purging, after all.

I met one author online who was promoting a book for a very specialized audience—dialysis patients. She said, "I wrote this book in hopes of reaching a very select audience and to offer some help based on my own personal experiences."

Other authors write in order to establish credibility in their fields. And then there's the writer who has a story dancing around in his head and he feels somehow compelled to share it with the world.

Once you've decided to write a book and you know why you are writing, how do you choose what to write? Will you follow your heart and write a children's story, a book of poems, or a novel? Perhaps you'll lead with your head and write a how-to book related to your business or your favorite hobby. Many professionals suggest writing a nonfiction book first. Yes, even if your heart's desire is to pen the next greatest novel, consider breaking into the publishing field with a nonfiction book. Why?

A nonfiction book is easier to write, and it's easier to sell both to a publisher and to readers. It doesn't have to be a huge tome. Produce a simple booklet featuring something you know well: a children's guide to recognizing constellations, 100 things you can fix with fishing line, what to do when you find an injured bird, a knitting guide for youngsters, tips for writing love notes, or the history of your local Independence Day celebration, for example.

Whatever your genre or topic, in order to obtain some level of success, you must enter into the project with ample knowledge and appropriate expectations.

Julie began writing for relaxation while working in the corporate offices of a banking company. She enjoyed writing so much that she decided to quit her job and write full time. It wasn't hard for Julie to choose her topic—she writes suspense novels related to the banking industry.

Sometimes the topic chooses the author, as was the case with Cindy. Her book captures her experiences as an island dweller living in a substandard cabin in a remote area with an array of animals (only some of them domesticated). Cindy wanted to share her unusual experiences with others. She told me, "I was bubbling over with this story. It became terribly important to me to share the lessons I learned as well as to entertain, enlighten, and inspire anyone who might venture to *drop out* as I did."

Get In Touch with Your Unrealistic Expectations

Most authors have an ideal or a standard by which they measure success. For some, success means becoming a published author. For others, they haven't succeeded until they've sold 100,000 copies of their books. I'm sure that some of us are never satisfied with what we achieve. The more we obtain, the more we desire. Isn't that what goal-setting is all about? Set a goal. Reach the goal. Raise the bar. It works for me.

> The Author's Guild has determined that a fiction book is successful if it sells 5,000 copies and a successful nonfiction book sells 7,500 copies.

Publishing isn't necessarily a money-making venture. If you self-publish a book that sells 5,000 copies, you might realize $25,000 to $75,000 in profits. If you published that book through a pay-to-publish company, you could earn anywhere from $5,000 to $10,000. And if you had collected royalties on that book, your earnings might be just $5,000 to $20,000. Keep in mind that sales could spread out over a five or ten year period.

> Embracing unrealistic expectations generally results in an unsuccessful and very disappointed author.

How does a hopeful author establish realistic expectations? By understanding something about the publishing industry. This is not to say that I (or any other professional) can teach you how to predict which book ideas will pay off in big bucks and which ones won't. Even the most experienced publishers sometimes miss the mark. But at least they make educated decisions. They're not apt to lead with their emotions (as an author will often do). Understanding the possibilities will give you enough wiggle room to help keep your expectations well within the realm of reality.

A book of poetry, for example, is extremely difficult to sell. If you want to share your poetry for the pure joy of sharing, that's okay. Just understand that this will be more a labor of love than a commercial venture through which you will receive enough royalties to retire on next year.

Having said that, I'd like to recommend two books designed to help poets sell their work: *Poet Power, The Complete Guide to Getting Your Poetry Published* by Thomas A. Williams, (Sentient Publications, 2002) and *How to Make a Living As a Poet* by Gary Mex Glazner (Soft Skull Press, 2005).

The author of a children's book said to me once, "The experience of publishing fell far short of what I initially thought it would be, and that was largely due to my unrealistic expectations and perceptions about publishing. Marketing is so far removed from the experience of writing that it is like this constant stranger who speaks a different language which I am neither equipped to nor have the desire to understand. Had anyone explained to me the ins and outs—the ups and downs—of marketing, I'm not sure I would have ever published."

Too many authors fail solely because they give up. Authorship is not designed to be a hobby. It isn't something that you can successfully manage as an afterthought. It demands your full attention. Your future in writing and publishing is almost completely up to you. If you do the necessary research and work, if you approach authorship as the business that it is, and if you exercise persistence, perseverance, and patience while maintaining realistic expectations, you will experience success.

How to Find the Very Best Publisher for Your Project

Most new authors make at least one of five mistakes when attempting to choose a publisher.

Five Common Authors' Mistakes

1: **Inexperienced authors write a book that is not publisher-friendly.** In other words, they write the book to suit their own emotional or altruistic needs without considering its commercial value. Once the book is completed, they try to find a publisher. What's wrong with this approach?

Most manuscripts that are written without concern for the target audience are not marketable, thus would not be profitable. A publisher may reject a manuscript featuring your grandfather's World War II experiences, but would welcome a book focusing on blacks in the armed forces during that time period. Your book on selling buttons through eBay may not appeal to a publisher, yet the public might be screaming for one featuring the most unique items ever sold online.

If you had written a complete book proposal first, your project would probably be more appropriately targeted. And if you'd submitted a query letter before writing your book, the publisher could have more appropriately directed you—greatly increasing your chances of becoming a published author.

2: **Newbie authors frequently send their manuscripts to the wrong publishers.** Much like doctors these days, some publishers specialize. More and more publishers accept either fiction or nonfiction. Some specialize in children's stories or textbooks while others focus their energies (and their finances) on true crime, poetry, romance, cookbooks, how-to, self-help, or business books.

There's no such thing as one publisher fits all. You wouldn't send your collection of poetry to DAW Books, but the editors at Red Hen Press might be delighted to receive it. These editors would reject your fantasy or science fiction manuscript on the spot, but those at DAW Books might welcome it. The publisher at Paulist Press doesn't want to see books in any of these genres, but send them a good children's or young adult book with a Catholic theme and you might score with them.

3: **Eager authors often set their hearts on being accepted by a mega-publisher.** In so doing, they miss out on more realistic publishing opportunities. I'm not trying to discourage you from starting at the top. I have no quarrel with you giving the big guys a whirl. But please develop a backup plan. Vow that if Random House and Simon and Schuster turn you down, you will lower your sights to, perhaps, a more realistic level and opt for publication with one of the many smaller publishing houses. Have you heard of Synerge Books? They publish forty to sixty fiction and nonfiction titles per year and offer fifteen to forty percent royalties. Cleis Press publishes around forty-five titles per year and ninety percent of them are from unagented authors. Untreed Reads produces as many as thirty-five titles each year in many genres and categories and eighty percent of them are from first-time authors.

4: **The most common mistake authors make when contacting publishers is to ignore their submission guidelines.** In fact, many inexperienced authors don't even study them. While there are basic standards for contacting publishers, there are also differences in submission requirements between publishing houses. Most publishers want to see a query letter first. If they are interested in your concept and impressed by your credentials, they will generally request your book proposal. Of course, there are exceptions to every rule, and this is why it's crucial to locate and study the guidelines for each publisher before approaching him or her. (See details for locating submission guidelines below.)

5: **Too many hopeful authors neglect to make a clear, concise, and clean presentation.** Some inexperienced authors believe that a publisher can see through a poorly written query letter to the magnificence of his story. Others are so eager to get their works into the hands of a publisher that they simply don't finish dotting all of their i's and crossing all of their t's. I'm here to tell you that your chances of winning a contract with any publisher are extremely slim when you submit an error-riddled, disorganized, rambling query letter, book proposal, or manuscript.

In order to be successful in this business, you have to stop looking at your project from an emotional place and start thinking like a professional. Don't worry; you can adopt a business persona without losing your creative edge. In fact, if you want to be published, it's necessary to shift from artist to businessperson on demand.

Publishers are bombarded with hundreds of query letters and book proposals each month. Scribner, an imprint of Simon and Schuster, receives thousands of queries each year and publishes only seventy to seventy-five titles. Strider Nolan receives 1,000 to 2,000 queries per year and publishes five to ten titles.

The news isn't all bad, however. Check out some of the smaller publishing companies. Barricade Books receives just 200 queries per year, and they publish twelve titles. Puritan Press receives only twenty-five queries in a year, and they publish five titles.

Whether you decide to approach a mega-publishing house or a smaller one, vow to give nothing less than your most polished presentation. Think about it: What is the point of leading with your second or third best shot when there may be 300 other authors soliciting this publisher with equally good ideas and highly polished presentations?

Why Choose a Publisher Now?

Locating and landing a publisher can take time. Most hopeful authors, after devoting several months or years to writing the perfect manuscript, don't want to spend another several months in search of a publisher. It is at this juncture that many authors make their second major mistake. They go with the first publisher who expresses an interest in their project without considering the consequences or the cost. If you have a few appropriate publishers in mind before writing your book, you could save time, money, and heartache.

Your first choice of publishers might have some specific requirements that you need to know about before writing the book. I know one successful author who forged ahead with her book without considering her publishing choices. It took her only five or six months to find a publisher, but he wouldn't publish her book without a major rewrite designed to more appropriately focus the content of the book. This extra work might have been avoided had she put more effort and thought into a publisher before writing the book.

Choose a publisher before you write the book and you may get an advance. Yes, a publisher might pay you a fee to write the book. This amount would then be deducted from future royalty earnings. Generally, a publisher will pay half of the advance when you sign the contract and the remainder upon satisfactory completion of the manuscript. While publishing advances are sometimes in the thousands of dollar range, it is rare for a first-time author to receive more than $500 or $1,000.

Keep in mind that publishers generally won't issue a contract based on a query letter by an unknown, unproven author. An excellent book proposal for a viable book including chapter summaries and sample chapters just might generate that contract, though.

Here are some key things that you need to know before you start writing:

- What are your publishing options for this particular book? Are there publishers who produce books like yours, and if not, are you willing to self-publish or go with a pay-to-publish company?
- What is the general word count for a book like the one you want to write? Some publishers have word count requirements. One publisher might want no more than 40,000 words while another won't publish anything less than 70,000 words. There are strict word-count guidelines for children's books based on the age group. And few, if any, publishers will invest in an oversized novel by an unknown author.
- What does the publisher need or expect from you? Does the publisher of your choice want to see the completed manuscript, a synopsis and two sample chapters, or just a query letter? What specific information does the publisher require from hopeful authors?

Manage the Maze of Potential Publishers

I receive the same question from hopeful authors many times each year. "How do I find a publisher?" Another even more important question might be, "What is a publisher?"

A **traditional royalty publisher** assumes the expenses involved in publishing a book and gives the author a percentage of each book sold. Depending on the policies of the publishing house, royalties are figured on either the retail or the wholesale price and generally range between five and eighteen percent.

Subsidy or vanity and **co-publishers** produce your book for a fee. This publishing model has changed in recent years. Under the original premise, the vanity or subsidy publisher was hired to produce books for authors who didn't want to establish their own publishing companies. With the advent of the digital age, a new model of subsidy publishing began to take shape. And today, there's a blurred distinction between the old vanity press and the modern-day all-inclusive pay-to-publish services.

Pay-to-publish services (formerly known as fee-based POD publishers or self-publishing companies) charge anywhere from a few hundred to many thousands of dollars to produce your book, and then they print the number of copies that you need as you request them and charge accordingly. They also offer various promotional packages and advantages for additional fees. These companies are extremely popular right now, but they are also the brunt of numerous complaints. I maintain that this is due mostly to the authors' lack of industry savvy and unreasonable expectations. (Read more about pay-to-publish services in Chapter Three.)

Self-publishing means that you establish a company through which to produce your book and you arrange for and pay for all of the necessary components—copyright, ISBN (International Standard Book Number), barcode, cover design and so forth. You audition printing companies and hire one for your project. You also promote, distribute, and ship your books. (Read more about self-publishing in Chapter Eleven.)

How to Find the Right Royalty Publisher for Your Project

Traditional royalty publishers are everywhere—not just in high-rise buildings in New York City. They reside and work in practically every state in the U.S. So how do you find out about them?

Start in your home library. You probably have books on the topic or in the genre that you will be writing. Look at those books. Who published them? Would your book idea fit into their list?

Visit local bookstores and locate recently published books similar to the one you have in mind. The publisher's name and contact information is usually on the copyright page and/or the back cover of the book.

New authors typically say, "But there is nothing out there like my book." Then consider this: Maybe it is not such a good idea. If you can't find any books like yours, perhaps there's no market for it. This reality check ought to help you develop a more open mind when seeking your book's rightful place in the scheme of things. Now, go determine where your book is likely to be placed in bookstores. Who published the books in that section?

I met a man at a writer's conference in Northern California a few years ago who told me there was nothing on the market like the book he was writing. It was a book of recipes and stories handed down by his German ancestors. Out of curiosity, I did my own search and immediately located a book featuring recipes and stories handed down by the author's German family.

Publishing Industry Reference Directories

Extend your research for appropriate publishers, their contact information, and their submission needs and requirements by studying some of the world's most comprehensive and useful publisher directories:

- ***Writer's Market*** is located in the reference section of your public library, for sale for around $30 in most bookstores, and online for a fee at http://www.writersmarket.com. The print book is updated annually and distributed each September.
- ***Literary Market Place*** is located in the reference section of your public library. You can also purchase this volume for $329. Get a discount for standing annual orders. There is also limited free access to their online directory: http://www.literarymarketplace.com.
- **Online publisher directories.** There are several online publisher directories you can access for free. Just do an Internet search using keywords: "publisher" + "directory."

The publishing industry seems to be in a constant state of flux these days, so make sure that you access the most updated volume available. And always double check the data you glean. Information in print guides can be more than a year old. Databases aren't always kept current. With every convenient resource comes the possibility of error or omission. What is an author to do?

1. Always verify publisher information by visiting the publisher's website.
2. Locate or request a current copy of the publisher's submission guidelines.
3. Call the publishing house for address verification or to confirm the name of an acquisitions editor.

Publishing Industry Periodicals

Stay on top of industry news, changes, and trends through periodicals. This is the best way to learn about new launches and failed publishing businesses as well as tips for successfully navigating the industry and resources to help in your journey. You can subscribe to *Publishers Weekly* for around $250 per year. Or subscribe to their free daily enewsletter at http://www.publishersweekly.com. Here are additional newsletters I recommend:

- ***SPAWNews***, a free monthly enewsletter produced by SPAWN—Small Publishers, Artists and Writers Network. (http://www.spawn.org).
- ***SPAWN Market Update***, a meaty monthly online newsletter posted at the SPAWN website for members only. Join SPAWN at http://www.spawn.org.
- ***IBPA Independent***, a print periodical for members of Independent Book Publishers Association (formerly PMA). (http://www.ibpa-online.org)
- ***Publishing Basics Newsletter***, a free online newsletter featuring topics related to all aspects of publishing and book marketing. (http://www.publishingbasics.com)
- ***A Marketing Expert Newsletter***, Penny Sansevieri's free email newsletter for authors with books to promote. (http://www.amarketingexpert.com)
- ***Marketing Matters Newsletter***, Brian Jud's free enewsletter for authors. http://www.bookmarketingworks.com.

Join authors/publishers online discussion groups to help you stay abreast of industry trends and changes. Most are free. Visit http://www.publishedauthors.org or http://www.writerspace.com. Click on "bulletin boards." Locate others by using keywords "publishing forum," "authors discussion group," "science fiction forum," etc.

Join SPAWN (Small Publishers, Artists and Writers Network) at $65/ year and participate in SPAWNDiscuss. http://www.spawn.org. Join SPAN (Small Publishers of North America) at $60 to $150/year and participate in the SPANnet Online Community http://www.spannet.org.

What Can You Learn from a Publisher's Website?

I recommend spending time poking around at publishers' websites. Here's what you want to know:

- **What type of books does he publish?** Read the submission guidelines, but also look at the publisher's online catalog and see if your book idea seems to be a fit. If this publishing company is a definite possibility for your project, review some of their books as a guide to writing yours. I can't stress enough the importance of following this advice. In fact, you'll see this tip posted often in publishers' listings in *Writer's Market* and at publishers' websites.
- **What does the publisher want from you?** Does he prefer receiving a query letter first, a book proposal, or the complete manuscript? Will he accept this material via email or USPS only? Is he open to receiving submissions all year around or only during certain months? Locate this information in the submission guidelines or, perhaps, on the "Editorial Page."
- **What is his contact information?** Go to the website "Contact Us" page to find out this publisher's mailing address, phone number, and email address.
- **What's the name of the acquisitions editor?** Always address the appropriate individual when submitting your query letter or book proposal. A large publishing house may have several editors—each with a different focus. Note which editor is most suited to your project.
- **Who are some of this publisher's authors?** You may want to contact them and inquire about their working relationship with this publishing company.

Tips for Using Search Engines to Locate Publishers' Websites

What if you can't find a website address listed for this publisher? Do an Internet search using Google, AltaVista, Yahoo!, or any other search engine.

Here's how:

- Type the name of the publishing company and click the search button. If they have a website, their listing will generally appear on the first page.
- Use an Internet search to locate additional publishers that may not appear in the resource materials you've studied. To find publishers who accept books in your particular genre and topic, type "science fiction publisher," "romance novel publisher," "publisher dog books," "publisher fantasy," for example.
- Search for publishers who may not be listed in the usual reference guides, yet. Your best bet for locating new publishers is to subscribe to industry newsletters (such as those listed earlier in this chapter) and to search online publisher databases such as http://www.writersmarket.com.

Tips for Locating Publishers' Submission Guidelines

- Once you have found several appropriate publishers, visit their websites for more specific information. Print out a copy of their submission guidelines (or "editorial guidelines" or "writers/authors guidelines"). Sometimes the guidelines are difficult to find. If you don't see a link button to the submission guidelines, click on "About Us" or "Contact Us." If you don't see the guidelines on either of these pages, look for a new link on that page. Sometimes there will be more link options available to the left or across the top of that page. No luck? Go back to the home page and search links within links. Put your cursor on the available link buttons and see if a menu appears. Read the selections on the menus. Also check the links that sometimes appear at the bottom of the home page.
- If you cannot locate the guidelines at all, email the editor and ask for a copy. Or send a letter of request for submission guidelines in the mail along with a self-addressed-stamped envelope (SASE). That is, an envelope with your name and full address as well as enough postage for the return trip.

Can You Name That Genre?

Genre is a French word for *kind, class, form,* or *type*. If you're confused by what comprises a genre, you're in the majority. Even publishers lack unison when categorizing genre.

While some say that genre is the classification of a book, others argue that it is a species within the category. One thing is for sure: There are many more types of books recognized now than ever before.

Is your book a novel, novella, romance, historical fiction, or a how-to book? Is it considered commercial fiction, chick lit, or true crime? Perhaps it's a young adult novel or a self-help book. As I said, more and more publishers specialize, and the specialties have become even more diverse. It is sometimes difficult to define your genre, but it is important to do so in order to attract the right publisher. How would you pigeonhole your manuscript?

Fiction Categories

Commercial Fiction encompasses books featuring popular contemporary issues for a general audience. Commercial fiction might include westerns, romance, and mysteries. Books in this category are generally highly marketable works that interest a wide range of readers. Look at books published by the major publishers in America. These are generally good examples of commercial or mainstream fiction. Think John Grisham and Danielle Steele.

Literary Fiction typically appeals to a smaller audience than does commercial fiction. Books in this category are less conventional and more creative. Not only are the stories generally more complex, the writing style is less rigid. It is said that literary fiction creates challenges for the reader instead of offering pure entertainment. Think *Da Vinci Code* and *Memoirs of a Geisha.*

Mainstream Fiction could describe either commercial or literary fiction if the book presents a modern day scenario relating to a universal theme. Mainstream fiction generally appeals to a more diverse audience. When you see books on the bestseller list, these are generally considered mainstream fiction. Think James Michener, Amy Tan, Joyce Carol Oates, and Sue Grafton.

A ***Novel*** is a story encompassing at least 50,000 words. A ***Novella*** is a short novel of just 7,000 to 50,000 words. Your novel or novella might be considered mainstream fiction or commercial fiction. It could also be categorized a romance, western, or mystery. There are young adult novels, adventure novels, Christian novels, detective novels, gothic novels, and historical novels, for example.

Fiction Genres

Historical Fiction. The author uses fictional characters to tell a story related to actual historical events. Sometimes he uses real characters and fictionalizes some of the events. St. Martin's Press publishes historical fiction, as do Untapped Talent, Soho Press, and several publishers of children's books.

Science Fiction features future-based plots using scientific principles and theories. Think *Star Trek*. If you're seeking a publisher of science fiction, consider Tolling Bell Books, Ravenhawk Books, and Vivisphere Publishing.

Fantasy is a departure from reality. Publishers of fantasy include several children's book publishers and Greenwillow Books, HarperCollins, Flying Pen Press, and Gauthier Publications. Subgenres include epic fantasy (or high fantasy), fairy tales, and sword and sorcerer. Examples of high fantasy include *Alice in Wonderland, Harry Potter,* and *Gods of Pegana.*

Romance is considered escapist fiction by some. For the most part, romance books are formula love stories. Publishers seeking manuscripts in this genre include Ellora's Cave Publishing, Diskus Publishing, and Avalon Books.

Mystery books usually focus on murder. Publishers include Bancroft Press, Alpha World Press, WindRiver Publishing, Diversion Press, and at least one hundred others.

Chick Lit is a relatively new genre. Stories usually border on modern literature for and about single women. Helen Fielding's *Bridget Jones's Diary* is a good example of chick lit.

Additional genres and sub-genres include horror, thriller, techno-thriller, suspense thriller, political thriller, futuristic, time-travel, and paranormal.

Category—Nonfiction

Nonfiction is, of course, factual—just give me the facts ma'am. Nonfiction is more widely read, and there are hundreds more publishers for nonfiction than fiction books. Genres include the following:

Creative Nonfiction might also be referred to as literary nonfiction. It's a form of storytelling focusing on actual happenings. A memoir written with flair could be considered creative nonfiction, as might a personal essay or a biography. Those who publish creative nonfiction include Archimedes Press, Harbor House, and Dram Tree Books.

Narrative Nonfiction is a nonfiction account that is narrated throughout.

Your nonfiction manuscript might be classified as a how-to, short story collection, self-help (or prescriptive nonfiction), humor, historical, ethnic, New Age, juvenile, reference, science, or regional, and the subject might be parenting, pets, medicine, gardening, hobbies, or computers.

Let's say that you are writing the true story of a murder that occurred in your town in 1894. This book would probably be classified as a nonfiction true crime book. But it's also a history.

A book telling how to prune your rose bushes would fall into the category of a nonfiction how-to book on gardening.

Your book on how to be a less stressed parent is nonfiction. It is a self-help book and the subject is parenting.

Some manuscripts need further definition in order to target the right publisher. Would you contact a publisher of history books, romance stories, or regional materials for your book featuring a turn-of-the century romance set in your hometown? Maybe all three! The story of your ancestors striking it big in Nevada's silver mines might interest a publisher of memoirs, a regional publisher, or a publisher of history books. Contact Mystic Ridge Books, Heritage Books, Loft Press, or University of Nevada Press.

If the story carries a spiritual message throughout or the miners had paranormal experiences while working the mines, you might focus on religious or New Age publishers such as Sterling Publishing or Hay House.

While several publishers produce how-to books, your manuscript might not appeal to any but the most specialized publisher. The good news is that sometimes it's possible to pinpoint your ideal publisher almost immediately, but only if you can clearly identify the category, genre, and subject of your book.

Here are a few examples of publishers who specialize: Ball Publishing produces how-to and reference books, but only those related to agriculture and gardening. They would not be interested in seeing your book on how to teach wheelchair sports. Nursebooks produces books on subjects related to nursing. There is a remote possibility that they would be open to your book on wheelchair sports.

Diskus Publishing produces fiction only, so don't approach them with your book on how to win a decathlon—unless you decide to write a fiction story around the lifestyle of a decathlon competitor. Breakaway Books, however, might accept either of your decathlon ideas as they only publish books (both nonfiction and fiction) that relate to sports.

If you're still not sure how to classify your book, find books similar to the one you propose. Look on the top left corner of the back cover. Some of them have the classification (genre) and subject printed there. It might say, fiction/historical, nonfiction/writing, history/autobiographical, cooking, religious/philosophy, self-help/inspirational, or nonfiction/personal finance.

Your ABC List of Publishers

It's unlikely that your first choice of publishers will accept your book, especially if you are a first-time author. However, it is possible, particularly if you use the correct criteria in making the choice.

The more thoroughly you research publishers, the more realistic you are in choosing one, and the more stringently you adhere to their guidelines and requirements, the more likely you are to receive a positive response.

BUILD YOUR "A" LIST OF PUBLISHERS

Who is the ideal publisher for your project? Most authors start at the top of the publishing chain. And that's okay. Keep in mind, however, that few of the major publishing companies will entertain a proposal without representation by an agent. (Read how to find and select an agent in Chapter Eight.)

Advantages of Landing a Big Name Publisher

- You pay no publishing costs.
- You are validated as an author.
- There's prestige associated with this partnership.
- Your book will most likely be available in bookstores.
- Your book has a greater chance of becoming a bestseller.

Disadvantages of Landing a Big Name Publisher

- You will wait for a year or more to see your book in print.
- Your book may have a very short lifespan. Typically, major publishing houses give a book a year or less to prove itself. If it isn't paying its way, they will not reprint it.
- Communication is often difficult. The company is so large that your itty bitty problem or miniscule request can become quite insignificant.
- You have to rely on someone else to get your books to signing events on time and to send out review copies within deadline. Even the largest publishers are sometimes lax when it comes to amply supporting an author's promotional efforts.
- You are expected to help promote your book.
- You earn only a small percentage on sales.

CREATE YOUR "B" LIST OF PUBLISHERS

Your B list might include some of the many appropriate medium and small traditional royalty publishing houses. Time spent researching these publishers is definitely time well spent.

Advantages of Working with a Small to Medium-size Publisher

- You pay no publishing costs.
- You are validated as an author.
- Your book will most likely have a longer shelf life than if you go with a large publisher.
- The publisher will participate to varying degrees in promoting the book.

- The publisher may have access to important promotional avenues such as bookstore sales.
- Smaller publishers seem more loyal to their authors.

Disadvantages of Working with a Small to Medium-size Publisher

- The publisher is less well known—there may be minimal name recognition.
- You could wait for a year or more before seeing your book in print.
- Author/publisher communication is sometimes a problem.
- You must rely on the publisher to ship your books to bookstores for signings or to get copies to you in time for a book festival.
- There's a greater chance that a new publishing company will go out of business.
- You are expected to promote your own book.
- You earn only a small percentage on sales.

DEVELOP YOUR "C" LIST OF PUBLISHING OPTIONS

Pay-to-Publish Company

You could pay a company to produce your book. While there used to be few subsidy publishers and few people used them, there are now at least 100 of them, and thousands of people publish through them each year. But with advanced technology and an increase in new authors, the paradigm has changed considerably. And the contracts come in a wide variety of patterns. In most cases, you own the copyright and, depending on the company, you may get some assistance with promotion. Different companies offer different packages. I know of one co-publisher who becomes a royalty publisher after the author has sold 1,000 copies of his book.

The general description of a pay-to-publish company is a subsidy publisher that uses digital technology to produce books when you need them. This is a popular means of book publication these days. Some pay-to-publish companies try to confuse you by advertising that they are royalty publishers or that they will help you to self-publish your book. I urge authors to exercise caution when considering a subsidy publisher. I can't stress enough the importance of heads up research before signing any publishing contract. Read Chapter Three for a more detailed explanation and evaluation of this modern day publishing model.

Advantages of the Pay-to-Publish Company

- You are guaranteed that your book will be published.
- You'll have a book in weeks rather than months or years.
- Your book stays alive for as long as you promote it.
- If you sell enough copies, you may be able to interest a traditional royalty publisher in your book.
- You don't have to store boxes and boxes of books.

Disadvantages of Pay-to-Publish Companies

- It is generally costly.
- Yours may be one of the countless books that are riddled with errors.
- Your book won't be welcome in bookstores unless you can bring in enough customers to warrant them carrying it. And this is enormously more difficult than you might think.
- You may be asked to sign away the rights to your book for a period of time. (One such publisher holds your copyright for seven years.)
- You are expected to do the majority of the book promotion with very little help. What help you do request from the company will cost you.
- Some reviewers and booksellers still reject pay-to-publish books.
- Books are often priced above market value making them difficult for you to sell.

Self-Publishing

You establish a company through which to produce your book. You obtain your ISBN (International Standard Book Number), barcode, etc. You arrange for the page layout and cover design work. You hire a printer. You accept total responsibility for writing, producing, and marketing your book. (Learn how to publish your own book in Chapter Eleven.)

Advantages of Self-Publishing

- You'll definitely see your book in print.
- You could have a product in weeks instead of months or years.

- You are in charge of every aspect of production and sales.
- You can keep the book alive for as long as you promote it.
- You have a book to show around to publishers. If it does well, you may land a royalty publishing contract.
- You keep all of the profits.
- You have legitimate tax breaks.

Disadvantages of Self-Publishing

- Self-publishing can be costly.
- You are in charge of every aspect of production and sales; promoting a book is extremely hard work.
- You are also the distributions manager, shipping clerk, PR person, and bookkeeper.
- Some bookstore managers and book reviewers may shun your book.
- Unless you use POD (print-on-demand—digital) printing technology, you may have to store boxes and boxes of books.

The Ebook

An ebook is a digital book posted online for consumers to purchase and print out, download onto a handheld electronic device, or read online. While some feel that ebooks are the wave of the future, others do not believe that their time has come. Keep an eye on the growth of ebooks at the International Digital Publishing Forum: http://www.idpf.org.

Advantages to Publishing an Ebook

- There is no or very little cost. Generally $0-99.
- You do not have to store or ship books.
- You can make changes to an ebook at any time.
- You keep all of the profits, except for any royalties you pay to web hosts of sites where the ebook is sold.
- There are more support companies than ever before for authors of ebooks who want to convert them to Kindle, Nook, MS Reader, iPad, etc. or who want to distribute them through wider channels.

Disadvantages to Publishing an Ebook

- They may not be well received within the genre or topic of your book.
- You may not bc taken seriously as an author when you produce only ebooks. (Self-publishing of print and ebooks will be discussed in Chapter Eleven.)

How to Meet a Publisher Face-to-Face

There are numerous writers' conferences, book festivals, and trade shows held all over the world throughout the year. Many writers attend these events as a way to meet publishers. Some conference organizers will arrange a meeting for you with a publisher for an additional fee. This is as much to the publisher's benefit as the author's. Publishers are as eager to find good material as you are to locate a publisher for your project.

To locate conferences near you,

- Do an Internet search. Type in "writer's (or writers') conference," "publishing conference," "writing conference," "writer's (or writers') conference California," "writers' (or writer's) conference Virginia," etc.
- Check with your local arts council, library, or writers groups for conferences held in your area.
- Keep an eye on the arts section of your local newspaper.
- Read writing/publishing-related magazines and newsletter.
- Access writers' conference directories:
  http://writing.shawguides.com
  http://www.allconferences.com
  http://www.newpages.com/writing-conferences.

How to Get the Most from a Meeting with a Publisher

Your first introduction to a publisher is usually through a letter or an email. And every writing professional will advise you to make a good first impression. This is even more crucial when you have that rare opportunity to meet a publisher face-to-face. I'm not trying to make you so nervous that you faint at the mere sight of the publisher. But I strongly encourage you to give this opportunity your best shot. How?

Before the event:

- Find out which publishers will be at the conference.
- Do a little research to learn what type of books they publish and what titles they have published lately.
- Plan to approach or meet with only those publishers that are appropriate for your project.
- Prepare and practice reciting a thirty-second commercial—a brief description of your project. (More about this below.)
- Create a promo package including a color image of your proposed book cover, a brief synopsis or overview of the book, and information about yourself. What is your writing background, why are you the person to write this book, and what is your platform? (Read more about platform in Chapter Six.) Provide your complete contact information including website and email address. The more compact the package, the better. I recommend creating a six by nine postcard.

Make a Good First Impression

When you meet a publisher, be gracious and professional not timid and desperate. Come across as a potential business partner with an excellent product, not an emotional writer who will crumble in a pool of tears if you don't find a publisher.

Every conference is operated a little differently. You might get anywhere from sixty seconds to twenty minutes with a publisher. Whether you are fortunate enough to have an audience with a publisher or you just happen to get a brief opportunity, the best advice I can offer is, be prepared.

When you finally manage that chance (or planned) meeting with a publisher, use your time wisely. Introduce yourself and your project with clarity. Make it interesting. Describe your proposed book through your intriguing thirty-second commercial.

Initiate questions and respond succinctly.

Before ending the conversation, hand the publisher your promo postcard to take with him.

Have the handout ready to hand out. Don't ruin a perfectly professional moment by rummaging through your purse or briefcase in search of the material. As I keep saying, preparation is key.

Your Thirty-Second Commercial

Some publishing coaches recommend that authors develop a one or two-sentence description of their book—something that they can recite should someone ask. This is a good idea for those brief opportunities with a potential publisher, agent, or customer. As you will learn in a subsequent chapter, this brief description is also valuable for the author during the book proposal stage and when writing the back cover copy. But a prepared thirty-second commercial gives you even more marketing ammunition.

Why should you develop a canned speech? While you may love talking about your book, it's not always appropriate to carry on and on about it. You may only have limited time to make a pitch and you definitely want to make a positive impression by sharing only the most pertinent points.

A short, prepared speech can be used at a class reunion or business meeting where you have snippets of time to discourse with classmates or colleagues. If you should be fortunate enough to have an audience with a publisher or even talk to a publisher by phone, you want to be ready with a brief description of your book.

It isn't as easy as it sounds to create and rehearse a thirty-second commercial. But it is an excellent exercise.

Two Examples of Thirty-Second Elevator Speeches

"*Spanner's Journey Into the No Time Zone* is a spiritual fantasy chapter book for children ages eight to eleven. Spanner, a spotted zebra, grew up as an outcast, leaving him somewhat naïve and vulnerable. All he wanted was to be loved. One night, through a strange incident, he finds himself catapulted into a series of unexpected adventures during which he meets Kakakaka, the lizard; Yamu, the eagle; and MaKa, the snail. Each one uses clever riddles, innuendos, and illusions that ultimately lead Spanner to greater understanding. Slowly, he begins to realize how to attain the elusive love and happiness he so desperately desires." (Author, Alexandra Monique)

"*Walking Through Jello* is a memoir. It's the story of my 'coming out.' When I turned fifty, I decided that it was time to grow up. My philosophy of life became to do as much as possible outside my comfort zone that was fun, reasonable, and safe. This new and daring perspective served to release me from depression and thoughts of suicide and transform me into a joyous woman filled with insatiable curiosity and the courage to satisfy it. This is the story of my journey from dependency and timidity to freedom and adventure." (Author, Paula Spellman)

Can you see how each of these descriptions would create interest and curiosity and elicit questions which would lead to a deeper conversation about these books?

How to Work a Book Festival So It Works for You

You can also meet publishers at book festivals and book trade shows. The larger the event, the more publishers in attendance. You probably won't meet major players in the publishing world at hometown book fairs and festivals. But there are almost always small to medium-size publishing houses represented at these events. Book Expo America is the largest and most prominent such event here in the U.S., and it is held in late May of each year sometimes on the east coast and sometimes in the west. http://www.bookexpoamerica.com.

A book festival or trade show is where authors, publishers, writing/publishing organization leaders, and booksellers rent booths for the day or the weekend to promote their books, their companies, and themselves. It is a great place to meet publishers, and it also provides a good opportunity to network with other authors.

If you have a book in the works and you want to meet publishers at a book festival in your area, plan ahead. Learn who will be there. Find this information published in your local newspaper or online at the festival website. As a last resort, pick up a copy of the festival program and booth map the morning of the event. Sit down somewhere with a latte and a muffin and study the program. Read about each publisher and note those who are likely candidates for your book. If in doubt as to what the publisher produces, visit the booth and see what they're promoting. If this publisher doesn't produce books in your genre, ask him or her for references.

Visit author booths. Ask who published their books, if they like working with the publisher, and how their books are selling. Sometimes an author is embarrassed to talk about book sales. A better question might be, "Are you pleased with the results of your publisher's efforts?"

A festival booth can get busy. Never lose sight of the fact that the reason this publisher or this author is there is to sell books. If you approach him or her to talk about *your* book, please be considerate of their time. I love talking with freelance writers, authors, and publishers who visit my booths at book festivals. But I resent people who try to monopolize my time for more than a few minutes when there are potential customers attempting to browse.

If you have the opportunity to make contact with a publisher at a book festival or trade show, state your polished and rehearsed spiel. Be prepared to respond to a few questions. Ask him or her if you can send your manuscript or book proposal. Before you exit, pick up the publisher's business card or a brochure and ask if you can leave him or her some of your information.

When you get home, jot this publisher a note, send an email or, if you were invited to do so, send your book proposal or manuscript with a note reminding him that he met you at the Austin Book Festival or the Central Coast Festival of Books.

By now, you're getting the idea that authorship is not as easy and straightforward as simply sitting down and writing a book. There are crucial decisions to be made, thus the need for the information and perspective that fill the pages of this book. As I tell hopeful authors, publishing is not an extension of your writing.

A major new player in the publishing game is the pay-to-publish service. To find out what they bring to the table, read on.

Recommended Reading:

Writers Market (Writer's Digest Books). A new edition of this publisher/magazine directory is published each September.

The Good, the Bad, and the Ugly Facts About Pay-to-Publish Companies

They are called POD publishers, fee-based POD publishers, POD partnership publishers, POD subsidy publishers, and "self-publishing" companies. Many professionals now refer to them by a title I coined: pay-to-publish companies. Who are they, where did they come from, and what do they do?

First, you should understand the distinction between POD publishers and POD technology. POD stands for print-on-demand—a digital process used to print books and other materials one product at a time. While companies using offset printing techniques generally won't take on jobs of less than 1,000 copies, those using POD technology might print as few or as many as you want—from 1 to 999 or more. Some traditional royalty publishers use POD technology for their book projects. Many independent publishers (self-published authors) use POD printing companies. The major benefits are a quick turnaround and fewer books to store. The downside is you generally pay more per book, thus decreasing your profit margin.

So a basic difference between the old subsidy publisher and the new pay-to-publish company is the printing method.

What about quality? While some believe that the quality of digitally printed books is not as good when it comes to images, the overall quality of digital printing has improved considerably in recent years. One measure of this is the fact that few booksellers continue to reject books on the basis that they were printed using digital technology.

The History of the Pay-to-Publish Company

The new wave of pay-to-publish companies came about in the late 1990s. With the event of digital technology, a few innovative businesspersons took the print-on-demand concept, linked it with the old subsidy publishing model and started a new sort of company. Others soon followed. These forward-thinking businessmen and women began promoting the heck out of their companies, and they were promptly noticed. They succeeded in opening doors for hopeful authors who might otherwise never realize their dreams of publishing a book.

Within less than a decade, the number of pay-to-publish companies has increased significantly. Dehanna Bailee lists over one hundred such companies in her free access pay-to-publish database. (Link below.)

Some pay-to-publish contracts trick the author into believing that he is entering into a self-publishing agreement. No, no, no. Self-publishing means that you obtain the ISBN and barcode, you hire the page and cover designer, you arrange for the printer. You are in charge. It is your publishing company and you reap the benefits. The only similarity between signing with a pay-to-publish company and self-publishing is that you are responsible for promoting, selling, and distributing your books. (Read more about self-publishing in Chapter Eleven.)

Is POD Getting a Bad Rap?

As recently as four years ago, booksellers had a policy against carrying any digitally produced books and reviewers would not review them. This policy came about in an effort to create a distinction between pay-to-publish and self-published books and traditionally published books. As technology improved and more and more traditional publishers began to use digital technology, however, the stigma began to lift.

Elizabeth Burton is executive editor at Zumaya Publications, a traditional royalty publishing house that uses POD technology. She told me in 2006 that the publishing scourge had affected her company's ability to do business. She explained, "Local bookstores refuse to even take our books on consignment for no other reason than the way they were printed. We've been told that our books lack editing—by people who not only haven't read any of them, but refuse to do so. Why? Because they believe that POD books are written by people not good enough to get a *real* publisher and are badly prepared for printing."

Burton set out on a mission. She told me then, "I'm trying all sorts of things to persuade bookstore owners that they CAN stock one or two copies of our books and they should because ours are of comparable quality to anything they'll get from New York—and, in some cases, better."

Important transitions have occurred within the publishing industry and now Burton reports: "Since 2006, the mainstream publishers have embraced POD (digital printing) as a more cost-effective way to handle backlists. As a result, more and more bookstores are agreeing to stock copies of books by local and regional authors regardless of how they were printed. It's fair to say that at least some of the stigma that kept 'POD books' on the sidelines is wearing away."

Since pay-to-publish companies came into being, there have been hundreds, if not thousands of complaints launched against many of them. I believe this is primarily an author issue. Few newbie authors take the time and exert the effort necessary in order to truly understand the publishing industry or even a single publishing agreement. This is why I strongly advise, buyer beware—buyer be well informed. Before entering into any publishing contract, know what to expect and what is expected of you from start to finish.

If you are contemplating hiring a pay-to-publish company, I highly recommend that you access Bailee's database. She lists the features, services, and costs of around 100 such companies. I urge hopeful authors to research a company before signing with them. Bailee makes it easy for you to make important comparisons. Go to http://dehanna.com/database.html. I also urge you to read Mark Levine's book, *The Fine Print of Self-Publishing* in which he rates and ranks some of the largest fee-based, "self-publishing" companies.

Generally, pay-to-publish companies will accept any manuscript submitted to them with the possible exception of pornographic or racist material. Having your manuscript accepted by one of these companies is not necessarily a statement of its value or worth. This premise was tested once by a disappointed pay-to-publish author. She deliberately submitted an unfinished, inferior manuscript with numerous organizational flaws and blatant errors to a well-known pay-to-publish company and promptly received a letter of acceptance. It read, in essence, "We are happy to inform you that your wonderful manuscript has been accepted for publication with XYZ Publishing."

The majority of pay-to-publish companies do nothing to promote your book. Think about it: Once you've paid a fee to have your book produced, what is the incentive for the publisher to promote it? Most of these companies have add-on packages inviting you to pay extra for promotional services, however. One author claims that he paid his pay-to-publish service $4,500 for three months of promotion. To say that he was unhappy with the results of this service is an understatement. "I didn't even break even," he laments.

> No matter what type of publisher you land, you must promote your own book. An author's ignorance of the book promotion process will keep even a good book from the public eye.

According to Robert Olmsted at Dan River Press in Maine, "Anyone with a job can have a book published, but having a book published is not what authors need. Readers are what authors need. Paying a subsidy does not get an author even one reader."

There is a wide array of publishing contracts issued by the large variety of pay-to-publish houses. Typically, for your money, you get an International Standard Book Number (in the pay-to-publish company name), barcode, standard page layout and cover design package, printing, and a percentage of each book sold. Generally, you will be asked for additional money if you want editing services, custom page and/or cover design, special formatting, promotional packages, and the printing of any graphics and photographs, as well as any corrections or changes needed along the way.

As I said, this is a typical scenario. There are numerous creative options. Along with many other professionals, I urge you—before you sign a contract with a pay-to-publish company, make sure that you understand it. For example, some of these contracts contain statements similar to this one: "We will make your books available to bookstores nationwide." Sounds good, right? But it is more than a little misleading. What you'd like to think it means is that your book will be shipped by the truckloads to bookstores everywhere. What it actually means is that if a bookstore manager contacts the publisher requesting a book like yours, they would certainly tell him or her about your book. They'll fulfill bookstore orders, should a customer request a copy. But no one will request a copy of a book they've never heard of.

At least one pay-to-publish company charges $800 extra for what they call "returnable insurance." The managers of this company are convincing authors that all they need in order to get their books into bookstores is proof of this returnable insurance. But, trust me, unless you do something to generate a lot of bookstore sales, your subsidy published book will not be available in bookstores anywhere.

I did my own survey involving a cross section of bookstore managers to find out how valuable the returnable insurance is to an author. Apparently, not very. While most of the managers I spoke with appreciate the returns concept, this is not enticement enough to sway them to accept books by authors who lack a following.

One independent bookstore owner told me that most pay-to-publish companies with a return policy do not pay cash money for returns, they offer credit. He said, "The last thing I want from a subsidy publisher is credit."

How Much Does It Cost?

My research shows that the price you can expect to pay for a basic package with a pay-to-publish company averages around $800. You may also be required to pay as much as seventy-two percent of the cover price for the books you purchase. Yes, for your own books. With this in mind, you would have to sell roughly 100 copies of a $20.95 book in order to break even. According to figures from some of the most well-known pay-to-publish companies, their authors average just 100 books sold, total.

Of course, your publishing experience could vary dramatically from the average. The highest price I found for the services of a pay-to-publish company was $7,200. The cheapest price is $120, and this includes ten books, which is ideal for folks who just want to produce a memoir for family members.

Most of these companies have several add-on services you can purchase. Many authors refuse to pay a pay-to-publish company the extra fee for editing services. This is fine with me if, instead, you hire your own excellent book editor. The going rate for editing services through pay-to-publish companies is $30–$60 per hour or $5–$7 per page. Hire your own editor and you'll pay about the same. I've heard from numerous authors who were extremely disappointed with their pay-to-publish company's editing services. One author told me that she feels she paid editing fees for amateur proofreading skills. But her disappointment didn't end there. She was eager to have this book published without spending additional money, so she okayed the edits. She says, "When the proof copy came to me for my approval, it was full of the original errors."

Keep in mind that those who own pay-to-publish companies aren't in the business of selling books. Their main focus is selling their services.

One of my clients decided to go with a pay-to-publish company. At first, he was happy with the contract and the publisher. Everyone was treating him well. He sings a different tune now. He had practically single-handedly sold the first run of 1,000 copies of his book, but the publishing house was not paying the agreed upon royalties. He said, "When it came time for them to start paying royalties, they were all of a sudden unavailable. They're breaking every clause in the contract. It has been a nightmare trying to deal with them. Thank heavens my contract is up and I can move on. But if I do, I wonder if I'll ever get paid. I figure they owe me around $6,000, but they've only paid me $400 so far."

There are some excellent books produced by fee-based publishers—there's no doubt about that. But many of the worst books on the market also come through these channels. Let's examine who's to blame. I fault a company that produces books indiscriminately. But I also hold careless, uninformed authors responsible. It's a shame to see what these combined efforts have contributed to (or taken away from) literature. They've tainted the reputation of all pay-to-publish and self-published books.

What Is the Lure of the Pay-to-Publish Company?

Why are so many people hiring publishers for their book projects? There are many reasons. Most inexperienced authors don't know how to find or approach traditional royalty publishers. Some aren't aware of the numbers of publishers seeking quality manuscripts. Others just grab the first opportunity that comes along, and pay-to-publish companies are out there advertising in all of the most prominent places. Hopeful authors, who notice these ads in prestigious magazines, newsletters, and at the top of the Google search list, see no reason to look any further for a publisher.

Pay-to-publish companies make the process of publishing seem easy. This is extremely attractive to an author who has just spent several months or a couple of years researching and writing a book. Suddenly, you have found someone who believes in your project, seemingly, as much as you do. And they vow to handle every little detail of production for you. All you have to do is send money. Most hopeful authors find the publishing maze all too overwhelming, and the pay-to-publish model seems like an easy way to approach success. In the end, many authors are left feeling compromised and disillusioned. But it's not necessarily because the pay-to-publish representative did anything wrong. It has more to do with the author's ignorance and unrealistic expectations. Most authors, who are facing the world of publishing for the first time, neglect to do sufficient research.

One first-time author sent his novel manuscript to just six traditional royalty publishers. When he didn't receive a contract within a short time, he went a different route. He says, "I found one of the 'self-publishing' companies online. I did not research at all. They were so very nice upfront. After they had my money, it all changed. Why did I choose this route? I had never heard of this concept before, and I thought it was the answer to my prayers."

This author now has numerous complaints. He says, "They charged me $300 extra for an editor that I thought was part of the deal. She did only a mediocre job, and it took her so long to complete her work that it delayed publication of my book by four weeks. They ruined my pictures, my font, my dedication page, and my about-me page. They left out pictures and started text half way down the page. They left blank pages in the middle of the book, they changed font style mid-sentence, they put commas in the middle of the title on the cover of the book, and they put the title in quotes. The headings and footers are not coherent with the text. It's a mess. Now they want me to pay to make the corrections."

This brings up another problem among many new authors. As writers, we are usually pretty good with words. We know how to use our favorite word processing programs. But how many of us are also adept at page layout and design? There's a technique to preparing a manuscript for a printer. I don't do Adobe PageMaker. Nor do I know how to operate my Microsoft Word page design program. Since I know there are definite tried and true methods of manuscript preparation, I always hire someone to design my books and to communicate accurately and expertly with my choice of printers. I wonder how many of the numerous design problems I hear about in pay-to-publish books occur because of author ignorance and miscommunication.

Is the pay-to-publish concept here to stay? Probably. But I predict that there will be fewer such companies in the future. Those companies that survive will refine and polish their services, and it could also follow that more booksellers, distributors, and reviewers will begin accepting books on merit, not by publishing status.

When Is Pay-to-Publish the Right Choice?

I suggest using a fee-based publisher ONLY if:

- You have some understanding of the publishing industry.
- You know what is expected of you once you become a published author.
- Your project is simple—without photographs, graphs, and tables, for example.
- You completely understand and agree with the contract.
- You hire your own editor.
- You prepare the manuscript accurately for the printer and stay on top of quality control.
- You demand close communication with your company representative and the tech people and stay informed and aware each step of the way.
- You have developed a marketing plan for your book which you are willing and able to implement.
- Your book is pretty much non-publishable through traditional channels.

I met a man with a basically unpublishable project last year at a book festival. He was a first-time author with a novel that encompassed more than 800-pages. He asked me, "How do I find a publisher for this book?" I explained the basic process of locating a publisher and he said, "I've done that. I've even had publishers interested in my book, but they all tell me that I need to cut it down. They won't publish a book of this size by a first-time author. How can I find a publisher for my book?"

I said the obvious, "You cut it down."

He responded by saying, "I can't cut it down. That will ruin the story." And, again, he asked me to tell him how to go about finding a publisher for his novel.

This man is a candidate for a fee-based publisher, but I would recommend this only if he is willing to do his homework: spend at least a couple of weeks or months researching the publishing industry, study contracts from several pay-to-publish companies, have an intellectual properties attorney explain the contract to him, hire an experienced editor, hire an experienced page layout designer, and have a complete understanding of his responsibility for promoting the book.

I know some authors who use the pay-to-publish model quite successfully. One is a professional in her field and she periodically produces books related to her industry. She frequently speaks on topics within her expertise and promotes her books at the same time. She also promotes them through a company newsletter. She has accurately targeted the audience for her books and uses specific methods to reach them. When she needs a supply of books quickly and doesn't want to take on the responsibility of self-publishing, she hires a pay-to-publish company.

While writing is usually emotional, the decisions related to producing that book should be all business. It's when we are desperate to have our book published that we make mistakes. Lead with your head when looking at publishing options. Educate yourself. Become informed. Don't hand over your money and your future without knowing exactly what you're getting into.

Recommended Reading:

The ABC's of POD: A Beginner's Guide to Fee-Based Print-on-Demand Publishing by Dehanna Bailee (Blue Leaf Publications, 2005).

The Fine Print of Self-Publishing by Mark Levine (fourth edition Bascom Hill Publishing Group, 2011).

Bite the Bullet and Write a Book Proposal

I remember the first time a colleague suggested that I write a book proposal. I reacted as if she had asked me to jump out of an airplane. I saw no reason to write a book proposal when I had a perfectly good manuscript. I didn't know what a book proposal was. Just the term intimidated me. It sounded like way more work than I was willing to do.

I now understand the importance of a book proposal. And since that time many years ago, I have written over a dozen book proposals of my own, and I've helped write dozens more for clients.

> In today's extremely competitive publishing climate, a book proposal for a nonfiction manuscript is essential and is recommended for fiction.

Why Write a Book Proposal?

- Publishers and agents do not generally issue contracts based only on a great book idea or outstanding writing skills. The information in your book proposal helps them to more realistically evaluate whether your project is a good business investment.
- A well-organized, complete book proposal helps you to ascertain if you actually have a publishable book and, if not, how to revise it so you do.

- A well-researched book proposal helps you to understand your responsibilities as a published author and how you will ultimately and successfully fulfill them.
- A good book proposal is an extremely useful guide to writing the book.

Many a book has changed direction during the book proposal process. And this is a good thing! Forge ahead and write the book and you may miss an opportunity for success. It's through the book proposal process that you learn whether or not your great idea is truly a great idea. That's why I suggest writing a book proposal before writing the book.

The only possible exception to this "book proposal first" rule is the novel or a children's book. If there's a story bubbling up inside you and your muse is sitting on your shoulder shouting in your ear, go ahead and write. Take advantage of every creative moment. But don't forget to consider your audience. There may be steps you can take and editorial decisions you can make to enhance your readership base while in the writing process. So it is wise to at least understand what goes into a book proposal before you start writing the book.

A publisher or agent needs certain information to help him/her determine whether or not this book will make them some money. It may surprise you to know that not every publisher is looking for the next bestseller. Some are hoping to discover a stable, long-term product. One publisher told me during an interview last summer that he is interested in publishing books that he can be proud of.

Melvin Powers at Wilshire Book Company confided in me a couple of years ago by saying, "We are searching for books that will be successful in the marketplace. We need you to write what we can sell." But all publishers are not the same. Powers may be one of only a handful of publishers with outlets for your 60,000-word book on horsemanship, for example.

Harold Carstens over at Carstens Publications wouldn't know where to begin evaluating the market for a book on horses. But bring him a book on model airplanes or railroads and he'll know right away whether it is a valid product with a target audience.

Elder Signs Press doesn't accept nonfiction. But submit a proposal for a good science fiction book, fantasy, or dark fiction thriller and some assertive marketing ideas and they may issue you a contract.

A book proposal is the first step in writing a book. It is through the process of writing a book proposal that you will define the scope of your book and respond to the publishers' most burning questions.

The Query Letter—An Introduction

You may wonder, "Can't I write a query letter instead?" In a word, No! A query letter is your introduction. It's your first chance to make an excellent impression. But, I recommend creating a book proposal even before writing a query letter. Why? Most publishers, after reading your intriguing query letter, if they're interested, will request a book proposal. You want to have yours ready.

Why write a query letter when you have a polished book proposal? There's no need to unless the publisher requests it—and most do. Some publishers receive hundreds of submissions each month. Reading a query letter consumes a fraction of the time it would take to read an entire manuscript or even a proposal. This is why most publishers prefer to screen projects through the query process.

Whether you prepare the book proposal first or last, you will most likely, at some point, be required to write a one to two-page query letter. A successful and complete query includes a provocative or interesting lead (whet the publisher's appetite), a brief synopsis (describe your book and your target audience), a little about yourself (your writing experience, credits, and expertise in the area of your book topic), and something about your platform (how will you attract readers). As a next step, the publisher will most likely either request your book proposal or pass on your idea altogether. (Read more about writing a query letter in Chapter Nine.)

What Is a Book Proposal, Anyway?

A book proposal is a business plan for your book. A well-designed book proposal is a remarkable tool for convincing a publisher of your project's worth. Think of it as a sales pitch for your book.

I know, I know, you are not a salesperson, you are a writer. And the more pride you take in your writing ability and your great idea, the more difficult it becomes to land a publisher. A publisher may not be particularly interested in how well-written your book is—at least initially. His primary concern is marketability. What is the potential for sales? Is this a good investment of his time and money? Yes, publishers are more interested in their bottom line than in your talent or, by the way, your feelings. A publisher wants to know:

- Who and how wide spread is the audience for this book?
- How does your book compare with similar books already on the market?
- What makes this book different—better?
- How will you promote the book?
- What are your credentials (related to this topic and as a writer)?
- What is your platform—your way of attracting readers—your marketable skills—your connections?

A book proposal is pretty much required for a nonfiction book and requested more and more often for novels, books of poetry, and children's books. The only exception to this rule might be if you are a celebrity of note or you have a story that is guaranteed to be of major interest to the masses. By this, I mean a story that has already received national or international attention—something that is in the news and is of interest to many people.

A book proposal is also a useful tool for you. It helps you determine whether your original focus for your book is on target or if you need to tweak it a little. Here's how a book proposal can help you write the book:

- A book proposal will tell you whether you have a book at all. If you can't write a synopsis or come up with chapter-by-chapter summaries, you don't have a handle on your book idea, yet.
- A book proposal will give you information about your competition. You might find that there are numerous books on your choice of subjects, but none covering a certain niche aspect of it. Having done that important research, you might decide to refocus your book and, in turn, create a more viable product.
- A book proposal helps you to clarify the audience for your book and define the extent of potential buyers.
- An effective book proposal is a guide for writing the book.

- A book proposal helps you to better understand the scope of your book so you can more succinctly and successfully pitch the book to agents, publishers and promote it to consumers.
- Through the book proposal process, you will become more educated about the publishing industry.

The first book proposal is the hardest one to write. Once you break through the barriers of fear, insecurity, and ignorance, you've created the mold and future proposals will go together more easily.

The Nonfiction Book Proposal

A nonfiction book proposal consists of the following:

- Cover letter introducing your proposal package. Generally, one page.
- Title page. One page.
- Table of contents (for the proposal—not for the book itself). One page.
- Synopsis or overview of the book. One and a half to around four pages.
- Marketing section. (Identify your target audience and reveal strategies for reaching them.) Two to six paragraphs.
- Promotional ideas. (How do you suggest this book be promoted and what will you do to promote it?) One to three pages.
- Details about your platform. (How widespread is your following—people who know you as an expert in your field or as an author? What connections do you have? What promotional activities or programs do you have in place?) Use as much space as it takes. Impress the publisher.
- Market analysis or comparison of competitive works. One or one and a half pages. (Compare your manuscript with five or six similar books.)
- About the author. (What makes you the best person to write this book?) One to three paragraphs. Be sure to add your list of published books and books in the works.
- Chapter summaries. Approximately 100–400 words per chapter.
- Sample chapters (if requested).
- Samples of illustrations, photographs, etc. (if appropriate). Also include a list of the experts you will be interviewing and the companies, agencies, etc. you will be researching for this book.

The Fiction Book Proposal

There are fewer parts to a book proposal for a novel and a children's book. You will include:

- Cover letter. (Generally, one page.)
- Title Page. (One page.)
- Synopsis or overview. (Two to four pages.)
- Promotional plan, including your platform.
- Market Analysis (optional). If you can, make a case for the popularity of books like yours.
- About the author.
- Endorsements. (Some publishers request endorsements—testimonials about your proposed book from experts in the field. In the case of a novel, this might be experienced, well-known authors or mentors.)
- Sample chapters, if requested, or the first 100 (or so) pages.

Presentation and Formatting

While it might be tempting to fancy up your book proposal so it stands apart from the rest of those in the perceived slush pile, most professionals advise against this. You want your book proposal to stand out from the rest, but your focus should not be on packaging. The way to get the publisher's attention is with a professional presentation, not frills and fireworks.

Many publishers now accept query letters, proposals, and manuscripts via email. Before clicking "send," check the publisher's submission guidelines. Does he want the proposal embedded in the email or sent as an attachment?

Be cognizant of what you put in the subject line. Publishers who accept email queries and proposals will often indicate (in their submission guidelines) what to put in the subject line. It might be, "Requested Proposal," "Query re: book on car repair," etc. If you have had previous communication with this publisher and he or she knows who you are, and that you are going to send him something, your name might be appropriate—"Charlotte David's Military Fiction Proposal," for example.

For the proposal sent via the post office, use plain white 8.5 × 11 paper, typed, double-spaced on one side of the page. Some experts suggest double-spacing every page of a book proposal except the synopsis. I single-space lists: listings of my published books and books in the works, for example. And the cover letter is single-spaced. For greater reading ease, use 12-point Times New Roman and leave 1 to 1 ½ inch margins.

While it is okay to use a paperclip or a binder clip to hold the pages of a book proposal together when submitting it, publishers do not like staples. Use one paperclip or binder clip to hold the entire proposal. Do not separate and clip the various sections of the proposal.

Number the pages. It helps the publisher to keep the pages in order if you type your name and the title of your book at the top left hand corner of each page.

Make a neat and organized presentation. Do not paste post-it notes all over the proposal with arrows for the publisher to follow. Do not write in the margins and do not draw on the pages of the book proposal.

Your primary concern in preparing a book proposal is that you conform to the form and style that the particular publisher has requested and that it is presented in the most convenient mode possible.

How to Write a Cover Letter

The cover letter identifies and introduces your book proposal package. Use your letterhead. If you don't have letterhead, type your name and contact information at the top of the page. Include your website address (if applicable to your writing skill and/or the topic of your book). Date the letter and address it to the appropriate editor/publisher. (Read more about approaching a publisher in Chapter Nine.)

Your cover letter should:

- be single-spaced.
- remind the publisher if he/she requested your proposal.
- describe your book in one or two paragraphs.
- introduce you as the author and include a brief list of your qualifications for writing this book. (Or mention that this information is included on page eight, for example, of the proposal.)
- mention your target audience (optional, as this is covered in another section).
- say whether the manuscript is completed or not. If not, what is the projected delivery date? (When do you think you could submit the complete manuscript?)

- ask for what you want—"Please review the book proposal and let me know if you would like to see sample chapters or the complete manuscript."
- be signed by you.
- note enclosures by listing each part of the book proposal.

Sample Cover Letters

This cover letter reflects a proposal for a spiritual self-help book. The author explains the purpose and function of the book, how it will serve readers, and how she came to write the book. She offers a peek into her credentials and a little about why she is the right person to write this book. Her backstory related to a well-publicized and tragic case gives her project added interest. Finally, she indicates that the book is completed, and she directs the publisher to other sections of the proposal for the additional information he will need.

Date

First/Last Name
Publishing company name
Address
City/State/Zip

Dear Ms. (or Mr.) [Last Name]:

Enclosed please find the proposal for my book, *The 7 Laws of Inner Peace: How to Have What You Want Without Struggle or Conflict.*

I teach conflict and problem-solving workshops and I use *The 7 Laws of Inner Peace* process, which is featured in this book, to help clients and students choose peaceful solutions in even their most conflicted situations. This is a book about change. It is designed as a guide to help readers expand and balance their personal power so that their greatest hopes and dreams can come true. I frequently tell my students and clients, "As your level of inner peace increases, so does your satisfaction and joyfulness." It is through the ability to experience inner peace that our desires can become reality.

As a lawyer, I might seem an unlikely author for a book such as this. In fact it was my affiliation with the highly publicized and controversial Terri Schiavo right-to-die case that prompted me to write it. The inner conflict I experienced after our first big win in court prompted me to close my law practice, leave my law partner/husband, and set up housekeeping in the mountains of Colorado. I embarked upon a search to find my own truth and discovered *The 7 Laws of Inner Peace*. For example, the fourth law, *The Law of Alignment,* showed itself to me while I was meditating in an airliner 30,000 feet in the air. One law became crystal clear to me during my only visit with comatose Terri Schiavo. While I didn't comprehend the revelation at the time, the awareness I experienced that day led to my eventual understanding of the first law, *The Law of Unity.*

Throughout this book, I share *The 7 Laws of Inner Peace* and how they came to be. Each chapter includes guidelines and exercises so that the reader can easily adapt these laws to start the process for improving his or her life forever. Through these exercises, readers can shift from conflicted to peaceful, from enraged to giving, from fearful to loving. By using *The 7 Laws of Inner Peace* process, individuals can experience healthier relationships, more normal stress levels, greater career and personal successes, more positive outlooks, and anything else they desire.

Each *Law* is accentuated by a real-life story illustrating how others used the law to change their lives for the better. Probably the most poignant stories are those related to my emotional struggles during the Schiavo case.

Information about my platform and marketing ideas are on page 8 of the proposal.

Please review the enclosed proposal and let me know if you'd like to see the completed manuscript.

Sincerely,
Constance d'Angelis
Enclosures: Synopsis, Market Analysis, Marketing Section, Platform, About the Author, Chapter Summaries.

The following cover letter adequately introduces the subject of this regional historical memoir, his significance to the history of Southern California, and the author's connection to the story. The author gives credibility to the material used in this book and suggests that there could be additional books to follow. He describes his ideas for designing the book and compares it to one that this publisher produced. He gives a completion date for the book, invites the publisher to become involved in this project, and lists the major parts to the book proposal, which he has enclosed.

Date

Name
Company
Address
City/State

Dear Ms. [Last Name]:

Enclosed please find the book proposal for *Coming of Age in Early California: The Adventures of Ike Frazee.*

Isaac (Ike) Jenkinson Frazee was my great grandfather. Not only have I inherited volumes of writings by and about this remarkable man, I've spent years researching his life. This book traces Ike's early life from the age of fifteen, when he accompanied his family from Indiana to Riverside, California through his mid-twenties, when he and his young bride settled in the wilderness near what is now Escondido to raise a family.

This is the true story of a young man's life and travels in nineteenth century Southern California, told through his own journals, poetry, and sketches. Ike Frazee, who's writing and artistic talents are clearly evident in these early journals, would later make important contributions to Southern California as a respected artist, poet, dramatist, and Indian authority. Today Isaac Frazee is remembered as a high-minded, slightly eccentric visionary whose art, poetry, and personal philosophy helped to shape the cultural life of Southern

California during the late nineteenth and early twentieth centuries. He was one of this state's first local artists.

While this book contains some narrative and a fascinating memoir by his beloved wife, Bettie, it features Ike's journals written in the late 1800s during three important stages of his life—life as a college student in 1875, what it was like to be a ranch hand in the wild West, and his solo trip to Yosemite on horseback. As you can see, *Coming of Age in Early California* will finally put many important historical documents under one cover, and will refer the scholar to other sources of Frazee documents and memorabilia, many of which are housed at the Huntington Library.

I envision this book measuring eight by ten in order to accommodate Ike's drawings and poetry on the outer edges of the pages. In size, this book would resemble the *Voyage to California: The Journal of Lucy Kendall Herrick,* published in 1998 by your press.

In preparing this proposal for you, it has become obvious that this might only be the beginning. I have enough material to write two additional volumes; one, perhaps, featuring a more detailed account of family life in the Pamoosa Valley castle and the famous Indian Pageant that Ike wrote and presented at his wilderness home. The second volume might focus on the events that led up to establishing the first California community of local artists.

Coming of Age is more than two-thirds complete. We could submit the entire manuscript to you within six months of your request.

I look forward to working with you to produce this book.

Sincerely,
Craig Walker
Enclosures: Overview of the book, About the Author, Marketing Ideas, Chapter Outline.

How to Use These Samples

Having shared these actual cover letters, let me say that yours might be quite similar or very different, depending on the subject matter of your project, the genre, your focus, your background, your motivation for writing it, the material you have collected, and many other factors. When you look at examples, such as I've provided throughout this book, make sure that you do so from an information/configuration perspective. Don't try to copy the terminology—it may not be appropriate for your project. Avoid attempting to follow these examples too closely in style and format. What you want to take away from the examples is the purpose of the document/letter and how you can best portray your book project using these as guides.

The Title Page

Include a title page similar to a title page in a published book. Type the title of the book centered about one-third of the way down the page. Below that, type, "by" and your name. At the bottom of the page, type your projected word count.

Okay, I know what you're thinking, "Hey lady, how do I know how many words I will have until I write the book?" This brings up another of your responsibilities—determining the appropriate word count for the type of book you're writing based on the publisher's requirements.

Change the projected number of words in your book proposal according to the guidelines of the particular publisher you are contacting. If ABC Publishing is looking for novels of between 60,000 and 80,000 words, estimate your projected word count at around 75,000. If this is the publisher who requests your manuscript, you will write it to conform.

Steps to Selecting a Perfect Title

A title is extremely important so take your time in choosing one.

> While intriguing titles sells novels, a nonfiction title should define the book.

When contemplating your title, think about the audience you want to attract. Let's say that your book features the practice of dressing dogs. Yes, there are people everywhere who purchase large wardrobes for their dogs and delight in dressing them for outings and occasions. If you want to attract people who already dress their dogs and people who might if they knew more about it, *Doggie Dress-Up* is probably a good title. If your book is a collection of stories about Hollywood celebrities who dress their pets, you could call it, *The Best Dressed Dogs in the West.*

If you want to get cute, clever, crazy with your title and choose one that isn't very descriptive, let your subtitle do the necessary work. For example, you may desperately want to use the title, *For Heaven's Sake.* You would need a subtitle to explain what this book is about. Is it a religious novel, a book of surprising facts, a book of poetry or, perhaps, a collection of sayings and where they came from? How about choosing a subtitle such as, "100 of Your Grandparents' Favorite Lines," "Little Known Facts and Fables," or "A Memoir—My Life as a Quaker."

Protect yourself. Before writing your title in stone, check book titles that are already in use. This ought to be fairly easy now with the advent of the Internet and our friend Google. You can do a quick search at amazon.com. But the best gauge of what's in print and what's soon to be in print are current editions of *Books in Print* (BIP) and *Forthcoming Books in Print.* I spoke with a representative at RR Bowker, the company that produces these directories. He said that the best way to view these books for this purpose is at your local library or by using the library's remote access for patrons. If you want to check the BIP database for your own titles occasionally, you can do that at http://www.booksinprint.com.

You should also check your perfect title to make sure the words or terms you want to use in your title have not been trademarked. Learn more about trademark searches here: http://www.uspto.gov.

Titles for Fiction Books

Novelists have more creative license when it comes to selecting a title. However, I still recommend that you consider your readers. You, too, want to attract the appropriate audience. If yours is a mystery, include the word *mystery* in your title or subtitle. If it falls under the chick lit category, use a title or subtitle indicating that this is a girly story. How? Presumably your book features issues of interest to women—romance, comfort food, buying and owning shoes, collecting designer handbags, dating men, and so forth. Make sure that this is evident in the title. Here are some titles for current chick lit books: *The Guy I'm Not Dating, The*

Secret Life of Becky Miller, Undomestic Goddess, and let's don't forget *Bridget Jones's Diary.*

Some authors of historical fiction include a date in their title to show the era. Or they use terms signifying a historical time period or place. Others use subtitles to show genre. For example, *Poison: A Novel of the Renaissance; The Last Illusion, A Molly Murphy Mystery* or *Escape: A Wyoming Historical Novel.*

Now, Create a Magnificent Synopsis

A synopsis is an overview of your book. This is where you describe your story or the theme and purpose of your book in one to four pages (double-spaced). Each synopsis (or overview) has a little different flavor. A synopsis will answer some or all of the following questions: What kind of book is this? What is your book about? What is the focus and scope of your book? Why did you decide to write this book? Who will be interested in this book and why? How large is your target audience? What makes your book different/interesting? Will you include expert quotes? Who are your experts?

If the task of compiling a synopsis seems a bit overwhelming, try writing a one or two-sentence description. A brief sentence or two description might give clarity and spark ideas for the synopsis. Some authors discover their descriptive sentence only after writing the synopsis. Which one should come first? I suggest writing the one that comes easiest for you.

The One-Sentence Challenge

Here are some examples of one and two-sentence book descriptions:

A Year of Sundays is the true story of my year-long travels through Europe with my blind wife and our cat. (By Edward D. Webster, VanderWyk and Burnham Publishers).

Ma Duncan, a true crime featuring an uncommonly evil woman whose incestuous relationship with her son impelled her to have her daughter-in-law and unborn grandchild killed. (By James Barrett, Riverview Press)

Murder With a Twist is the story of my son, a serial rapist, a convict, and a murder victim. (By Marian Clayton, MC Enterprises)

The 7 Laws of Inner Peace is a clear and practical guide that shows you how to cultivate inner calm and tranquility no matter what is going on in your life. (Constance d'Angelis, JD, distributed by DeVorss and Company)

The Black Dog and the Cyclone Racer is a guide for companions of people with depression and bipolar disorder. (Jerry Malugeon)

It's not always easy to describe your book in one or two sentences. But this task will serve you in four important ways:

1. It will help you to focus on the scope of your book.
2. It will become the theme for writing your synopsis.
3. It may help you to decide upon a title and/or subtitle.
4. It will be useful in pitching and promoting your book.

What can you say in one sentence that describes your book? If you can't clearly describe your project in one or two sentences, you probably don't have a handle on the topic of your book. Take a time-out. Read other books in this genre/topic to discover what is out there, what is missing, and what you could provide. Perhaps you are trying to cover too much territory in your book. Maybe you just aren't good at paring down an idea into a nutshell. In this case, have someone else read your book and ask them how they would describe it. Brainstorm with members of your writers' group.

Let's Write That Synopsis

A synopsis is like a book in that it has a beginning, middle, and end. Your synopsis is generally the next thing a publisher reads after your query letter. He has opened the book proposal package, tossed aside your cover letter, title page, and table of contents. You now have your second best shot at attracting his attention and convincing him that your book is a great idea.

There are many ways to approach a synopsis. I recommend the following: For nonfiction, try to grab the publisher's attention in the first paragraph. Sometimes this can be done using a rather shocking statement or statistic ("America's children are in crisis . . ." or "Tonight, one out of every three children will go to bed in a home without their father in it . . ." or "Over four million cats and dogs are euthanized in shelters each year in the US . . .")

The first paragraph of a fiction or nonfiction synopsis should also identify the project. ("This is the story of murder and mayhem set in an unlikely place—a convent in the California foothills . . ." or "*Spitless* is a book of quips, phrases, and quotes unknown to anyone who is under thirty . . ." or "*Lost and Found* is the story of a family torn apart by disaster, and who begin to find their way back to one another through the most mysterious of circumstances . . .")

For a nonfiction book synopsis, summarize the content. What is the point of the book? What do you hope it will accomplish? Will it teach, provide comfort, entertain, inform, educate, inspire? Who is the audience and how widespread are they? How will the information be presented? Give your credentials for writing this book. This might involve education, a strong interest, research, experience, and/or training, for example.

Assume that the publisher is ignorant of the topic you are presenting. And in some cases he/she is. For the Doggie Dress-up book, for example, tell him what percentage of the $31 billion pet industry comprises clothing and grooming aids for dogs and how many dog owners dress up their pooches. Let the publisher know that you have done your homework. For help in locating information and statistics, read the section on research tips and techniques in Chapter Ten.

Sample Nonfiction Synopsis

This is a synopsis for a nonfiction self-help book with a spiritual twist and some rather interesting statistics related to a rather common everyday activity. With humor and wit, author, Louis Lapides attempts to use the concept of standing in line to teach life skills techniques. And he gives examples of the type of reader who could be positively influenced by this book. (This proposal was prepared in 2008.)

> How much time do you think you spend waiting in line? A June 2007 nationwide survey reveals that the average person spends two to three days every year waiting in line. Considering data collected by the national Center for Health Statistics, the average life expectancy is 77.9 years. Therefore, once a person leaves the stroller and is capable of maintaining a place in line, seventy two hours a year or 213 days of his lifespan will be spent standing motionless in line. Taking into account we will squander 5,112 lifetime hours tapping our feet waiting for a line to move forward, a book about making the most of our time in line is a welcome tool.

What if we turned our moments waiting in line into opportunities to discover new life lessons? That's exactly what Louis Lapides suggests in his book, *Lifelines, Is Your Life Waiting in Line*? Occasions in line provide a backdrop for the author to share amusing and invigorating encouragement to those who seek a lift when their life pursuits have come to a standstill. In fact, *Lifelines* takes a Seinfeld perspective by pointing out the humorous aspects in a most mundane human activity—standing in line.

Each chapter describes an extraordinary or amusing anecdote. Following that is a life application the reader can take away from the story. The application is tied into common behavior and choices that hinder people from experiencing their lives as a smash hit. In addition, many chapters connect the spiritual side of life where people grapple with unanswered prayer or patiently look to God for direction.

The readership for this book is the everyday man or woman who wants to move through life without many gridlocks. The author speaks to the hearts of people who set goals for their lives, are eventually compelled to put their dreams on the backburner, and are now seeking helpful advice. This might include the aspiring student who wonders if all his studying is worth it, the bored accountant who needs to know he makes a difference, the anxious engaged woman worried about her future. And it speaks to the person who needs to laugh when they feel unable to move forward.

Readers will be surprised to learn that by merely standing in line they are paralleling what is taking place in their own lives—*Why is my life not moving forward? What can I learn during this temporary stopover*? As you can see, people in all kinds of waiting patterns can benefit from the life-giving message in *Lifelines*.

As a popular Christian speaker, Lapides has been featured on several television and radio talk shows. He is included as an expert on biblical prophecy in *The Case for Christ* by Lee Strobel, he served as senior editor of FaithMD for several years, and he is the author of *The Jesus Family Tomb Controversy*. He has recently created ScriptureSolutions, a publishing and distribution center for his print materials and recorded messages. (*Lifelines: Is Your Life Waiting in Line* by Louis Lapides, is as yet unpublished.)

Sample Synopsis for Fiction

A synopsis for fiction is typically more about the flow of the story. It's important for the novelist to be able to describe his or her story succinctly. Also try to give some sort of proof or indication illustrating the popularity of a book like this. Here is Roy Raynor's synopsis for his action-packed and touching romance adventure story.

> ***Chameleon Man*** is a western action romance novel. Two Rivers was born in 1907 of mixed blood—his mother, an American Indian and his father, a rancher of French and Seminole ancestry. A brutal murder and a heartbreaking suicide claim Two Rivers's parents before he experiences his first year of life, and his Indian grandparents raise him to manhood. Hidden deep in the northwest wilderness, his home and his life are sheltered from the emerging twentieth century.
>
> His grandfather, Stone Heart, teaches him about the spiritual world, and this becomes his life path. Stone Heart, well known as a great warrior of past Indian wars with the encroaching European whites, and for his vast wisdom, enlightens his grandson on many life issues. He encourages young Two Rivers to leave the village and experience the wilderness alone. After several challenging encounters, the boy returns a brave. Later, Stone Heart introduces Two Rivers to Sun Mother, a Cherokee woman whose lovemaking rituals change him forever. Stone Heart's guidance also gives Two Rivers the courage and cunning he needs in order to avenge his parents' deaths.
>
> All the while, Two Rivers learns from the Chameleon how to live as a free man in the new world and blend in. But it's the devastating hardships he endures, his connection with nature, and the beautiful kinship he has with the women he loves that shape the man he has become and the feelings he holds deep in his heart.
>
> While part of his story is told against a natural wilderness backdrop, it also reflects his growth and change as Two Rivers transitions from his native roots and comes of age in modern America. In the end, his participation in a world war tests his spiritual resolve and his courage. (*Chameleon Man, His Women, His Journey*—Book One by Roy Raynor, R.A.R. Publications, 2009)
>
> Both of these synopses could definitely be expanded to include more detail, to show greater definition with regard to the sequence

and the scope of the text and the story. We chose the abbreviated renditions of these synopses because they demonstrate the heart of the books they represent in a neatly succinct way. When you develop your synopsis, follow the guidelines we've outlined for you within this chapter. We urge you to use these examples to create your synopsis, and then flesh it out in order to give the publisher a more complete mini-version of your story or nonfiction book.

About the Author—That's You!

The publisher wants to know who you are, your level of writing experience and what makes you the best person to write this book. This section typically encompasses anywhere from a paragraph to a page or so.

If you have expertise in the topic of your book, mention that first. For example: "I've been playing doggie dress up with my terriers for ten years." Or "I'm one of about thirty-five people in the United States who makes and sells clothing for dogs." Or "I earn my living as a groomer specializing in costuming and creative grooming for dogs."

Talk about your writing experience, especially where pertinent to this topic. You might say, "I've been writing articles for pet magazines and industry trade magazines for about five years, having been published in *Pet, Your Dog, Fancy Dog*, and in several online newsletters and websites. I write my own monthly print newsletter, *Dressing Doggie* for the doggie dress-up community."

Of course, the publisher wants to know about any previously published books. List each title, publisher, date of copyright (include every edition of each book) and add a little description.

List your planned books and books-in-progress to illustrate that the well isn't likely to run dry with this project. If this book is successful, the publisher wants to know that you can make a repeat performance. You never know when information like this is going to bring unexpected results. I've had publishers turn down the book I was pitching and ask to see proposals for books on my list of works-in-progress.

You'll need to convince the publisher that you can write, that you understand and can meet deadlines, that you are flexible and easy to work with, and that you are able and willing to promote your book. How do you assure him of your worth? Mostly by example.

Rather than telling the publisher that you are a great writer, prove it. Instead of promising that you will be an asset to his stable of authors, illustrate some of your past and current publisher or editor/author-relationship successes. Maybe you are pitching a fantasy. Tell him about the ebook that RST Publishing produced in 2009 and the fact that you sold 1,500 copies. Reveal your ongoing work with two well-known fantasy magazine editors over the last five years. Explain the positives that make up your platform—your way of reaching your particular audience. Perhaps you write a regular column for a fantasy newsletter, you have a slot on a radio station and/or you travel frequently on business and could use this opportunity to promote your book throughout the U.S., for example.

Sample About the Author—Paula Spellman

This is an excellent example of the about-the-author section of a book proposal. This author adequately introduces her unique abilities and affiliations. Her impressive work with a variety of organizations goes a long way toward convincing a publisher that she is well-rounded and that she can follow-through on projects and meet deadlines. Her life experiences make her seem interesting—she definitely has something to write about. And her writing ability and experiences are evident here and throughout her proposal. The fact that she added something about her marketing skills and connections as well as her willingness to promote this book is a big plus.

> I have worn many hats as a nonfiction author, speechwriter, literary consultant, and public speaker on memoir and ghostwriting. After being born, raised, and educated in Los Angeles, I continued school at the University of Southern California earning degrees in Speech Pathology and Elementary Education. I later became a graduate of the Jefferson Institute of Business.
>
> Extensive travel experience has led to a diverse background as a citizen diplomat in the former USSR: a participant in the Kazakh-American Research Project (an archeological dig) and coordinator of the (then) Soviet Economic Development Program. In addition to touring a vast number of countries, sailing on the majestic QE 2 to the fiftieth anniversary ceremonies of D-Day, and riding on the Trans-Siberian Express, I continue to explore new and unique options such as digging in the dirt with heavy-duty equipment in the

Northwest and dancing at a Viennese Ball in Austria. I'm a blue-jeans and ball gown woman who loves it all.

After being a participant for many years at the Santa Barbara Writer's Conference, I presented a workshop on memoir and ghost-writing there in 1997. Recognized as an Ojai Living Treasure, I later served as executive director for the organization (a local mentor and role model program), which was eventually embraced by Rotary International. I was a member of Rotary International for six years; former chair of the board for the A.S.T.E.R. Foundation (Abuse Survivors Treatment and Education Resource), a local program; and was recognized as one of Two-Thousand Notable American Women by the Board of Registrars of the American Biographical Institute of the United States of America. In addition, I was the first place recipient for short story fiction from the Church of Latter-Day Saints—Ventura Stake and wrote speeches for a congressional candidate and also for a member of the international board of Rotary International. Recently I've been approached to adapt a short fiction piece of mine to screen.

Writing is a sensual experience for me. Much like a sculptor moves the clay, I move the words and mold and remold them until they find their angle of repose and I am satisfied. It is a passion that takes center stage in my life. I am also a pastel artist and am in the process of developing a line of note cards. In addition, I am the "as told to" author of *Code to Victory: Coming of Age in WWII*, a memoir written for Arnold Franco. Poetry is something that my muse must write occasionally and several of my poems were published in the poetry anthology *Electric Rain*. I received the Silver Pen Award for articles appearing in the *Ojai Visitor's Guide* and the *Ojai Valley News*. A real kick in my writing career was having senior editor John Wood of *Modern Maturity Magazine* contact me for permission to include one of my cover letters in his book, *How to Write Attention-Grabbing Query & Cover Letters*.

Living life to the fullest is a must for me, and I continue to delve into unique adventures and local causes. I have the time, energy, and desire to promote *Walking Through Jell-O*. My many current and past affiliations give me a step up that can be used in the marketing process. Because of experience in front of the camera as well as

> doing book signings, service club talks, and radio interviews, I am very comfortable with marketing and personal presentations. (Author of *Walking Through Jell-O*, Paula Spellman)

Sample About the Author—Corrie Woods

This author also knows how to present herself to a publisher. Here, she focuses on her education, accomplishments, and associations related expressly to the book she is pitching. And she does a good job of listing her previous writing experiences—again, all related to the theme of her book. You'll notice that, while Spellman wrote her synopsis in first person, Woods has chosen to write hers in third person.

> Corrie Woods is the author of *The Woman's Field Guide to Exceptional Living*, published by Morgan James Publishing in April 2008. She is a women's life coach, a certified retreat leader, a speaker, and a woman whose work centers on supporting women in designing and living lives they love. She reaches women in a variety of ways: through one-on-one coaching, workshops, tele-classes, mini-retreats and weekend wellness retreats, as a speaker, and through her writing.
>
> She is a graduate of the world-class coach training program, CoachU, a member of The International Coach Federation, and founder and host of the ICF Self-Care for Coach and Client Special Interest Group. She is an administrator of the Myers Briggs Personality Indicator Assessment and a Certified Seasons of Change Facilitator. In addition, her professional experience includes work in a non-profit organization as a program evaluator and designer, serving in a top management position for a multi-million dollar corporation, as well as being a stay-at-home, homeschooling mom.
>
> **Previous Writing Experience**
>
> Book
>
> *The Woman's Field Guide to Exceptional Living*, published by Morgan James Publishing in April 2008.
>
> Articles/Ebooks
>
> Numerous articles and e-books by Corrie Woods can be found online and in print. These are currently featured on the following websites:

- The National Association of Baby Boomer Women
- Divine Caroline
- Women-at-Heart
- Leadership in Everyday Life
- I am Thankful For
- Holistic Network Exchange
- The Women's Growth Network
- Meditations for Women
- Sure Woman
- Everyday-Wisdom
- WomansFieldGuide.com

Print periodicals include: *Women On Purpose*, *Western North Carolina Women*, *Madam Chair Magazine*. See attached list of reviews, testimonials, and other publicity related to the original book in this series. (Author of *The Woman's Field Guide to Exquisite Self Care and Long-Term Vitality*, Corrie Woods)

Why a Book Proposal for Fiction?

If you're still wondering about this, let me say that roughly half of the publishers of fiction that I researched want to see a query letter first. One-quarter will ask for the complete manuscript and another quarter are adamant about receiving a book proposal. (Read about writing a query letter in Chapter Nine.)

While the query letter is your foot-in-the-door, the book proposal is the deal maker (or breaker). And you're not finished yet. In fact, you've just scratched the surface of the professional book proposal.

Recommended Reading:

Write the Perfect Book Proposal: 10 That Sold and Why by Jeff Herman and Deborah Levine Herman (John Wiley and Sons, Inc., 2nd edition, 2001).

Write the Right Book for the Right Audience

You've described your wonderful book. Now you need to convince the publisher that there's a market for it—that it is a sound financial investment. The publisher wants information about the commercial merit of your book and he needs facts and figures—not your uninformed opinion or wishful thinking. And this information is also an important part of your book proposal.

While there's no crystal ball to tell us which books will sell and which won't, there are techniques and tools for determining whether or not a particular book might have a future. We can guestimate by watching trends. The Association of American Publishers (AAP) comes out each year with a report on industry net sales. And they even break sales into categories.

If you are currently planning a book, you might consider writing a children's or young adult book as they have reigned in the industry for the last several years. While they aren't rising in sales as fast as they were in 2004 and 2005, the paperback versions are still in the running as far as potentially good investments. Teens particularly choose young adult books with sequels. Adult hardcover books were up in 2009, higher education books showed an increase in sales and ebooks continue to flourish, but not for the younger set. Keep an eye on book sales by visiting the Association of American Publishers at http://wwwpublishers.org.

Choose a Marketable Topic

Marilyn Ross is the cofounder of About Books, Inc. and http://www.SelfPublishingResources.com and the co-author, with Sue Collier, of the 2010 edition of *The Complete Guide to Self-Publishing*. She is also co-founder of SPAN (Small Publishers Association of North America). In a previous issue of the *SPANet* newsletter, she commented, "The first and most important step any potential businessperson takes is to decide what product or service to offer customers. Whether you're an author or publisher, you must determine your 'vehicle.'" And she reminds us that, "Some forms of writing hold more promise for commercial success than others."

I believe that many authors miss this important point. We don't think our projects through thoroughly enough. We just launch out and trust that everyone will love our book as much as we do. I have no problem with an author following his/her passion. Write the book that's in your heart. Enjoy the process. But if you hope to make money on that book, you must consider more than just your desires. You have to think like a businessman/woman. And this needs to be your mindset before your book becomes a book. If you intend selling copies of your book, choose a marketable subject.

As Ross says, "A marketable subject is vital both for trade publication and self-publication." What makes a marketable subject? According to Ross, commercially viable books are "usually about hot, timely subjects." She continues, "Choosing a marketable topic is the first step toward the bestseller dream to which all authors aspire."

In order to write a book that's hot and timely, you must stay alert. Ross uses the story of the first crockpot cookbook to illustrate this point. "The author attended a trade show and noticed that several manufacturers were introducing these new devises. Presto! The lights flashed. Would cooks need new recipes and guidance on how best to use their new cookware? You'd better believe they would. Since *Mabel Hoffman's Crockery Cookery* came out in 1975, more than three million copies have been sold."

Ross cautions writers to differentiate between a fad and a hot topic. But even a fad can make you some money, if you're on your toes and bring it out at the right time. Of course, I would go along with Ross and advise focusing on a trend rather than a novelty. One way to do this, according to Ross is "Ask yourself if a lot of people are likely to still be interested in the subject in a year or two. Think whether other ideas in this field have tended to flash and die or whether they've lasted at least long enough for a book on the subject to be written, published, and find an interested readership."

Ross explains, "I'm reminded of a few topics that were hot two years ago and still are: spirituality and religion, diet and exercise. There are, however, hundreds of books on these topics. It would make no sense to come out with another run-of-the-mill tome on dieting. If you are clever, though, you may find a new way to ride the wave of interest others have generated."

Address large segments of people such as teens, pet owners, working moms or the largest one of all, currently, baby boomers. What might their interests be? How about managing personal finances, volunteerism, aging gracefully, health and fitness for the senior, part-time self-employment, and how to write a memoir?

Ross urges writers to become "lurkers." By this she means visit chat rooms, discussion groups, online bulletin boards. Find out what people are talking about, concerned about, wondering about. She says, "Check out Google to determine what search terms are the most popular. When you see a pattern emerge, you've just learned about a need you might want to fill. As you climb the sheer cliffs of publishing, watch for tiny crevices that have been passed over by the big guys."

As you can see, there's more to producing a book than just fulfilling your desire to write from the heart. In order to become successful, you must also engage your brain.

Too many new authors are more focused on what they want to write about than what is wanted/needed. They think about what they can say best rather than what someone might want to read. They are more interested in entertaining their muse than in entertaining or informing a potential audience.

Authors, I urge you to get out of *me* mode while writing for publication and concentrate on your audience. Your readers should be primary in your mind throughout the writing process.

Who Is Your Target Audience?

How difficult can it be to find readers for your terrific book? Reading is still one of America's favorite pastimes. Everyone enjoys reading a good book, right? Not necessarily.

According to the Jenkins Group, fifty-eight percent of adults claim they have not read a book since high school and forty-two percent of college graduates never read another book. However, there still seems to be ample readers for our books. A 2010 American Booksellers Association (ABA) survey reveals there are an estimated 62.4 million avid readers in the United States. Add to this number those readers who seek out books only on occasion in order to educate or inform themselves on a certain topic of their interest.

What segment of the population is most likely to be interested in your book? Everyone who reads? Tell a publisher that and you're practically guaranteed a rejection letter. Only the most naïve, inexperienced, short-sighted author believes that his book will appeal to everyone. Reality check! Your audience does not comprise all of humanity.

Targeting your audience can be just about as difficult as taming a wild buffalo. But there are techniques that will help. We often write something that we would like to or, perhaps, need to read. Thus, the audience for your book might be made up of people like you—people who enjoy a good novel, who want to learn to knit, who need help with an emotional problem, or who collect cookbooks.

The fact is that most first-time authors give little thought to their audiences until after they write their books. They have a book in them and they just want to get it out. I met one such author at a recent book festival. Gerald wrote a book focusing on what he perceived as scientific proof that there is no God. He paid to have it published. When I met him, he was borderline despondent. His book wasn't selling. He came to my booth asking for help. Putting my personal convictions about the subject aside, I asked Gerald, "Who is your audience?"

He quickly and confidently responded, "Everyone."

I said, "So you think that everyone will want to read this book?"

He said, "Well, everyone ought to." Isn't this how we all feel about our lovely and important words?

After some discussion, Gerald and I isolated his target audience—those with the same theory as his. This might include some scientists and philosophers, atheists, agnostics, and those who are on the fence but leaning in the direction of Gerald's beliefs. We talked about where he would find these people. Together, we determined that it would be pretty much the same places where Gerald hangs out—lecture halls where speakers talk about this theory, and websites and publications devoted to atheism and science versus theology.

This isn't what Gerald hoped to hear. He wanted a quick and easy entrance into bookstores as an outlet for his book. More than anything, he is interested in changing minds. Whether or not he took my advice and started soliciting appropriate magazines, newsletters, and websites, I may never know.

If Gerald had written a book proposal, he would probably have altered the focus of his book. He might have realized that his approach—trying to convince readers to change long-held traditional beliefs—would turn off the very audience he wanted to attract.

Let's say that you dream of making a difference in the world through your book on living a more Christian life. Your goal is to reach the sinful masses. In reality, however, your audience will most likely include Christians who want to do an even better job of being Christian—people like you. Your target audience probably read the same books and magazines you read. They attend church. They visit Christian websites. But it isn't enough to say this in your book proposal. The publisher wants to know how many people you're talking about.

Your job is to find out how many Christian churches there are in the world and calculate the combined attendance. How many Christian bookstores and websites can you locate? Again, find books similar to yours and ascertain the number of sales. This will help you to define and calculate your target audience.

What segment of the population will embrace your book? Who are you writing for? Who will seek out a book like yours for the entertainment value? Who cares about what you have to say? Who wants the information or guidance you offer in your book?

As authors, we sometimes want to do more than just write. We hope to alter perspectives. We yearn to teach and to share. It's when we set out to change minds that we lose sight of our true target audience.

The audience for a how-to book is probably somewhat easier to ascertain than those for self-help books and books without a message. Your book on tax tips for authors would attract authors who are making or who expect to make money selling their books. Do you know how many people this is? Neither does the publisher. It's up to you to find out. Use statistics to illustrate the percentages and numbers representing key segments of people who might be interested in your book. Always double check that figure, if possible, and provide the sources for your statistics.

Find statistics in a current *Information Please Almanac* (or at http://www.infoplease.com, http://www.askanexpert.com, or http://www.demo

graphics.com), through reference or informational books on the subject, and/or do a Google search. (Learn more about conducting research for a book proposal or a book in Chapter Ten.)

A book featuring pet photography techniques would probably draw beginner and intermediate photographers as well as people who want to learn how to take better pictures of their pets. For your book proposal, seek out facts and figures to demonstrate the huge increase in camera use throughout the world and the wider availability of computer photo enhancing programs. These figures, combined with those related to our fondness for pets, would certainly help to make a case for this book.

I happen to know that there are around seventy million pet cats and sixty million pet dogs in the U.S. alone. One in four households has at least one pet. While not all pet owners are interested in photography and not all photographers want to learn about photographing pets, demographics such as these give you a good starting place in determining your audience.

Now see if you can more precisely pinpoint your readers. How many people subscribe to photography magazines, pet magazines—are there any pet photography magazines or websites? How many people subscribe or visit? How many other books are there on the subject? How are these books doing in the marketplace?

Your Target Audience for Fiction

How does one target an audience for a novel or a children's book? First, you might get some statistics related to the number of novels or juvenile/young adult books sold each year (http://publishers.org). Then see what you can find out about the public's interest in the particular type of book you want to write or the subject of your story. Your historical romance novel won't appeal to all fiction readers. Your audience might comprise those who have purchased similar novels, who rent similar movies, who subscribe to certain magazines, and who visit related websites. Get these figures and tally them.

To acquire information about sales for books similar to yours, check amazon.com and other online bookstores. Ask the managers at several traditional bookstores how a particular book is selling. Snoop around at author and publisher websites. If a book is in its third printing, it is pretty clear that it is selling. Mention this in the marketing section of your book proposal. Study authors' website media pages to find out if they have announced the number of books they've sold in any of their press releases. Also study their media pages, appearances pages, blogs, and marketing material to discover who they are promoting their books to. You may even get an author to tell you how many copies of his book he has sold. It would be convincing, indeed, if you could say, "Arthur Author's, *Hattie's Crush: A Victorian Novel* (XYZ Publishing, 2008), sold 20,000 copies after only ten months." Or "Wanda Writer's historical fiction has sold 5,000 copies."

Provide numbers to illustrate the popularity of books like the one you are pitching. But also see what you can find out about the readers. What are these authors' promotional tactics and who are they targeting with their marketing messages? Spend some time at the authors' sites and you may discover that they specifically address visitors to certain related blog sites and websites. They advertise or write articles for key periodicals. They've had their books reviewed by the most popular Internet reviewers. And they go out and speak to women's groups regularly.

Can You Attract Readers?

Why would anyone buy a book on your chosen topic written by you? Do you have a following in this field or in this genre? If so, this may be a plus. The fact that you have expertise may supersede the fact that there's a near glut of books out there on your subject.

Let's go back to the idea for a book on pet photography. Be sure to reveal your connections—you've been specializing in pet photography for ten years, you produce an enewsletter and have 8,000 subscribers, you have over a thousand friends on Facebook and 1,500 followers on Twitter, and you get 50,000 hits per month on your website. Not only does this demonstrate that you have a following, but that you know how to market yourself.

Your Bonus Audience

Sometimes you get a bonus audience when you produce a book. Let's say that you wrote a book featuring your local pioneer cemetery and the earliest burials there. You intended it for residents, history buffs, and others interested in the history of your community. What you didn't expect, however, was that it would also appeal to genealogists with ancestors buried in the cemetery and individuals who harbor a fascination with this nation's cemeteries. This book might sell well to genealogy libraries and even on eBay.

While developing the marketing section for your book proposal, ask yourself:

- Who is my target audience?
- What do they need or want from a book like this—information, tools, entertainment, inspiration?
- Do they have a problem? Do they want to make a lot of money? Do they need help understanding digital cameras, rose gardening, death?
- What do they worry about? What do they want to know?
- Why would they care about what I have to say?

Sample Marketing Section—Your Target Audience

These co-authors fairly clearly identify and describe two primary markets for their book and give some statistics in order to illustrate an ongoing need for a book like this. Everyone can either identify with or knows someone in both of these common categories.

> **Markets for *Challenging God: Ordinary People, Extraordinary Answers***
>
> **The Disillusioned**
>
> The first of two primary markets for *Challenging God* encompass people who have experienced tremendous loss. They are bitter and angry about their lives, and either don't believe there is a God, or think they've been abandoned by him. This individual is male or female, at any level on the income scale, and any age. He or she doesn't understand or respect God, and has a lot of trouble with the whole idea of there being any rhyme or reason to the universe. This book invites people who would love to rage at and have an argument with God. These are the people who look to God (if there is one), shake their fists, and ask "why?"
>
> The numbers of people who have suffered severe losses has risen in recent years. There have been many social and environmental catastrophic events: earthquakes, erupting volcanoes, terrorist attacks including 9/11, and hurricane Katrina, to name a few. According to

Wikipedia, Katrina alone killed at least 1,836 people, making it the deadliest U.S. hurricane since the 1928 Okeechobee Hurricane.

In addition, there are millions of people who have suffered loss due to the tragic or violent death of a loved one, loss of physical health or mobility, loss of employment, loss through drug abuse and addiction, or loss of income and lifestyle. Many of these people represent a viable market for this book.

Cultural Creatives

The second primary market consists of "Cultural Creatives," who usually look for books under "self-help/inspiration," and buy thousands of books each year through major retailers and local neighborhood bookstores. *Cultural Creative* is a term used by Paul Ray and Sherry Anderson in their new millennium book: *The Cultural Creatives: How 50 Million People Are Changing the World.*

Ray and Anderson based their conclusions on twelve years of survey research, 100 focus groups, and dozens of interviews. This market, which the authors say consists of about fifty million people, crosses all classes, races, social backgrounds, education, and income levels. Characteristics include: openness to self-actualization through spirituality, psychotherapy, and holistic practices; strong concerns about the well-being of families, a desire for quality relationships, and a concern for all people in the world. These people are more interested in authenticity, world peace, and social justice than in "keeping up with the Joneses." Eight percent of the Cultural Creative market, according to Ray and Anderson, consists of "New Agers." This particular section may have the potential for even more sales from those who are apt to buy psychic or channeled books and who frequent New Age bookstores. (Authors, Kellie DeRuyter and Laurie Gregg.)

Here's how Lola Brown, Ph.D. handled the target audience portion of the marketing section for her book, *Joyful Mondays: How to Find Passion and Joy in Your Work*.

While this book is meant to serve a wide audience, the primary target would be college and university students who are undecided in their major and future career goals. This book will also be of interest to early careerists (ages 25–34) who are having difficulty getting launched in their careers. Another audience is the mid-careerists (ages 35–50 and beyond) who have become disenchanted with their work or who may be facing termination of employment duc to the recent economic downturn.

A. Primary Market: College and University Bookstores; Workforce Centers
There are approximately 2,100 four-year colleges and universities and over 1,655 community colleges in the U.S. Most of them have bookstores with career or self-help sections. This book will be extremely useful to the college student and it will serve as an excellent resource for outplacement centers and institutions that have workforce training.

B. Secondary Markets: College Courses
Because this book is targeted toward college courses such as Career and Vocational Exploration and Career Development: Adults in Transition, it will serve as a supplemental text to any of the many texts currently used in these classes. It would also serve as a primary text if accompanied by a vocational assessment package and computerized career guidance program such as Eureka™.

Career development courses have changed in recent years to reflect electronic means of dissemination. For example, a number of career development courses are now being taught online versus through the traditional classroom approach. This book would be an excellent source for this approach. (*Joyful Mondays*, by Lola Brown, Ph.D., Dog Ear Publishing, 2011)

What's Your Competition?

Now that you know how to focus your book and who will buy it, you need to find out what else is out there like it. What is your competition?

- Are there other books on this topic?
- How similar/dissimilar are they to the one you propose?
- What is special about your book?

- Why should the publisher invest his money in another book on this topic?

How do you check out the competition? Here's a guide.

Step One
Visit amazon.com and reference *Books in Print* (at your local library) to find listings for books similar to the one you propose. Visit local bookstores to locate additional books. Don't forget to check your own home library. Also study sites related to your topic to discover what books they are recommending, featuring, reviewing.

Step Two
Study books like yours and choose four to six recent titles that are most similar. If the book is also popular, that's a plus. Note the title, author, publisher, publication date, page number, size, type (hardcover/paperback).

Step Three
Compare each book to yours—noting significant similarities and differences in the design, scope, information, style, purpose. Perhaps yours is more well organized, is more comprehensive, provides an easy-to-follow guide, includes diagrams and graphs, and/or has an index. Maybe your book for horse owners is unique in that it is for beginners and it provides tips for trail riding skill and etiquette. Possibly yours is the only craft book with instructions for the popular hand crocheting technique for kids. Perhaps none of the other books you found on fatherhood and fathering feature true life stories.

Also consider the pluses of books that are similar to yours. In the case of fiction, for example, if Christian fiction with a message is selling well, compare yours favorably to others that are popular. Young adult fantasy has been topping popularity charts. Show the publisher how yours compares favorably to those already on the market.

Never, never make the mistake of claiming that there is nothing out there like your book. There may not be another book on how to handle rattlesnakes without getting bit, but there are books on rattlesnakes, reptiles, and taming wild animals. Your book on losing weight by living in the moment may be unique. But you can compare yours with others in the self-help section and those on dieting.

You must convince the publisher that there is a place for your particular book. Is there truly a need for another book on snakes? What would your book add to a perceived glut of books on weight loss?

> Is your book timely enough to be accepted and different enough to be noticed?

Authors must guard against trying things that are ultra unique. There's a fine line between what will be accepted in the marketplace and what will be rejected. Thus, most publishers tend to shy away from things that are too different.

I know a first-time author who planned to write a book about a particular scientist's study revolving around flotsam (wreckage and/or cargo found floating in our oceans). After doing her comparative study, she realized that there was more promise for a scientific account of the ocean's currents as it relates to flotsam. It's practically the same book, only with a different focus. Yes, she found a publisher.

Marilyn Ross suggests, "Look closely at the competition. Do the existing books leave a gap your book could turn into a target? If your book is to stand out from the pack, it must have a fresh angle, offer a unique approach or information to persuade a prospective reader to buy it rather than one of the others."

Sample Market Analysis—Your Competition (for a Children's Book)

Spanner's Journey Into the No Time Zone

Even with the recession, the book market shows an increase in sales for spiritual books in recent months and an increase of children's book sales of 14.1 percent. (Note: this proposal was compiled in 2008.)

Recently, Eckhart Tolle's *The New Earth* has brought millions of people globally into a new stage of awareness. Oprah Winfrey has contributed to this awareness by promoting his book to such an extent that several new spiritual TV and radio shows have been created through her company. After a demanding request from parents, Eckart Tolle has just published his first spiritual book for children, *Milton's Secret,* which is being heavily promoted by Oprah and Amazon.com. It will be interesting to watch this book flying off the bookshelves into the hands of children. With this in mind, the market shows few spiritual fantasy chapter books for children on the bookshelves. Below find some examples of books which could be relatively compared to *Spanner.*

The market is open for this kind of new genre of books. A good example is the picture book *I Love You More* (Sourcebooks Trade, 2007), which has presently sold more than 200,000 copies, making it one of the top-selling illustrated children's books in this country. *I Love You More,* by Laura Duksta and Karen Keesler (grade K and up) is a cleverly conceived flip book, which ends in the middle and starts from either side and shows what love looks like from both a child's and a parent's perspectives. This book features a simple, touching story, rhyme and rhythm, and vibrant child-like illustrations. Even though this is a picture book, the story emphasis is on love and respect—a message similar to the one *Spanner* embraces. Only, *Spanner's* message is on a more profound and deep level of the word.

The Temple of Wisdom (for grade 6 and up) by Karin Alfelt Childs (Fountain Publishing; 2nd edition, 1997) is a lyrical tale of spiritual growth with an especially strong emphasis on the young person's coming of age. The quest goes deeper than the search for the scepter, as its main characters, Brandun, Kempe, and Larke each journey forth to forge an identity, to find a place in the world, to find and fight for values, and to discover the power to act for the good of one's self and others. This book is more faith-related than *Spanner.* The story invites the reader to ponder on the meaning of one's purpose and life—another aspect which is included in *Spanner.* But *Spanner's* life purpose is more predominant. I believe that children of all ages will be more able to relate to the message in *Spanner.*

Animalkind by Sean P. Griffin, grade four and up. (PublishAmerica, 2008.) This is the story of Thane, a typical teenage boy who lives in a medieval world where all beings have two forms: one human and one animal. This children's book offers adventure, suspense, and a message of hope and determination with the presence of animals and human, which is, to some extent, comparable to *Spanner*. Nevertheless, *Spanner's* story delivers a similar message of hope through a more gentle approach—without the use of violence or war.

Return to Rairarubia by W. Royce Adams (Rairarubia Books, 2001) is an intriguing story mix of real life and fantasy action centered around two grade school children. This story is also laced with challenges that children can relate to and life lessons that will assist them in their real life world. This is another story filled with fantasy characters and parallel messages, similar to *Spanner's* story. Even though this book is self-published, it has done quite well and is widely publicized on the web.

All of the books mentioned above present stories filled with adventure and similar points for understanding, love, peace, hope, and the search for truth. *Spanner* is unique because more than one message is offered to the readers. My book is not only filled with excitement, but also wisdom. (Author, Alexandra Monique)

Sample Market Analysis for a Nonfiction Book

The Black Dog and the Cyclone Racer: A Guide for Companions of People with Depression and Bipolar Disorder by Jerry Malugeon.

There are a number of books that address the mental illnesses diagnosed as *mood disorders,* and some of them have proved helpful for companions but in a limited way. Here are a few:

The Bipolar Disorder Survival Guide: What You and Your Family Need to Know by David J. Miklowitz (The Guilford Press, 2002). While possibly a source of information for those not knowledgeable of mood disorders, this book tends to minimize and oversimplify the many complexities a companion faces when helping a loved one with bipolar or depression. Much of the information is considered outdated and thought, by some, to be wasteful of time and energy. *The Black Dog and the Cyclone Racer* is more innovative and examines a large number of currently acceptable and recommended approaches a family member or companion can consider using. There are examples in each chapter that identify potential challenges with possible responses in effectively assisting a loved one through their challenges.

Helping Someone With Mental Illness: Compassionate Guide For Family, Friends and Caregivers by Rosalynn Carter with Susan Golant (Three Rivers Press, 1999). This work has too much emphasis upon hope and not enough on specifics to helpfully guide a companion in an intelligent exploration of alternatives. Also, much of Ms. Carter's book relies on medication with only limited suggestions pertaining to available supportive techniques. *The Black Dog and the Cyclone Racer* outlines and discusses a large number of additional options available to explore while helping a loved one regain their health (i.e., nutrition, exercise, rest, calm, stress-free and pleasurable activities, etc. to promote wellness.)

Loving Someone With Bipolar Disorder by Julie Fast (New Harbinger Press, 2004). This work is not particularly hopeful for companions who expect to see improvement in a loved one's condition. As medicine, treatment, and time once have their opportunities to work, companions hope to see a positive change in their loved one. Instead, some readers have found that this book leads toward the negative with low expectations for any changes for the good. Others find it depressing, promoting codependency, limiting, and sending some companions unhealthy messages. *The Black Dog and the Cyclone Racer* has an upbeat style, encouraging the reader to never lose hope in the belief that a loved one who is suffering from the effects of a mood disorder, may surely improve with proper treatment. It may not be easy, but faith, hope, and perseverance are essential if the companion is to be able to truly help a loved one.

The Depression Workbook: A Guide For Living With Depression and Manic Depression, second edition by Mary Ellen Copeland and Matthew McKay (New Harbinger Publishing, 2002). While possibly helpful for some, this book can be a tough read for companions seeking immediate suggestions in supporting a loved one in the throes of a serious illness. This book is mainly for those suffering from an illness and not necessarily aimed at readers searching for ideas on how to help such a person. *The Black Dog and the Cyclone Racer* was written directly for those actively seeking supportive ideas and potential ways out of the confusion, worry, and often chaos of loving someone with a potentially life-threatening illness.

Talking to Depression: Simple Ways to Connect When Someone In Your Life is Depressed by Claudia J. Strauss and Martha Manning (NAL Trade, 2004). The information in this book is mostly already known. While it presents a summary of such information, it also suggests a specific path of treatment to follow that seems a narrow point of view. There are many tried and successful approaches to helping a loved one with a mood disorder, a fact that certainly demands exploring. This book does not do that. It appears to suggest that cognitive therapy is the only really successful method in overcoming the effects of these illnesses. Again, *The Black Dog and the Cyclone Racer* points out many paths for exploration in locating those methods or techniques that may be especially useful for that particular reader and his or her loved one. Not everyone benefits from the same method or technique. Many approaches must be considered and many need to be explored. And this is a key benefit of *The Black Dog and the Cyclone Racer* that many of the other books on the market do not offer.

Recommended Reading:
The Fast-Track Course on How to Write a Nonfiction Book Proposal by Stephen Blake Mettee (Linden Publishing, 2008).

Dazzle 'em With Your Marketing Savvy

Now that you have a marketable topic, you know who your audience is and where they are, how do you plan to reach them? "What" you ask? "I have to promote my book, too? Won't the publisher do that?"

This is where the inexperienced, naïve, unaware hopeful author makes his biggest mistake. He expects the publisher to handle promotion and sales. Unfortunately, it doesn't work that way anymore. At least, not until you establish yourself as a bestselling author or can attract a large following for your line of books. Until then, the publisher is counting on you to actively generate sales. And this information should also be a part of your book proposal.

Few people even consider the promotional aspect of authorship. Until we enter into the field of publishing, we have no reason to know what goes on behind the scenes. If you want a book, you go to the bookstore and buy one, right? You see others in the same bookstore buying books. And you assume that once your book is published, it will have its spot in bookstores nationwide and enough readers will buy it to support your writing habit for years to come. Ahhh, wouldn't that be nice?

Well, enjoy the fantasy while you can, for once your book is published, you will be required to promote it.

After the synopsis and your proof of marketability, the promotions portion is probably the most important aspect of a book proposal. A publisher wants to know that you understand the concept of book promotion and that you can and will participate in promoting your book. This section of your book proposal is important for you, too. You need to have a plan.

You must understand what it takes to promote a book and be willing to commit to it. There is nothing easy about book promotion.

Too many authors disregard this aspect of a book proposal. They so believe in their project that they expect sales without effort. Don't fall into this trap. Reality check: You must be prepared to promote your book and you have to convince a potential publisher that you'll be successful in this endeavor.

But I Write Fiction

Authors of fiction works are expected to help with promotion, as well. Times are changing at a rapid rate. With bookstores closing by the dozens, publishers are scrambling to discover new methods of promoting books. And even fiction publishers will rely more on their authors now that their main outlets for sales is on shaky ground. Thus, more publishers will request marketing plans for fiction.

Tell the publisher that since your novel is set in the state of Georgia, you see this book as a good regional seller and that you plan to promote the book to historical societies at the state and city levels, at libraries, through museum gift shops and, of course, Georgia-based bookstores. You might let the publisher know that you'll be available to do book tours throughout the state and beyond once the book is published.

Maybe your romance is set in a senior home. You can surely promote your book by doing readings in such homes as well as through articles and excerpts published in senior-related magazines, websites, and newsletters. Research the circulation figures for these publications and share them with the publisher. Many newspapers have columns devoted to senior interests. Find out how many and assure the publisher that you will contact each of these columnists to solicit interviews and book reviews.

What Do Publishers Really Want?

I interview publishers regularly for the *SPAWN Market Update* and I usually ask them, "What sort of authors do you most like working with?" They almost always mention those with time, energy, ideas, and the ability and willingness to promote his or her book.

Some publishers even post their expectations on their websites or in their submission guidelines.

Mystic Ridge Books advertises that they want writers who are good self-promoters. They state in their submission guidelines, "Authors must be willing to be aggressive and proactive regarding doing publicity and book events on their own. Books do not sell without author-self-motivated marketing efforts. This, in the twenty-first century, is your job." They go on to say that, "More and more booksellers want to know, BEFORE buying a book: what is the author doing on his or her own to attract publicity?"

Editor Donna German writes in the guidelines at Sylvan Dell Publishing, "This is a very bizarre business and if you are still waiting for your first break, I recommend that you start reading books about how to market your book. That might help you in understanding what it is that editors/ publishers are looking for when they select manuscripts. Don't forget that this is a business—not just your art of writing. The authors who survive (and thrive) in this business are the ones that truly understand that and commit to doing what it takes."

Betterway Home Books guidelines state, "We prefer authors who already have established marketing platforms for their work."

Robert Olmsted at Dan River Press says, "Tell me how big your mailing list is, how many readings you can do, and how many books you've arranged to place in bookstores."

The guidelines at Intervarsity Press read, "We need authors who will bring resources to the table for helping to publicize and sell their books."

Floricanto Press editors state simply, "Develop a loyal audience."

Publishers today need your help in promoting your fiction and nonfiction book. And many of them are seeking, along with excellent manuscripts, authors who are bold promoters and who are not afraid to be in the public eye.

It's Never Too Soon to Think about Promotion

From the time you first conceive your book idea, you should be thinking about promotion. In fact, I generally start a file folder for promotional ideas from the get go which I add to over the duration of the project and beyond. I might write myself a reminder note to contact school districts once my *Young Writer's Handbook* is completed. I may note a particular teachers' magazine editor who expressed an interest in reviewing the finished book. And, of course, I'll start collecting data on newspapers nationwide with literary arts and/or kids columns. I'll want to send out press releases to each and every one in hopes of initiating reviews or interviews.

Become Acquainted with Your Target Audience

Once you have determined your target audience (per the guidelines in Chapter Five), you must take time to get to know them. What do these people read? What magazines do they buy? Where do they purchase books? What associations and groups do they join? Do they attend workshops, lectures, church? Do they travel, exercise, diet, have pets, knit, go fishing? What do they care about? Do they support a particular cause? You've used these prompts to isolate your target audience, now you must figure out how to reach these people. What ploys do you have up your sleeve to attract readers from your perceived demographic pool? How do you envision prompting these people to purchase your book? You'd better figure it out because the publisher wants to know. If you plan to go it on your own and self-publish, this information is even more vital to your success.

You don't have to go into great detail about every promotional idea that strikes you. The publisher just needs proof that you understand the job of promoting your book and are willing and able to take it on. Tell him about any important contacts you have.

What Is Your Platform?

We hear a lot about *platform* these days. What is it and why do you need one? Your platform is your way of attracting readers. It's an indication of your following. It's your connections related to the theme/genre of your book. Elements of your platform for your vegetarian cookbook might be the fact that you have been a vegetarian for twenty years. You teach vegetarian cooking classes at a local cooking school. You have a popular blog on vegetarianism. And you head up a national Internet organization for vegetarians. You may also have contributed numbers of articles on this subject to several appropriate magazines and newsletters over the years.

Are you involved in an area of expertise related to your book? Do you have a reputation or a measure of influence within your community or beyond?

Karen Stevens is founder of All For Animals and the author of a book by the same name. She has a large following of animal advocates through her website, and she also appears on a local weekly TV segment with the "Pet of the Week." She writes for several animal-related publications. A publisher would probably accept her book of animal stories based largely on her impressive platform.

Debbie Puente was working for a well-known kitchen store when she started pitching her book on how to make crème brulee. She gave the publisher a letter from the store buyer confirming that she would place the book for sale in all of their stores once it was published. This was a major factor in Puente receiving a publishing contract for *Elegantly Easy Crème Brulee and Other Custard Desserts.* While Puente didn't have a following of her own at that time, she had a connection to a business with a huge customer base.

Be sure to tell a publisher if you have a meaningful association within the area or field of your book subject. Maybe you're a CEO for a company that sells knitting supplies. What publisher of craft books wouldn't be interested in your book featuring the latest and greatest projects to knit or one called, *Knitting Nostalgia*?

Maybe you can afford to hire a publicist, your brother-in-law produces a major catalog and has agreed to feature your book in it, or you have a strong marketing background. These are all good selling points for your project.

Face it, even if you're well-known in your field and you've just written the best book of the century, it will take some effort to entice people to buy it. People will not come just because you wrote it. It will take time, work and strategy to get news of your book out there so it is noticed. Tell the publisher how much time you will spend promoting your book every day/week.

When Jim Barrett made the rounds with his second book proposal, he was on the verge of retiring. He told the publisher that he would be available to promote the book practically full time at that point. The publisher believed him and has not been disappointed. Barrett's connections and experience as a peace officer helps to sell copies of his true crime book. And he continues to put in the time and energy to get the word out.

It's discouraging to know that seventy-six percent of all books published do not make a profit (Jenkins Group). What is behind the sales and success of the other twenty-four percent? A little bit of luck, perhaps. But mainly it is persistence and work.

Sure, a traditional publisher will offer some promotional assistance. He might include your book in their annual company catalog, showcase it on their website, offer review copies to three or four dozen reviewers, and send press releases to their list of periodicals. The publisher may also set you up with their marketing agent once your book is published. When you locate someone willing to review the book or when you are scheduled to do a book signing and need books, you let this person know and he or she will make necessary arrangements. Some publishers will also arrange for shelf space for your book in bookstores. But if you aren't bringing in the customers, your unsold books will be returned to the publisher rather quickly.

Some of the main selling points for pay-to-publish companies are their promotional packages. Hopeful authors are thrilled to think that their publisher will go out of his way to promote their books. Sure, it costs the author an additional $300 to $2,000, but it's worth it. Isn't it? Probably not. To date, I have not met nor have I heard of a pay-to-publish author whose company sold more than a handful of their books whether they bought the promotions package or not.

What type of promotion are you paying for? The pay-to-publish representative may use a service to send out cookie cutter press releases announcing your book to a general audience. You could hire the service yourself for less money. But I'd rather see you send your own press releases to a more appropriate, targeted list.

The sad truth is that you cannot rely on your publisher or anyone else to take over full responsibility for promoting your book. Think about it, no one else knows your book as intimately as you do. And no one cares about it as much as you do.

Build Your Platform

You may already have the beginnings of a platform. This is the time to evaluate your skills, connections, etc. so you can build on them. Do you have a mailing list? Have you been collecting business cards everywhere you go? Do you have a reputation related to the topic of your book? Perhaps you circulate a newsletter to a large number of your potential readers—they already know you as an expert in your field. And maybe you have been presenting workshops in your field (the topic of your book) for several years.

Build on that platform or start establishing one even before you write the book. Some of you have already written your books, and that's okay. You'll just have to play catch-up. How do you build a platform where none exists? Become visible within your field or genre. For example:

- Compile a massive email and mailing list. (Read more about using your mailing list in Chapter Thirteen.)
- Build a website related to your topic or genre and provide tons of resources. (More about this in Chapter Thirteen.)
- Ask site visitors to sign up for a free report or free gift related to your book topic/theme and add their names to your mailing list.
- Introduce yourself to appropriate website and organization leaders and ask how you can become involved.
- Establish a blog in your topic/genre. Post regularly and encourage comments.
- Be a frequent guest blogger at other related blog sites.
- Get involved in social media networks—Facebook, Twitter, etc. Make friends and encourage followers.
- Write articles in your field or stories in your genre for appropriate web sites, magazines, newsletters, and ezines. Their readers are potential customers for your book.
- Go out and speak to groups on behalf of your topic/genre.
- Rent booths at flea markets and book festivals and handout material related to your topic. Always have a sign-up sheet for visitors.
- Make news in your field or genre and tell it to the media.

Do whatever it takes to get your name out so that your public knows you exist. Be creative, consistent, persistent, and patient. Even with a fairly solid platform, it still takes effort and energy to promote to your audience.

Build Marketability Into Your Book

Whether your book is a novel or work of a scientific nature; whether it will appeal to artists, is meant to entertain, is important to psychologists, or significant to history buffs, you can build promotional opportunities into it.

For Nonfiction

Write What People Want to Read

Choose a topic that has a large target audience or a strong niche audience. Add aspects that could attract additional readers. For example, if your book features summer activities for kids, include a section on inside activities for rainy and snow days, as well. Maybe you plan to write your military memoir. Consider enhancing your book by weaving some military history throughout. You'll surely attract another segment of readers who might not be interested in a book about your life. Add graphics or photographs to a book of poetry and it may appeal to a larger audience. Your dessert cookbook will tempt additional readers if you insert a section on low-calorie dessert recipes.

Involve Others

Practically everyone likes to see his or her name in print. Most people will buy one or more copies of a book in which they're quoted, and they'll talk about it to others. Mention a particular organization, charity, or company and they might actually help promote your book. Here are some ideas for involving people in your book:

- Quote experts in the text.
- Mention agencies and organizations in your resource list.
- Share true stories about real people (with their permission).
- Create an acknowledgements page and list everyone who contributed to your book through information, resources, stories, etc.
- Ask experts in the field of your subject to write testimonials (or endorsements) for the back cover or pages inside the book. Also post testimonials at your website.
- Include a bibliography, plenty of resource material, and an index and you will entice another level of readers—researchers, the media, and librarians.

Get Permission

For a nonfiction book or even a book of fiction in which you've actually used true anecdotes, be sure to get permission to print a quote or a story. I generally type up the quote or the story exactly as I wish to publish it and send it to the individual along with a permission slip for them to sign. Most people simply sign. Others might make slight changes before signing. While I've never had anyone refuse to allow publication of their quote, I would rather get a refusal before the fact than a law suit after.

I've discovered that an email "okay" is a suitable permission, as well, and much easier to obtain.

For Fiction

Choose your setting carefully. Make sure that it is conducive to promotion. Select a city that is interesting—one in which the citizens take pride. Provided your story portrays a positive view of the community, residents of this town are apt to welcome you for author events. Write about a run-down town where nothing is happening and the residents are depressed and you probably won't get friendly invitations to promote your book there.

Involve your characters in current issues: autism, gang activity, politics, school bullies, peanut allergies, or childhood obesity, for example. Why? This gives you additional impetus for promoting. Your audience base, in this case, might go beyond the typical mystery or romance reader. Someone who typically reads only nonfiction might pick up a novel if it involves something they're interested in or familiar with—such as protecting the wild horses in America, an adult with ADHD, or an almost fully functioning deaf cat, for example.

Premiums and Incentives

Companies sometimes purchase large numbers of books to give away to customers. Your book might be chosen as a premium item if it mentions a certain product. A historical novel might be of interest to a bank or another large business in the area where the story takes place. A major sporting goods store might carry your book on small town Little League players who made it to the big time or quotes and quips from umpires and referees.

Your Book as a Special Interest Item

Write a novel or a children's story that will appeal to a specific group of people. Give one of your characters an illness, a horse, a disability, a motorcycle, a convertible, a set of twins, or an affiliation with a well-known agency, for example. The American Diabetes Association might be interested in promoting a book with a character that provides a positive diabetic model. Child health professionals and advocacy groups might purchase quantities of your book on how to help slim down our overweight kids. School administrators might purchase numbers of books that relate to subjects taught in their classrooms or one on taming the classroom bully.

Several copies of Betty Middleton Britton's first book, *Promises! Promises! Adventures of Jose Joaquin Tico, Cataluna to California 1766–1802*, were purchased by the California school system for classroom use. Not only does this book reflect early California history, it gives an excellent Spanish lesson throughout.

What's Your Plan?

You truly won't know much about the process of promoting your book until you get involved. Most first-time authors find it is more difficult than they had imagined. A book proposal forces you to think about promotion way before you ever write that book, thus to be more well-prepared.

Think back to the information you gleaned while working on the marketing section of your book proposal. Where are your primary customers? What do they buy? Where do they shop? What do they read? What newsletters do they subscribe to? What's the best way to reach them?

Perhaps your ideal customer reads travel magazines. You'll want to offer excerpts from your book and write articles for such magazines. This would be great exposure for a book like Edward D. Webster's travel memoir, *A Year of Sundays* and Chantal Kelly's book, *Gelato Sisterhood on the Amalfi Shore*. As I understand it, those who travel, read travel magazines, but so do an equally large number of armchair travelers.

Maybe you plan to do back-of-the-room sales during professional conferences throughout the world. This is a good promotional plan that many authors use to sell books related to their professional expertise. When you explain this to your potential publisher, be sure to give details: where, why, how often, numbers of attendees and so forth.

I recently worked with a client who had grandiose ideas for promoting his fitness book. Jonathan wrote in the promotional section of his book proposal that he was planning a conference next summer and that he would travel the world speaking to groups on the subject of his book. This looked good on paper, until it came to proof. I challenged him to offer the publisher something concrete. I asked him to describe the upcoming conference: where would it be held? What celebrities would be there? How many people did he expect? He had nothing. So I asked him to tell about similar conferences he has organized in the past. He admitted that he had never done anything like this before. I suggested he give a few examples of his successful speaking engagements. Well, guess what? He had no such experience. He had not even tested his fitness idea on anyone.

Imagine how a publisher would view this portion of Jonathan's book proposal. Do you think he would take this author seriously? Would he trust that the author would follow through with these ideas? Wouldn't the publisher be more impressed and convinced if Jonathan could give some particulars—"The conference is tentatively called, *Feeling Good, Being Fit.* I've reserved a hall at the Hilton Hotel in Los Angeles for June 30, 2012 and I have commitments from Suzanne Somers and Queen Latifa to be presenters. I've also contacted Richard Simmons, John Basedow and Dr. Phil McGraw. I expect this event and this line-up to draw at least 1,000 people. We have provisions for 1,500."

I would vehemently advise against Jonathan or anyone else inventing details such as these. I would suggest, instead, that he hold off sending his book proposal until he had something concrete to share with the publisher.

However, if he had a track record, he could use that as proof. He could say, for example, "I teach fitness workshops nationwide. For the last five years, I've presented workshops in twenty-five cities including Denver, Baltimore, Los Angeles, New York, and Portland. Last year, I was a featured speaker at the Fantastic Fitness Fantasy Expo in Chicago with 800 people in attendance. I created a test book for this event and sold all 150 copies I printed. I'm scheduled to speak in Seattle this spring before a group of colleagues at the World Fitness Council Conference and believe I could sell a thousand copies of this book there."

Don't blow in the wind, people. Give the publisher something to hang his bank account on. If you don't have anything, maybe you should postpone your book. Spend the next several months testing your idea, making contacts, developing a following, creating projects, and honing your public speaking skills. (Read more about public speaking in Chapter Thirteen.)

You don't need to share all of your promotional ideas in your book proposal—just the best ones. Try to come up with a few really good short-term, get-this-book-off-the-ground ideas and a couple of great long-term ideas. Those initial ideas might include: sending review copies to appropriate websites and publications and circulating brochures to key organizations that might be interested in using your book as a premium or employee incentive. Perhaps you've already reserved a booth at a trade show related to your topic. Name names. Be specific. In other words, say, "I've reserved a booth at the annual Business and Technology Expo in Philadelphia next spring." List some of the most prestigious publications you plan to contact for reviews and the names of some of the organizations you will contact or are already involved with.

Long term ideas might include spending two hours every day sending press releases to newspapers or starting a charity related to your book topic. Say, for example, that there are 325 newspapers with senior columns nationwide and you will contact each columnist about your book featuring 100 fascinating seniors who are still in the workplace.

If your expertise relates to the theme of your book and you have enough personality and skill to pull it off, consider launching a local radio show. If you're good and if you're lucky, it could even become syndicated. Possible topics might include cooking, travel, pets, computers, finance, automobiles, senior or family issues, child-rearing, health, or even writing. Radio personalities, such as the ever popular Dr. Laura Schlesinger and Bill O'Reilly, sell a lot of their books to their listeners.

I know a published poet who landed a spot on a literary-focused public radio show. This led to her own one-hour show. As often as she can, she mentions her book of poetry.

Strategies for Promoting to Your Audience

Social Networking for Authors

A well-known book marketing expert told me recently that "the jury is still out" on how effective the whole social media movement is for book promotion. But she agrees with most other professionals that this is an avenue authors should pursue.

As an author, you should saturate the airways with news and information about your book through frequent and regular blogging, a Facebook page, and maybe Twitter, LinkedIn, and other accounts. While the typical author does not receive a lot of feedback from these efforts, they are getting the word out, people do find them, and they do sell books.

Before setting up your blog and before posting at your Facebook and other social media pages, spend some time researching those that seem to attract a lot of traffic. What makes these sites popular? It might be their controversial posts or their free offers. Penny Sansevieri, a marketing expert, says that the key to success is "Be helpful." In other words, don't come on strong with a sales pitch. Offer your expertise where needed/wanted. Thoroughly study the social media sites you want to participate in so you know how to navigate them expertly.

Create Your Own Newsletter

Many authors write newsletters to promote their books. Newsletters have been informing readers rather inexpensively for a long time. Even insurance companies, hospitals, utility companies, and investment companies send newsletters to their customers. While blogging seems to be edging newsletters out, some people still appreciate receiving a newsletter. To be successful with your blog site or your newsletter, never ever look at it as a means of selling books. Instead, your focus should be to position yourself as an expert in your niche, be helpful, and offer something of value to your readers.

Keep on Promoting

I tell hopeful authors that your book will sell for as long as you are willing to promote it. So consider book promotion a commitment similar to that of raising a child. You created the book; now you're responsible for it. Nurture it and it will flourish. Neglect it and it will falter and fail.

Keep in mind that it isn't necessary to convince a publisher that you can turn hardened nonreaders into book buyers with your marvelous book and sell 50,000 copies in the first year. Most publishers are savvy enough to know that even though there are an estimated forty-four million dog owners in the United States, only a percentage of them will actually purchase a book on dog ownership. Let's say that you can convince a publisher that you could potentially sell 10,000 books. He might be interested in taking the risk. After all, a $5 profit on 10,000 books is a cool $50,000.

Should You Hire a Publicist?

Sure, if you can afford to and if he or she is experienced in working with authors of books in your genre/topic. Hire a good publicist and you will sell books.

Don't think that hiring a publicist is a way out of promoting your book, however. A publicist does not do the promotion for you. Typically, a publicist will spend her time and energies making appropriate contacts. You will be expected to follow through by making appearances, doing book signings, giving interviews, and so forth. A good publicist will keep you very, very busy.

Here's my recipe for landing a good publicist:

1. Consider publicists who come highly recommended.
2. Be prepared to spend $9,000 to $15,000 for three months of a publicist's time.
3. Audition a potential publicist. What is her track record? Has she handled books like yours before? What was her level of success with these books?
4. Ask for references and check them.
5. Find out what her main marketing focus is and determine if this is compatible with your abilities and availability.
6. Once you hire a book publicist, expect to be extremely busy promoting your book for a year or more.

John Kremer lists over 125 book publicist and PR agency recommendations at his website: http://www.bookmarket.com/101pr.htm.

Sample Marketing Strategies

Chantal Kelly's "Marketability Statement"

As an independent travel agent for the last twelve years and the owner of an import linen business, French Elegance, I understand marketing.

I'm also comfortable before groups of people. For six years, I lectured adults on a series of travel destinations in community education classes. I was a frequent guest speaker at a local radio station to discuss travel and have appeared on Portland's "AM Northwest" television show to promote my linens which I sell through the Internet and at festivals. With my experience in generating sales, I am motivated to launch a promotional campaign for this book.

I plan to:

- Send press releases to the major national and metropolitan newspapers and dozens of large and small magazines such as the *Oregonian,*

Lake Oswego Revue, *Senior & Boomer*, *Travel + Leisure Magazine*, and *Condé Nast Traveler*, and raise interest through reviews.

- Contact travel-related radio programs and general consumer television shows to appear as a guest.
- Line up speaking engagement at travel conferences, NACTA (The National Association of Career Travel Agents), NWTP (Northwest Travel Professionals), Kiwanis and Rotary Clubs meetings and others.
- Contact major and independent bookstores, such as Powells, to set up signings.
- Offer to read in libraries and Italian restaurants.
- Promote this book on my website http://www.bonvoyagetravels.com, in my bi-annual newsletters to my 300-plus travel clients and to 1,200 French Elegance customers.
- Advertise *Gelato Sisterhood on the Amalfi Shore* on several tour sites at their invitation, such as Euro Connection, Barclay International Group, and Select Italy.
- Contact AAA headquarters to distribute the book through their 100-plus locations.
- Print 2,000 postcards and mail to friends, family, and clients. Send an additional 3,000 to the various businesses mentioned in this book who have expressed an interest in promoting it.
- Plug the book at Italian festivals and cultural events.

I also have a thousand pictures available for promotional use once the book is published.

(Author of *Gelato Sisterhood on the Amalfi Shore*, Chantal Kelly)

Example of the Marketing Section for Fiction

My marketing plan for my novel, *Love in the Darkness*, is many faceted. I have been blogging at "The Romance Novel Blog" for over a year and have a steady stream of comments coming in from readers. My Twitter account boasts 557 followers and my Facebook followers are 1,304 and growing. I have built an interactive website for romance novel readers and have it linked to some of the most popular sites for this audience. I will announce and promote my book at all of these sites.

> I've been submitting stories to literary magazines and several others that publish fiction since 1990. My articles have appeared in about three dozen different publications (see list enclosed with this proposal). I'm no stranger to public speaking, having been an active member of Toastmasters for ten years, the president of a large writer's group in St. Louis (250 members), and the facilitator of a fiction critique group. I also give presentations as part of my job. I plan to go out and speak to my audience and do readings in costume, for added interest.
>
> I already have half a dozen book festivals and writer's events in mind for 2012 and, once the book is published, I will sign up to participate as a speaker where appropriate.
>
> I will retire next year and will have even more time to promote this book and to tour at your request. I've already started writing the second in the series of at least four books planned. (Anonymous Author)

When you're writing the promotions section for your book proposal, be realistic. Be bold, be creative, and be clever. It is your job to convince the publisher that you can manage the promotion of your book every bit as successfully as you can the writing of it.

If you need more help coming up with specific promotional ideas, jump to Chapters Twelve, Thirteen, and Fourteen.

Recommended Reading:

1001 Ways to Market Your Books by John Kremer (Open Horizons, 6th edition, 2006).

Okay, Now Organize Your Book

One major reason for writing a book proposal for a nonfiction book is to find out if you actually have a book at all. The chapter summaries will tell the tale. It will also become your guide for writing the book.

Chapter Summaries

Why does a writer need to follow a guide? While a fiction story can develop almost as if by magic, a nonfiction book generally takes some manipulation to make it work. Many authors have difficulty putting the material for their nonfiction book in a logical order. In fiction, you are concerned with telling a good story in an interesting way. Nonfiction is successful when the material is worthwhile, thorough, and easy to understand and use.

Organizing a nonfiction book can challenge even the most methodical and orderly writer. It helps if you can break your book down into subjects, themes, steps, or techniques—each representing a chapter. Avoid presenting too many ideas at once as this can be confusing. Perhaps the following will help:

- Design a table of contents for your book, but don't become too attached to it. It might have many incarnations before it is set. Some authors write possible chapter titles on index cards because they are easy to shuffle. Divide a book on dog training into eight or ten steps, for example. A book on herb gardening might be separated into seasons, regions, or plant types. A memoir would probably be divided into historical time periods, one's age, or significant life events.
- Separate and file the material you've gathered. Whether you're writing a novel, a children's story, or a nonfiction book, you've probably gathered a variety of facts, figures, and anecdotes. You've collected

thoughts jotted on paper napkins, information printed from the Internet, magazine articles, lists of resources, and newspaper clippings. You've earmarked certain books that you want to use in your research. Much of this is probably held in one or two file folders and several additional stacks and piles. When you are ready to start writing, separate this material into subtopics and place it in appropriate file folders. These will, most likely, become your chapters.

- Evaluate each folder. Are they relatively equal in size? Consider splitting large file folders into two chapters.
- Arrange your file folders (or chapters) in logical order. Be sure to make corresponding alterations to your table of contents.
- Write your chapter summaries. For nonfiction, give each chapter a title. This is optional for fiction.

A Word about Chapter Titles

Have fun choosing intriguing chapter titles for a fiction book. For nonfiction, think service. Be practical. Devise titles and headings that are functional, not frilly. Help the reader to navigate easily through the information and steps you've laid out. Logical organization and succinct titles are two excellent methods of doing this.

This is not to say that you can't have fun with chapter titles. A little humor and some interesting innuendoes help to lighten up an informational book.

Techniques for Creating Your Chapter Summaries

This is your moment of truth. It's time to show the potential publisher that you actually have a book. If you cannot list at least five or six (or twelve to sixteen) stand-alone chapters and describe them, you probably don't have a book at all.

Your chapter-by-chapter summaries will help the publisher understand the flow of your proposed book. It will tell him whether your book has substance and relevance and whether you have the writing skill to carry off this project.

While some books seem to fall together naturally, others can cause a great deal of frustration when it comes to the task of organizing.

The point of chapter-by-chapter summaries is to reveal the purpose of each chapter and show how you will accomplish the goals you've set forth. How will you communicate your message, for example?

Additional Tips for Creating Chapters

- Evaluate other books on your subject as well as some outside the subject. What do you like/dislike about the way these books are arranged? Which aspects would you like to copy and which ones will you reject?
- Organize your chapters. Your detailed, well-written synopsis will be a useful guide in this task.
- Look at each chapter separately. Ask yourself, what is the purpose of this chapter? What will it teach? What information should it include? How will it inspire? What encouragement will it provide? Why is it important? Simply summarize the purpose and point of each chapter and reveal how you will accomplish the goals you've set forth for your book.

Describe Your Chapters

Once you have identified your chapters, describe them. Write a brief (100–400 words) overview of each chapter. Write more text where the material is complex, but avoid padding or rambling just to fill space. I see two common problems among book proposals. Some authors overstate their point and purpose in the chapter summaries and others withhold information. Avoid redundancy, but don't play coy with the publisher, either. Give him or her what they need in order to appropriately evaluate your project.

Most professionals suggest writing your chapter summaries in third person as you are describing each chapter to the publisher. However, first person is more appropriate in some cases.

Sample Chapter Summaries

Walking Through Jello **(Paula Spellman aka Glinka)**

Prologue

What you are about to enter is my life. Why am I inviting you? Because, as women, we share common threads that weave us together. Like patches of antique fabric, rich in experiences, we're united by the stories we tell. My story is common. My journey isn't. I looked into the mirror for a long, long time before finding the courage to do what I did. By coming with me, maybe you won't have to look for so long.

History molds men and women into roles which we often don't become aware of until later in life. We wake up one day to find that we don't like who we are or where we are. When boy meets girl our culture sends messages to the girl: abdicate your power, your personality, your identity. If it's not in our genes, it's certainly in our jeans, as we begin to dress and act to please others. We become husband and wife and eagerly enter our assigned roles as hunter and gatherer, thinking that we'll live happily ever after. But damn it, we don't. I tried to change "my" man. I tried to mold him into someone he wasn't. I wasn't satisfied with his good traits. I wanted him to be someone else. He didn't have a chance. Neither did I. Neither did we.

For thirty years I tried to make everyone else make me happy. And then, one day, I realized that there is only one person who can make me happy and I've finally met her. That person is me. And, so, at the age of 50, I decided to launch out on a journey and I vowed to do everything I wanted to do, outside my comfort zone, that was fun, reasonable and safe.

When I began my journey, I experienced times of intense fear and loneliness, but I never contemplated turning back, although doing so felt easier and safer. As I sifted through the process, I frequently felt as though I was walking through Jell-O.

Walking Through Jell-O is about self-empowerment. While this book reflects my own journey, I have included elements to help you recreate your relationship with yourself. This story is not about walking away, but about assuming responsibility. It is not about waiting for shining knights, but about polishing your own armor. You have the power. Acknowledging it will set you free. My choices led me in a direction that will be different from yours, but YOU can choose to make yours anything you want it to be. Plan to be scared. Plan to be joyous. There is a happy ending.

Glinka's Note

"Hey Mom, you're going to be a grandmother, but I've got a problem." My heart leapt with joy and lurched with apprehension. I waited silently to hear what troubled my daughter. "I don't know what to call you. You're not a typical grandmother, so all the usual words don't seem to apply." With relief, I began throwing out words that started with the letter G, and that might substitute for granny, grandma, grandmother, but none worked until I said *Glinka*, the name of a Russian composer. Bingo, that became my new name and my alter ego.

Chapter One

GLINKA LEARNS TO WALK

Obstacles

This chapter focuses on the events and circumstances that facilitate my transition from timid little Paula to a deeply depressed and suicidal young woman and then onward to Glinka, a vibrant and youthful grandmother engaging the world head-on.

Life has not been a cakewalk for me. It has been a trudge—sometimes feeling more like a walk through Jell-O. In this chapter, I briefly introduce "little Paula," a scrawny, underweight youth who has to sew fishing sinkers into her skirt to make weight for the Drum and Bugle Corp. I suffered terribly from low self-esteem resulting from my struggle as a dyslexic child in the first gifted classroom in the Los Angeles City school system. Having everything done for me by a loving father and never being expected to accept any sort of responsibility, I lacked self-confidence. I carried this almost debilitating dependency into marriage where it was perpetuated by a, perhaps, overly caring husband who knew how to maintain me physically, but not how to nurture me emotionally. Yes, I had a loving husband, healthy children and enjoyed a rather luxurious lifestyle.

When you have it all, life should be perfect, right? Think again. What about the suicide rate for people in this category? Marilyn Monroe certainly seemed to have it all; as did Ernest Hemingway and Amy Vanderbilt. These people lived sparkling lives. They were the envy of many. But they experienced such doubts, addictions, and horrendous depths of loneliness that they saw suicide as their only escape.

I, too, suffered from depression. In fact, I perfected Depression 101. It's a closet disease—one that we try to hide. Why? Because, to someone who struggles with depression, the clichés coming from well-meaning yet misdirected friends and family feel judgmental and insensitive. It's as if others believe that depression is voluntary. "You need to count your blessings," people would say to me. "You should think of others who are worse off than you." "Just pull yourself up by your bootstraps."

Grrrrrr. My bootstraps became so ragged from pulling and tugging that my boots fell off. My list of blessings was endless. My awareness of starving people was limitless. Did people really believe that I wanted to live like this? If they knew my thoughts, would they believe that I actually wanted to die? Unable to find understanding outside of myself, I went underground with my shame and my guilt, unable to plan ahead because I never knew if I could even get out of bed the next day.

I reveal, in this chapter, my own suicidal tendencies and the fact that, not only did I choose to live, but I chose to live life full steam ahead.

In this chapter, I show how perfect little Paula eventually transitions into Glinka, an energetic, healthy grandmother. Herein, I share my vulnerabilities and foibles as well as the life-changing thought processes that give me the courage and, in fact, the need to seek and face some incredible life challenges. These are some of the same challenges that confront many women. Few women have gone to the lengths that I did in order to meet those challenges, however.

Not only will this book inspire women, it is also a story of amazing events that are just plain entertaining. While this book reads more like fiction, it all really happened. That's what makes it so unique.

Chapter Two

GLINKA DIGS THE DIRT

Russia

Chapter two finds Glinka exploring her new-found philosophy designed to push herself outside of her comfort zone. Being one of only three Americans on a month-long Russian archeological dig, and the sole American woman, I sleep in a huge, glistening white, round tent right out of the time of Genghis Khan and bathe in a dishpan.

Before leaving on this expedition, I develop excruciating back pain and know that my mind is trying to sabotage my body, so I'll cancel the trip. As it turns out, I discover that my independence is just too threatening for my ego. Recognizing that, if I don't go this time, I'll never have the courage to try again, I commit to getting on the plane even if I have to drug myself and use a wheelchair. Only much later was the pain diagnosed as a herniated disk.

After meeting many challenges brought on by unimaginable inconveniences at the dig site, I discover a new sense of self-confidence. For hours, I sit with "my" 5,000-year-old friend in his grave and ask questions, hoping to gain some sense of where I fit into the universe and why I'm even here. For the first time in my life, I begin to see the immensity of the world but, as yet, I can't grasp it.

I grow increasingly proud of Glinka and her new sense of self until, toward the end of the excursion, a male acquaintance presents me with cognac and a longed-for bath. I decline the cognac and give up the idea of a relaxing soak because the door to the bathroom is nothing more than a strip of fabric covering only half of the opening. Realizing that my new-found confidence is waning, I do a quick dunk in the claw-foot tub and wonder how to yell *help* or *rape* in Russian.

My return home begins a year-long recovery from E. coli, Bovine Tuberculosis, and Giardia lamdia. If I had the strength and the sense of humor, I might have said, "Now, this is a fine mess you've gotten us into, Paula." But I am just too sick. After four months, having lost twenty per cent of my body weight, I clutch the edge of my hospital bed and make a decision to live. In fact, I make a bargain with God to never want to die again—a bargain, by the way, that I've kept.

Chapter Three

GLINKA CLIMBS THE LADDER IN A LONG RED DRESS

QE II

Recovery is slow. When I look into the mirror, what appears to be an emaciated refugee is looking back. My clothes and skin hang on my bones and my energy is barely existent. At first, I can't walk across my bedroom without help. Then I begin to force one foot in front of the other as I make circles in the pool each day. Finally, I'm able to walk down and get the mail, a 250-foot effort that requires several resting stops. I never regret going on the dig, but I do question my ability to heal and the drain on my family. My feelings of worthlessness return as my depression deepens. But as those of us who live long enough discover, things always change. And change it does, big time.

A friend invites me to help her pick out a mother-of-the-bride dress, and I come home with a slinky red spandex number that I have nowhere to wear. That changes quickly.

Three days before sailing, I discover that I can accompany my WWII veteran friends on the QE II to France to celebrate the fiftieth anniversary of D-Day. Now, I've never been a spontaneous person. I've always needed to know the itinerary. But I stop to think, what would Glinka do, and I decide to go for it. I throw together a suitcase of clothes, including the soon-to-be famous red dress, jump on a plane, and voilá, I'm in New York ready to board my fantasy; the luxury liner Queen Elizabeth II.

Through a series of events—some of my choosing and a little luck—from my bunk at the bottom in third-class, I *arrive* at the table at the top in first-class. Here, I sup in the Queen's Grill with a Kennedy family attorney, a blue-haired gentlewoman who puckers solemnly as she looks over the rim of her glasses at the lesbians seated next to her, a Brit who receives a fax that's he's being named an MBE (Member of the British Empire) by Queen Elizabeth, and Arnold Franco, a WWII vet who hires me two years later to write his memoir *Code to Victory*.

As I arrive for dinner that first evening, I walk the length of the dining room in my slinky red gown, passing William F. Buckley, Bob Hope, Walter Cronkite, Andy Rooney, Vera Lyn, and Vic Damon. As I approach my table, all the men stand and the attorney remarks, "Paula, I wish you could have seen how many men choked on their drinks when you entered the room." Considering the conservative nature of those in the room, I wasn't sure that their choking was a compliment, but it sure was fun.

Glinka discovers that there's a red dress in every woman and, throughout this chapter, she encourages all women to try it on. Life is a choice, and, much like the rungs of a ladder, if you take them one at a time you will get where you want to be.

Up to this point, I had never traveled alone to a big city, reserved a hotel room, or ridden a subway. I do it all and without getting mugged, raped, or murdered. In stark contrast to my experiences on the archeological dig, I live my fantasy life to the fullest in my slinky red dress.

Chapter Four

GLINKA RIDES THE RAILS

Trans-Siberian Express & Yukon Pass Railroad

Glinka realizes another dream of a lifetime when she takes the Trans-Siberian Express across the Siberian continent from Vladivostok to Moscow. But, instead of enjoying the journey of reliving tsarist times in contemporary luxury, I find myself deeply troubled by the surrounding devastation of rural villages wrought by the destruction of the collective farm system. In Mongolia, I am again challenged with unidentifiable food as I share a meal with a family in their yurt. After my experience on the dig, I have serious doubts as I contemplate the curdled something in my bowl. Afterward, although terrified, I ride a Mongolian pony.

The highlight of my day in Mongolia is finding serenity within chaos at a monastery and enjoying the beauty of the architecture. In this chapter, I also write about a stop at Lake Baikal, the deepest lake in the world, and a visit to a dacha, a Russian country house in the village on its shore. The lake is another place I've always wanted to visit because it once had some of the most pristine water in the world, had then become severely polluted by neighboring factories, and was now being restored. I was interested, not only in how much attention Russia is giving to the environment, but how they were going about it.

Chapter Five

GLINKA SEES ALASKA

Journey to the Frozen World

I learn that not everything has to be experienced just because it's there and that it's okay to say no. This chapter features Glinka's sometimes bold excursions into the vast frozen wilderness of Alaska. Starting by ship from California, I head north to the Inside Passage where glaciers line the shore and wildlife fascinates the eye. On board, I meet a countess and her brother. Having missed out on being a bona fide countess myself because the title went through the paternal line, I commiserate with the brother who lost out because, in his family, it went through the maternal line. The ship is pure luxury with no challenges other than which dress to wear to dinner. The scenery is spectacular, the crystal so thin I'm afraid a sip might shatter it, the cordon bleu menu fascinating, and the woman with a two-inch parrot hanging from her glasses a story in itself.

But once in Juneau I'm faced with anxiety as I soar for the first time in a helicopter. I've always been afraid to fly in one, but really wanted to because of all the unique places that can be reached and all the incredible things that can be seen. So I gave it the *test*, and it passed. It's only unsafe if we crash, right? Because the passengers are seated according to weight, the little ones are put in front where the world seems to drop away. Yeah! That's me. All fear falls away as the scene below unfolds into a magical splendor I had never imagined. In all directions, glistening white glaciers are cut deep by neon blue crevasses and I find myself mentally creating fanciful stories of climbers traversing through this treacherous frozen beauty.

We land on a vast ice field covered with plastic igloos for the dogs, and I drive a dogsled. I'm hooked and briefly consider entering the Iditarod. This thought lasts for only a moment when I put it to the *comfortable*, *safe* and *reasonable* test. It comes up *unreasonable* and very *uncomfortable*. I decide that I really don't want to begin, at the age of 64, training for a dogsled race that covers 1,150 miles through some of the most extreme terrain in the world and challenges the drivers to the limit. It would take years to prepare for and I decide that I have *miles to go before I sleep* and the miles aren't going to be in the Alaskan wilderness.

Out of Skagway, Glinka takes the Yukon Pass RR where, at the summit, she imbibes on very bad champagne and worse salmon canapés. But I do receive a brass "Christmas tree" ornament that says I've been there. Wow! What an expensive little decoration. It was a more than memorable event because I wet my pants on the way to the train when I couldn't get my zipper down and had to choose between missing the train or spending the journey in warm soggy ski pants. Fortunately, the pants were waterproof, but only from the outside. I never expected they'd have to be waterproof on the inside, too.

In her former life, Paula would have returned to her stateroom and missed the boat, literally and figuratively. But now she doesn't want to miss a thing, even for the sake of vanity.

Chapter Six

GLINKA GOES AWRY

Foibles, Fiascos, & Internet Dating

Some of the vignettes in this chapter belong in a plain brown wrapper—the rewriting of the manual on how to play a didjeridu, for example. Others are just plain fun, as Glinka works through the web of Internet dating and unusual experiences such as Celestine moments that reveal her vulnerabilities, flaws, and moxie.

After many years of singlehood, I hire a life coach to focus on the one area of my life that's missing; a soul mate. I try Internet dating big time and subscribe to five sites. A whole array of lovely men appear and a myriad of unique experiences transpire as I learn the system and how to cull from the herd before making contact. A two-month, in-depth correspondence with a man leads me to believe that he might be the one. During extensive communication he mentions that Alaska is the only state he hasn't visited and would I entertain the idea of sharing my stateroom with him on an upcoming cruise.

I decide that he would make an interesting companion and good dance partner, so I agree to meet.

I clarify the separate sleeping arrangements and stress that there is no hope of it changing. He agrees and goes home to pack. Three days into the cruise, he comments that his stomach is constantly hurting. When I ask if he knows why, he answers, "It's the Cialis."

"Cialis? Why are you taking Cialis?"

"So I can be ready when you are."

"What? I'm not going to be ready. I thought I made that clear."

"You did, but I've changed my mind."

(Partial Chapter Summaries from *Walking Through Jell-O*, by Paula Spellman.)

Tips for Sending a Proposal Package to the Publisher

Generally, you're going to start the process of approaching a publisher by sending a query letter. Once the proposal is requested, send it per the specific requirements that publisher has outlined in his submission guidelines or letter of request. Some publishers want to see sample chapters as part of the proposal. Others won't ask to see sample chapters until after reviewing the proposal. For a fiction proposal, it is common for a publisher to request the first 50 or 100 pages of the manuscript.

Send your proposal package by mail unless a publisher requests it sent by email. And then follow the publisher's guidelines. Do they want to receive it as an attachment or in the body of an email? For additional details on how to prepare your proposal package, refer to Chapter Four.

Publishers' Major Pet Peeves

Most publishers who have been in the business for any length of time believe that they have seen everything. Authors sometimes do some bizarre things to attract a publisher. And publishers tend to be annoyed by certain approaches. Here are a few actual publishers' pet peeves.

- Authors who send a manuscript when their submission guidelines call for a query letter first.
- Authors who don't bother to read the publishers' submission guidelines.

- Receiving pitches for books on the wrong topic or in the wrong genre.
- Proposal packages or manuscripts sent via the post office when the publisher prefers receiving email submissions and vice versa.
- Over-taping packages so they are difficult to open.
- Authors neglecting to read what the publisher produces.
- Sending pitches to the publishers' voicemail.

This is the end of our lesson on how to write a book proposal. Once you have completed your chapter summaries, it is time to start approaching agents and/or publishers.

But first consider hiring an editor who has had experience with book proposals in your subject or genre. This is a good insurance policy and generally well worth the $250 to $2,000 (or so) fee. (See Chapter Ten for more about editing.)

You want to produce the best book possible for your readers. And if you are going to seek a traditional publisher, he wants to see only your best effort. Here's what some of the publishers are saying:

The Harvard Common Press wants to see "Strong writing skills." Autumn House Press asks you to "Submit only your best work." Sweet Gum Press guidelines state, "Good writing is the most persuasive part of the submission." Tolling Bell Books editors advise, "Be sure your work has been proofread."

Recommended Reading:

How to Write a Successful Book Proposal in 8 Days or Less, by Patricia Fry (Matilija Press, print edition, 2005).

How to Approach and Work with Agents

Most authors, at some point in their careers, wonder, "Should I get an agent?" The answer to this question depends on a couple of factors. If you want to be published by one of the mega-publishers, you will probably need an agent. If your project would appeal only to small, niche publishers, you may not need one. In fact, some small to medium-size publishers prefer working with authors who do not have outside representation.

Random House and HarperCollins make it a policy to reject a submission unless it comes through an agent. Of course, humans make policies and they can change policies. You could be the lucky one who lands a contract by slipping one over the transom at Simon and Schuster, for example.

In fact, according to one source, just eighty percent of books accepted by major publishing houses are represented by agents. So, while I won't discourage you from trying to infiltrate the system by sending an unagented submission to a major publisher, I urge you to arm yourself with enough information so that you are operating within the realm of reality. Before venturing off into the unknown and crossing over long-standing barriers, at least be realistic.

Is your book actually one that would interest a large publishing house? Few of them would take a risk on a first novel. You might consider building a reputation and a following before approaching the Penguin Group. A book on bird-watching in the Ozarks or creative window dressings for a child's room probably wouldn't appeal to a major publisher. They wouldn't be interested in your memoirs, either, unless, perhaps, you have celebrity status.

What Does an Agent Do for You, Anyway?

An agent might help you to fine-tune your proposal or manuscript before sending it to a publisher. When it's ready, she will show it around to suitable publishers—especially those with whom she has worked before. She'll give a sales pitch. She'll follow up with a publisher, when necessary. And she'll bring you any contract that is offered. She'll also advise you in negotiating a better deal—a larger advance, perhaps, and a higher royalty percentage.

Agents sometimes run in the same circles as publishers and can get inside information. An agent might know what type of manuscript is currently being sought by a particular publisher. One author I know received a tip from her agent. She said that a certain major publisher was in the market for a book on a particular topic. The author quickly put together a proposal and promptly landed a contract. I've heard about other authors who were contacted because of their excellent blog posts or extraordinary websites on topics of interest to publishers, and who were asked to write books on those subjects. One involved a new slant on fitness training for women; another one had to do with self-promotion.

An agent sometimes elicits bidding wars in an attempt to get the author more money. She may show your manuscript to two or three publishers. If they're all interested in it, she may challenge each of them to up their antes.

An agent can sometimes get your manuscript read faster than when you submit one on your own. Some acquisitions editors prefer working with qualified agents as opposed to less savvy authors.

Once your book has been published, a good agent will make sure that your royalty checks arrive on time. After all, she has a vested interest. Your agent doesn't get paid until you land a publishing contract. Along with a percentage of your royalties, he or she may also receive a portion of the advance they negotiate for you and any escalators that might come your way.

If you choose not to use an agent, hire an intellectual properties or literary attorney to look over any publishing contract you might receive.

Before choosing an agent, understand that they don't all come with the same knowledge, experience, and values. While many agents are legitimate and have had years of experience working within the publishing industry, there are plenty of newcomers trying to ride the wave of opportunity at the expense of hopeful authors.

An agent typically signs with you for a year or two. This can create a rough road ahead if the agent is a poor one. It can tie you up for months and keep you from pitching your own manuscript.

A bad agent can be worse than having no agent at all. Here are some warning signs indicating that you may have contacted the wrong agent:

- She asks for money up front, usually in the form of a reading fee. Many agents will request a minimal amount to handle copies and postage. That's okay. It's when they ask for a reading fee or an advance against royalties that you should start to see red flags.
- He suggests that you turn your manuscript over to a particular book doctor or editor before he will start working with you. It's not uncommon for an agent to suggest that you hire an editor. Nor is it unusual for him to make recommendations. But if he gives you just one or two leads, he may be running a scam. Sometimes, people calling themselves agents are just operating editorial services. They don't have any actual agenting experience.
- He is unwilling to give references. Legitimate agents are pleased to share their successes. If the agent has never signed an author within the category of publisher you hope to land, this may not be the right agent for you. It's important that you find out what types of manuscripts he or she has placed and with whom. I suggest talking to some of the authors he represents to learn if this agent is professional and effective.
- She goes for long periods without communicating and will not respond to your letters, emails, or phone calls.

Some opportunists who masquerade as agents con unsuspecting authors out of hundreds or thousands of dollars. It would behoove you to thoroughly check out any agency you are considering before signing with them. It could take time to find the right agent. But it is important that you choose one who is legitimate, with whom you are compatible, and who believes in your project. Locate agents through the following channels:

- Access the Association of Authors' Representatives (AAR) database at http://aaronline.org. All 382 literary agents on this list have gone through a stringent screening process. All come recommended. Before signing with an agent, make sure that he or she is a member of this organization.
- Visit the Agent Research and Evaluation Company's free access agent database at http://www.agentresearch.com. They provide a new agent list for $75.00. For a $210 fee, they'll offer a more detailed search involving five agents of your choice.
- Find agents listed in *Writer's Digest's Guide to Literary Agents*. You'll also find lists of literary agents in *Writer's Market*, *Literary Market Place,* and a database of US and UK literary agents at http://www.1000literaryagents.com.
- Consider an agent who is recommended by another author who has a book similar to yours.
- Find agents listed in recently published books similar to yours. An author will often mention his agent on the acknowledgements page.
- Attend writers' conferences where agents are speaking and see if you can find a match.
- Set up appointments with appropriate agents at writers' conferences.

Tips for Choosing and Working with an Agent

The Association of Authors' Representatives website provides valuable information for the author seeking agent representations (http://aaronline.org/FAQ). Here, you'll learn how to connect with an appropriate agent, what an agent can do for you, and what questions to ask an agent before getting involved.

Some agents, like some publishers, specialize. Match your project to their expertise. Linda Konner at the Linda Konner Literary Agency in New York specializes in health, self-help, and how-to books, so don't bring her your latest novel. Elaine English and Kevin McAdams represent only novels through the Elaine P. English Literary Agency. And Michael Larsen at the Larsen/Pomada Literary Agency specializes in many nonfiction topics.

Beware of the newbie or wannabe masquerading as a literary agent. There is no licensing of agents, thus no industry standards. The screening at the Association of Author's Representatives is the most reliable method of choosing an agent today.

Many publishing authorities recommend soliciting an agent before you begin showing your manuscript around. They say that an agent will reject manuscripts that have already been submitted to the prime publishers.

On the other hand, sometimes it pays to distribute your proposal to a few appropriate publishers before contacting an agent. If you get positive feedback from a couple of publishers, you may have a greater chance of engaging the services of an agent. Tell the agent, for example, "ABC Publishing has asked to see my sample chapters. Would you represent this project for me?"

You approach an agent in much the same way you do a publisher—with a query letter and/or a book proposal representing your current project. Read the agent's submission guidelines for authors and comply. Generally, you will send a query letter to appropriate agents once your book proposal is completed. If yours is a novel, you might wait until the book is finished. Send the same query letter you would send to a publisher, only address it to the agent and refer to your desire for representation rather than publishing.

As with any query letter, keep it brief, professional, and to the point. The job of a query letter is to pique the agent's interest. If you adequately do this, she or he will ask to see your proposal and/or manuscript.

Working with an agent is similar to working with a publisher. You should strive for mutual respect and an air of professionalism.

Recommended Reading:

Jeff Herman's Guide to Book Editors, Publishers and Literary Agents, 2011: Who They Are! What They Want? How to Win Them Over by Jeff Herman (Sourcebooks, 2010).

How to Find a Publisher on Your Own

Can you find a publisher on your own? Absolutely. In fact, some publishers prefer negotiating without the interference of an agent.

You already have an A, B, and C list of publishers (see Chapter Two). You know which publishers you want to target. You have their submission guidelines. You understand which publishers prefer to receive your query letter, which want the book proposal, and which want to receive your complete manuscript as an introduction.

Give 'em What They Want

Perhaps you've submitted your manuscript to ten, twenty, or even fifty publishers without success, and you feel as though publishers are not accepting anything from anyone. Maybe you just haven't offered any of them exactly what they're looking for. One publisher told me recently that smaller publishers are looking for authors who will write outside the New York box. They want fresh voices that have something new to say. But first you must know what that is. This is where the submission guidelines come in.

Once you've decided which publishers to contact, solicit the most recent copies of their submission guidelines and follow them. (See tips for locating and studying submission guidelines in Chapter Two.)

The Query Letter Explained

You've seen the term *query letter* approximately two dozen times so far in this book. Expect to see it several more times. Why? Because this is one of the most important pieces to the publishing maze. As I said in Chapter

Two, a query letter is your first chance to make an excellent impression—it could be your foot-in-the-door.

Most agents and publishers request a query letter first. I recommend waiting to write the query letter until the book proposal is completed. By then, you'll have a clearer idea of the scope and focus of your book. A book idea can change right before your eyes once you've been forced to examine it through the process of writing a book proposal. Also, you will have a book proposal to send to the publisher should he or she request it.

The Format

Type the query on your letterhead. Make sure that your letterhead is up to date. Do not use an old version where you have to pencil in your website address or cross out your old email address and write in the new one. Technology is such that creating letterhead on your home computer is easy and inexpensive. There's no need to give less than a perfect presentation.

Adhere to the requirements of most publishers. That is, single-space your letter with an extra line space between paragraphs. Do not indent. Use 1 to 1 ½ inch margins. Keep your query letter to one page, if possible—no more than two pages.

Type the date toward the top of the page on the far left side. Leave one line space and type the name of the acquisitions editor (or agent), then the publishing company (or agency) name, and then the complete mailing address.

If the publisher prefers an email query, type the letter in your word processing program without the address block. You can also omit the date as it will appear automatically on your email. Do, however, include your full name, address and phone number at the bottom of the letter. Make it easy for the publisher to respond in the way that makes him or her most comfortable. When the letter is finished, do a spell-check and copy and paste the letter into the body of an email, unless the submission guidelines ask for an attachment. (Read about what to put in your subject line in Chapter Four.)

Making Contact

Make sure you are addressing the appropriate editor. Large publishing companies often assign certain topics/genres to different editors. Some companies have as many as eight or ten editors each representing different types of manuscripts.

There have been times when I thought I had the name of the current editor, only to have my query letter returned with a note stating, "This editor no longer works here." Now, why they didn't pass my submission along to the new editor, I don't know. My point is that you can't always rely on the universe (or a publishing house staff) to give you a helping hand or a leg up. Take charge.

While we're on the subject of being proactive, I'd like to caution you against using a submissions service that charges authors a fee for contacting editors and publishers. These services cannot be any more effective than you and are probably less so. I recommend that you do your own legwork and headwork when it comes to pitching your manuscript. If you're already working with an editor who has experience submitting to publishers, and you want to hire him or her to handle the submission process for you, go ahead. But I still prefer that an author strive toward heavy personal involvement throughout the submission process and beyond.

Okay, so we have the protocol out of the way. Now let's explore what goes into a successful query letter.

The Basics of a Successful Query Letter

Your magnificent query letter must:

1. Contain an intriguing beginning or a hook—something that catches the agent's, publisher's, or editor's attention. Don't fret over this—just come up with something that creates enough interest so the editor will keep reading. Don't try to be too cute or clever, you might come across as trite.
2. Identify this as a query letter and ask for what you want. Sometimes we become so involved in choosing the perfect words that we forget to focus on clarity. State or indicate early on that this is a query letter. Say, for example, "Please consider my manuscript for publication," or "I'd like to propose a book featuring . . ."
3. Describe your project succinctly and briefly explain (based on information from your book proposal) the need and/or desire for a book such as this.
4. Mention the highlights of your project and any special aspects.
5. Name a few of your experts. (You might want to include a separate list of experts, if it is extensive and impressive.)

6. Share something about yourself—your background in the subject of your book and as a writer. I sometimes include a separate page listing my published books or titles of any articles I've had published on the topic of this particular book.
7. Let the publisher know that you have a book proposal ready to send or a complete manuscript. I know, I told you to forget about the manuscript until after you've completed the proposal. But there will come a point when you have completed the manuscript and you'll want to mention that to the publishers you contact.

Should You Send Simultaneous Submissions?

It is perfectly okay to send out query letters to numbers of publishers at once. Some publishers even sanction sending a book proposal to more than one publisher at a time. I usually send my initial query letter to my first choice of publishers only. If he or she isn't interested in my project, I start sending out simultaneous query submissions.

Do not, however, send your manuscript to more than one publisher simultaneously. An exception to this rule is when a publisher holds your manuscript for a long time without responding. If you can't elicit a response after a reasonable waiting period, write or call and let that publisher know that you will be sending the manuscript to another publisher who has requested it. And then tell the new publisher that the manuscript is also being considered by XYZ Publishing House.

How Long Should You Wait for a Response?

What is a reasonable waiting period? My rule of thumb for a requested manuscript is two to four weeks past the projected response time for that particular publisher. Most publishers state in their submission guidelines when you can expect a response to a query, a book proposal, and a manuscript. FYI, the average response time for a query letter is one to two months; for a proposal, it's around two months and three months for a manuscript. Unless otherwise stated by the publisher, use these standards.

Sometimes, you'll contact the publisher with a *tracer letter* (letter of inquiry) only to learn that he has misplaced your submission or he claims he did not receive it. Don't throw yourself in front of a bus. Sometimes a perceived disaster such as this can work in your favor. Think about it:

Suddenly your project becomes a priority for that publisher. Re-submit it at his request and he will go out of his way to look at it this time.

A publisher might admit that he received your package, but he just hasn't had time to review it. There's still hope. Or he will tell you that it is being circulated among his editorial staff. This is a good thing. Publishers at most larger houses will distribute what they view as more promising proposals or manuscripts among the editorial staff and, sometimes, the marketing team. This can take time. Try not to get impatient with publishers who don't respond within minutes of receiving your manuscript. When a publisher responds promptly, it is often with a rejection.

Authorship is not for the weak, desperate, or faint of heart. There is nothing glamorous about rejection. There is nothing nurturing in negligence and abuse. If you're in this business long enough, you will experience all of the above, and it ain't a pretty sight.

If you think that writing is a lonely activity, just wait until you enter into the competitive field of publishing. You'll be ignored, shined on, dissed, talked down to, and even treated rudely. You'll sometimes feel like a second-class citizen. To get along, an author must be humble, patient, persistent, and always professional.

Surefire Ways to Get Your Query Letter Rejected

Here's a list of mistakes to avoid when developing and submitting your query letter.

1. Do not send your query letter to the wrong publisher. Christine Holbert is founder and director of Lost Horse Press. She publishes specialized fiction only. She says, "A writer needs to do a bit of investigative work before submitting a query or a manuscript to a publisher; find out what the publisher's vision is and what the previously published titles of that particular publishing house are. I receive hundreds of manuscripts of inappropriate genre that are a waste of my time and the author's effort."
2. Don't tell the publisher his business. In other words, don't say, "You've really got to add this book to your list if you hope to make a success of your publishing company." Or "This book will make you rich."
3. Do not threaten the publisher. It will do you no good to say, "If you don't buy my book, I will kill myself." Or "You're missing the book of the century if you pass on this one."

4. Don't claim that your book contains no mistakes. Have you ever picked up a book that had no mistakes? I don't think it is humanly (or even mechanically) possible to produce a book without a mistake. And from what I'm told by publishers, many authors who claim to have hired professional editors for their books, have been taken for a ride. Hire a reputable editor before submitting your book proposal or manuscript to a publisher. Make sure that it is the best that it can be and avoid making wild claims as to the pureness of your project.
5. Don't try to convince a publisher to accept your book by saying that your family and friends love it. This is a blatant, red flag sign of an amateur.
6. Don't tell the publisher that everyone will buy your book. A publisher will be more impressed by an author who has done his homework and is quite clear as to who his audience is.
7. Do not state that this is the only book you'll ever write. Publishers prefer working with authors who are likely to produce more than one good book. If your book is successful and you are a pleasure to work with, the publisher would just as soon accept another book from you than from someone he doesn't know.
8. Don't reveal that you've been working on the book for twenty-five years. There is nothing impressive in the fact that you have not been able to complete a twelve-month project in over two decades.
9. Do not try to bribe the publisher. Unless you can offer him a large sum of money or a free vacation in Tahiti, don't bother to entice his favor through bribery.
10. Avoid sending a query letter with spelling and grammatical errors.

Keep Current

Things change rather frequently in the publishing industry. Because of this, I suggest that you do not rely on submission guidelines that are more than six months old. In fact, I suggest writing the date on copies of submission guidelines as you print them out. Demonstrate your level of professionalism by keeping a close check on changes within the publishing companies of your choice.

Fairview Press, for example, a division of Fairview Health Services which is affiliated with the University of Minnesota, founded Deaconess Press in 1989. They originally published only chemical dependency and recovery materials. Then they expanded their list to include psychology, self-help, humor, reference, inspiration, sociology, parenting, child care, general health, and children's books. In recent years, the owners of the press have decided to focus on two main categories—health/ medicine and aging/end of life/death and dying/grief.

Treble Heart Books was established in 2001. Last year, they had three divisions: Treble Heart (romance, paranormal, metaphysical, science fiction, etc.); Mountain View (inspirational and Christian books) and Sundowners, which publishes Westerns. Their newest division at this printing is WhoooDoo Mysteries.

Sample Query Letters

(A query letter addressed to a publisher for a nonfiction self-help book.)

Dear Mr. or Ms. [Last Name]:

Over twenty million Americans suffer from mood disorders in any given year. Add to that, the number of loved ones who are also severely affected by these diseases and the figure could be as high as fifty million or seventeen percent of the population. I know how difficult life can be when someone you love has been diagnosed with a mood disorder. Depression, bipolar, anxiety, and suicide have taken an extremely difficult and sometimes grave toll within my own family.

In addition, I've spent decades working with patients of mood disorders and helping their companions cope with the ailments while they struggle to regain enough stability to have a joyful life of their own. My book, ***The Black Dog and the Cyclone Racer: A Guide for Companions of People with Depression and Bipolar Disorder***, is the outcome of these many experiences.

My years of personal involvement with the Depression and Bipolar Support Alliance (DBSA), both as a board member and office manager, have shown me how helpful an easily understood guidebook could be for companions of patients with mood disorders. As of now, there just isn't one. Without question, the need is there. My book will meet that need.

I know my target audiences and specifically how to reach them. I am passionate about the potential benefits of getting this book into the hands of as many people who need it as possible, and I have the time, energy, and ideas toward this goal.

The Black Dog and the Cyclone Racer has been whole-heartedly endorsed by three associations and groups that are directly involved with depression and bipolar disorders. The directors at Suicide Awareness Voices of Education (SAVE) and The Jed Foundation, as well as Terence A. Ketter, M.D., Chief, Bipolar Disorders Clinic of the Stanford University School of Medicine have all encouraged me to have this book published so they can use it in their work. The directors at SAVE even suggested that I contact your publishing company. I, and other professionals, believe that this could be an important contribution to helping the many people involved in caring for those with life-challenging depressive disorders.

Please request the book proposal or the completed manuscript for ***The Black Dog and the Cyclone Racer.***

Sincerely,
Jerry Malugeon

(A query letter for fiction addressed to a literary agent.)

Dear Mr. (or Ms.) [Last Name]:

Thank-you in advance for taking the time to consider representing *The First Gift*, my recently completed novel.

The First Gift is about first love, the loss of that love, which occurs twice over the course of the story, and the realization that there is a spiritual foundation to the love that is given and received in our lives. The narrative evokes a strong sense of place; the majesty of alpine meadows and wildflowers, untamed rivers, meteor showers and starlight, and an ancient observatory where love is found and spirit is made manifest.

As baby boomers realize their mortality, the timing of this novel is perfect because the story provides a different way of looking at aging and loss. It both respects and celebrates the wisdom and experience that comes with aging, while at the same time explaining that loss is connected to the spiritual underpinnings of a universe where love is the unifying force from which we came and to which we return.

The story's elderly protagonist, Walter Harrison, a well-known writer and scientist, combines the genius of Albert Einstein with a dash of Will Rogers. The narrative plunges back in time as, in the final days of Walter's life, he recalls a trip he and his dog, Buck, made into the mountains of Colorado in 1968 to reconnect with Walter's first and only love, Elena.

Buck's mission in life is to help Walter understand that there is no correlation between a dog's loyalty and human intelligence. As they travel, the dog has various exploits—some of them reckless and others endearing. The imaginary conversations Buck and Walter share about the nature of life on earth are interspersed with Walter's recollections of his blossoming love for Elena in the late 1940s.

After nearly two decades of being separated by war and illness, Walter and Elena meet again and rekindle their passionate love affair in an ancient and abandoned observatory. Like *Romeo and Juliet* and *The Notebook*, however, all great love stories need tragedy and separation in order to fully touch the reader. Walter and Elena's story is no exception. After being reunited, fate and life circumstances intervene, and they must separate again. In the depths of his despair over the loss of the one true love of his life for a second time, Walter experiences a spiritual revelation about love, loss, and about the ultimate loss we all face—the end of life. The theme of trying to reconnect with a first love and a lost love is, in many ways, a metaphor for all of our lives: First, after our birth, losing and then during our lifetime attempting to reconnect to *The First Gift* we receive—the spiritual love of the universe.

Appeal:

This love story is about an enduring passion and commitment that spans sixty years, but it also uses a rare and humorous relationship between a man and his dog to counterbalance the emotional impact of the story. This novel stands alone in two important ways. First, it is one of the few passionate stories about a couple committed in their love to one another, despite circumstances that forever separate them. Even more importantly, however, *The First Gift* is a love story that describes the spiritual love of the universe as the unifying force of our existence. The result is a moving eulogy to all of our lives—a story of love and loss that pretty much sums up the notable context of most people's lives. The novel will appeal to everyone who has ever been in love, those who have imagined reconnecting with a lost love, all of us who understand the unique relationship that humans share with animals, baby boomers who will relate to both the story and era in which the novel is set, and anyone who is seeking a greater spiritual awareness.

Marketing:
Buck is my real-life companion. He is a therapy dog who regularly makes the rounds of hospitals to spread the unconditional love that is demonstrated in *The First Gift*. Buck is the best marketing tool imaginable. Taking Buck on promotional tours will sell this book!

Similar Books and Authors:
A random review of any bestseller list reveals four equally pervasive American obsessions: getting rich, getting skinny, getting the love we want, and getting spiritual. Over the past few decades, in the love story category, readers have connected with the works of Nicholas Sparks and Gabriel Garcia Marquez. In the spirituality genre, people have devoured books by the likes of Richard Bach, Dan Millman, James Redfield, among dozens of others as literature of inspiration, if not modern scripture. This book is thus marketable to a wide audience as its timeless spiritual message is enfolded into a grand and passionate love story.

I have been writing for ten years and have a BA in English. My first novel, *The Silent One*, was represented by the Sandra Watt Literary Agency. I am the editor of a publication for a prominent local winery and my article about fundraising will soon be published in *Society Magazine*.

Please review the enclosed synopsis of *The First Gift*. May I send you my 65,000 word manuscript?

Sincerely,
Lyle McDonald

Your Query Letter

Obviously, your query letter will not look exactly like either of these query letters. Your subject is different, your writing style is different. Your experiences, connections, and skills will differ. You could look at a hundred query letters and never find one exactly like yours or one that you feel comfortable patterning yours after. That's okay. Just use the guides and examples provided here to design your query letter, keeping in mind that your goal is to adequately and succinctly describe your project and make a case for it.

Before sending your query letter to the agents/publishers of your choice, establish a way of recording each submission. Keep excellent records. Don't rely on memory. Know exactly when you sent a query or a proposal and to whom. Log each response and each tracer letter sent. Effective recordkeeping isn't just a convenience, it's a necessity.

A Word about Rejection

We write, we get edited, we get critiqued, and we sometimes get rejected. There is no such thing as a writer's life without editing or without rejection and criticism. Robert Olmsted, publisher at Dan River Press told me once, "The average writer thinks because he/she writes brilliantly, that publishing should follow. Not real. Publishing is a commercial activity engaged in for profit. Writing is art. If you are asking a publisher to invest in your art, give the publisher a reason and he will. All rejections happen because the publisher has other options on which he believes he can make more money."

What if you get that dreaded rejection letter? Here's a reality check. Publishers don't know everything. And they don't always recognize a Wow project when they see it. Some tremendously successful books were rejected many times before they were discovered. The first in the series of *Chicken Soup for the Soul* books was reportedly rejected by 140 publishers before Health Communications agreed to publish it. Since then, there have been more than 112 million copies of the nearly 200 Chicken Soup titles sold.

James Redfield's *Celestine Prophecy* was rejected by several publishers before Redfield decided to self-publish. He sold so many copies on his own, that Warner Books (now Grand Central Publishing) eagerly agreed to publish it. The book has sold millions of copies since.

While I want you to focus on the positive and believe in your project, I also stress the importance of realistic evaluation. Keep an eye on trends. Make it your business to know what is selling and what is not. Get into the minds and hearts of readers. Avoid being so emotionally attached to your project that you become blind to reality.

What Happens When You're Issued a Publishing Contract?

Not all correspondence from a publisher comes in the form of a rejection letter. There's always the chance that you will eventually receive a contract. When this happens, I urge you to read it carefully and thoroughly and then hire an intellectual properties or literary attorney to review it. He or she may point out areas that you'll want to discuss with the publisher. He might advise you to negotiate higher royalties or a better percentage for book club sales.

Yes, most contracts are negotiable—at least aspects of them are.

Some publishers today offer to purchase your manuscript outright. Probably two-thirds of those I researched for this chapter had the outright purchase option. What can you get for a manuscript? Publishers offer anywhere from $600 to around $20,000, with $2,000 to $5,000 being most common.

Royalties, for books governed by royalty contracts, are generally paid quarterly, but there are exceptions to this rule, too. Read your contract carefully. Are you getting royalties on the retail or the wholesale price? About half of those publishers I researched pay on the retail price and half, of course, on the wholesale price.

In May of 2007, I did a survey of thirty-five publishers and came up with twenty-four combinations of royalty percentages offered by these publishers. For print books, the percentages range from 2.5 to five percent on up to ten to twenty percent with every combination imaginable in between. One publisher offers five to twelve percent, another seven to ten percent. There were publishers giving a straight ten percent and a straight fifteen percent or 6.5 to fifteen percent. Still the average royalty percentage you'll find among traditional publishers is between ten and twelve percent. For electronic books (ebooks), royalties are in the twenty-five to fifty percent range.

Not all publishers will pay an advance. In fact, advances run from 0 to $50,000. The majority of publishers offer $1,000 advance in two equal payments: $500 at the time the contract is signed and $500 upon satisfactory completion of a manuscript. The advance is deducted from future royalties.

There are many new twists in the publishing arena. Some publishers today ask prospective authors to solicit funds among the corporate sector in order to finance their projects. If you can't land a publishing contract the traditional way, you might consider asking for some sort of financial support. Of course, the business will want something in return—either in the form of royalties, or an advertisement on the inside cover of your book. This may seem like an unusual idea, but if you can come into a publishing agreement with a chunk of money, just think of the difference it could make.

A contract is sometimes issued before the book is written. A hopeful author might be asked to write a book or several chapters on speculation (spec). This means that the publisher wants you to produce something tangible and to his liking before he issues a contract. At that point, he may give you half of the advance and a deadline.

Sometimes publishers demand changes to a manuscript. As authors, we have to decide how much we are willing to bend in order to satisfy a certain publisher. Do you really want to rewrite your young adult novel for an adult audience? Are you willing to alter the true story of your grandfather's war experience so that it reads like fiction? While I encourage hopeful authors to make the decisions necessary to get published, I also caution you against selling your soul.

How to Work Successfully with a Publisher

When you enter into a contract with a publisher, he has certain obligations and so do you. Your responsibilities go beyond the parameters of the contract. It is to your benefit to develop a good working relationship with your publisher for the life of your contract. For example:

- Give the publisher your best effort. Hire an editor before sending your manuscript to a publisher. Shortchanging your publisher in this area means shortchanging yourself.
- Respect the publisher's time and space. How? Respond with just the information requested and send just the materials required. Do not overwhelm the publisher with frequent phone calls. Don't send the first

twelve drafts of your manuscript unless, of course, he or she asks for them.

- Keep your word. The publisher is counting on you to meet agreed upon deadlines, to follow through with promotion, and so forth.
- Keep an open line of communication. Stay in touch regarding deadlines. If something changes and you can't meet a deadline, communicate that.
- Expect to do a rewrite. The publisher may or may not ask you to rewrite parts of your book. Most likely, he will send you an edited version of your manuscript for your approval. Study the edits carefully to make sure that the meaning of your message has not been altered.
- Be prepared to hand over control. A publisher may change the title that you have become so attached to. He may ask you to reorganize your chapters. Of course, you can question his judgment and maybe negotiate for what you want if it means a lot to you. But realize that the publisher probably has more experience with matters of book publishing than you do.

Recommended Reading:

The Author's Toolkit: A Step-by-Step Guide to Writing and Publishing Your Book by Mary Embree (Allworth Press, 2003).

Get Ready, Get Set, Write

This is what you've been waiting for—the opportunity to write your wonderful book. You've established that there is a market for it. You've decided on a publisher. You've sent out at least one query letter. And you've developed a chapter outline. It's finally time to shift into writer mode. But first let's do a little detective work.

Read What You Write

Before launching into your manuscript, I want you to read books similar to the one you plan to write. It surprises me how many new authors neglect to follow this vital step.

Familiarize yourself with the tone, format, and style of books in your genre. Read a variety of authors. If yours is a young adult novel, study half a dozen or so young adult novels. Pay attention to the language. What drives these stories? Identify the elements of the most successful books in this category and apply some of them to yours. I'm not suggesting that you copy these books, but use them as guides in organizing and writing yours. Concentrate on addressing the same audience.

Maybe you're writing a how-to book. Not everyone can write directions or a series of steps with clarity. Read instructional books on many topics. Notice how they are organized. What techniques seem to work and which ones don't? Do you prefer books with lots of shaded boxes and bulleted lists to break up the monotony of text? Perhaps you like how-to books sprinkled with humor. What types of illustrations are appropriate for a book on your topic?

Different genres require different approaches. And some genres have pretty specific requirements or guidelines. Children's literature is one of them.

If you are writing a children's book, you particularly want to read books at the age level of your proposed book. Note the language used in books for that specific age group. How many pages do these books run? What is the typical word count per page? Get involved with the Society of Children's Book Writers and Illustrators, http://www.scbwi.org. Also spend time at the Children's Writers Marketplace, http://www.write4kids.com. Both sites have numbers of resources for writers of children's books.

How to Get Beyond Overwhelm

The thought of writing a sixteen or even eight-chapter book can be intimidating. It's way easier to procrastinate than to dive in and start writing. But it's certainly not very productive. If you find yourself straightening your desk over and over, sharpening pencils until they are nubs, separating small paperclips from large ones, and testing the strength of the rubber bands in your desk drawer, stop it now!

Writers, listen up! Shut down that computer solitaire game. Stop checking your email. Turn off your phone ringer. And start writing.

If you feel a bit overwhelmed when faced with a large writing project, just knock it down to size. Perspective is everything. Rather than looking at the book as a whole, focus on one, chapter at a time. And, you don't even have to start at the beginning.

Start with the chapter that you feel would be easiest to write—the one containing the material or theme you're most familiar with.

I generally begin with the introduction because it helps me to focus on the point of the book. It reveals the purpose of the book and sets the stage for what's to come. Some authors write their introduction last on the theory that you can't properly introduce your book until you've written it.

If you're still having trouble getting started after an hour or so, consider writing a short piece or two for a local newspaper or a national magazine. This is a great method of building up your confidence while honing your organizational and writing skills. This is also an excellent way to test consumer interest in your topic and to establish credibility in your field and as a writer. (Read more about writing and submitting articles in Chapter Fourteen.)

Psychologically, writing an article or a stand-alone chapter is less overwhelming than the thought of writing a 60,000-word book. If you are comfortable writing a 2,000–4,500-word article, you should have no problem writing a chapter. Just look at your book as a series of articles or stories—each with a beginning, middle, and end.

How to Manage the Mountain of Material

There are a variety of ways to handle material while preparing a book. I file research material in file folders and store them in a large Stor-All box in hanging files throughout the duration of the writing process. Some authors type everything that comes across their desk into the computer immediately. Others use index cards to organize topics or a storyline. One writer I know pastes pages from her current book-in-progress all over her office walls. She likes having a constant and complete visual of the project.

The right way to proceed with a book project is the one that works best for you. And this might change from book to book. Here are a few ideas that might help.

By now you've probably written the first draft of your introduction. If not, here's a tip: start with the book description or the introduction from your chapter summaries. This description may, in fact, become your first few paragraphs. Bring material from your synopsis into the introduction, as well.

Don't give too much thought to style and grammar, yet. This is not the time to fret over sentence structure and punctuation. Just write. Document your ideas and thoughts along with the information you've collected. You can organize, fact-check, and edit later.

What about Fiction?

When writing a story, chapters may not be evident at first. It could take some contemplation and practice to learn where to make chapter breaks. Some breaks will be obvious, others will not. I like to see novelists start each chapter with a hook to pique the reader's interest and end it with a cliff hanger or at least an unanswered question to keep them reading. Chapters may be determined by a timeline, the introduction of characters or location, or the natural progression of events and occurrences.

Hone Your Research Skills

Just as there are varying ways to write and organize a book, the process of conducting research and interviews can differ. Some writers complete the research and interviews before starting to write. Others research as they move from chapter to chapter. For most nonfiction authors, research is an ongoing process.

Research is necessary for most nonfiction books and many fiction books. Even if you are an expert in your field, you'll want to bring in current information, statistics, and, perhaps, the opinions and experiences of others. If you're writing about something outside your realm of expertise, you'll be required to do more in-depth research.

I find that people either love research or they hate it. The fact is that, if you're a good researcher, you can actually write a book on a subject you know nothing about. You may be interested in writing an informational book on Alzheimer's disease or building a sod house, but you have no practical experience. Perhaps you want to write a novel reflecting the pre-depression era in New York City, but you're only forty-five years old and didn't experience it. Does this mean that you cannot write a book on these topics? Absolutely not. It just means that you will need to do a lot of research.

Most authors have a comfort zone when it comes to research. I'd like to encourage you to step outside that zone in order to provide your readers with the most complete information or the most exact historical accounts. Your reputation as an author and as an expert in your field depends on your accuracy. And you owe it to your readership to be precise and thorough.

Start with Books

Study books from your home library. If you're interested in the subject or genre that you'll be writing about, you probably have books to prove it. For nonfiction, gather ideas, information, statistics, and resources. Note the experts that were quoted and referenced. Contact some of them for fresh quotes and additional information.

Note the title, author, publisher, copyright date, and the type of material you found in each book in case you want to reference this material again. You may also consider including this book in your bibliography and/or your resource list.

For fiction, notice the writing style, the way authors handle dialogue, and what makes the stories intriguing, interesting, or suspenseful. What makes these stories work? Practice these techniques.

Visit the Public Library

The old-fashioned public library is still a great place to conduct research. While you don't find many new books in libraries these days, you're likely to locate some good sources for historical and statistical information.

Use reference books on your topic, the period, or the geographic location of your proposed story. Search out statistical data in appropriate reference materials. Locate current articles on the subject or location of your story through the *Reader's Guide to Periodical Literature*. This directory lists articles by subject and the magazines in which the articles appear. Use old newspapers on microfiche for factual data on once current events, the political climate back then, the cost of living in earlier times, and even the weather conditions during a certain time period.

There's more to a library than is immediately obvious, which is why I recommend that you seek help with your research. Make friends with the librarian. She/he can open up worlds of awareness which you never knew existed.

Step into the Bookstore

You can purchase books to use in your research from brick and mortar bookstores as well as online. There are many online bookstores today that sell new books at discounted prices. Start at amazon.com. Scroll down on the page where the book appears and you'll usually find some discount options. Or do a Google search to find a discount bookstore to your liking.

A Note about Plagiarism

I'm not suggesting that you plagiarize (copy copyrighted materials). Research means gathering and verifying information, facts, and statistics. It means locating expert sources for your book. If you wish to use a passage from a published book, you must get permission.

Write or email the publisher and request permission to use a specific passage or quote. I typically provide the publisher with the exact quote I want to use, information about how I'll use it, and, if by mail, a permission form to be signed. Sometimes there's a fee for such permission. And sometimes the information is worth the fee. I've never had a publisher ask for more than $100 for a paragraph or two.

Always give full credit for any material used. Just because you pay for it doesn't mean that you own it. In fact, most publishers and authors will specify that you have paid for or have been given permission for one-time use of the material, only.

If you want to use a statistic or just briefly paraphrase a quote or a concept, you may not need permission. But always give written credit to the author or researcher.

Pursue Computer Research

As writers, we have unlimited research resources at our fingertips. All we have to do is enter the information highway. Yet, still many people don't know how to find the onramp.

Google

Start with everyone's favorite search engine, Google. Type in the subject you want to research or a particular question and away you go.

Sometimes you'll find the answer to your question quickly and other times it takes a while. But the process can be rather interesting. Always be cognizant of unexpected avenues for information and data anytime you are doing a search.

If you stumble across something interesting and pertinent to your project, print it out and/or bookmark the site for later reference. Perhaps you're looking for information or statistics related to uniforms worn by a certain regiment in the Civil War. While searching, you discover a page describing plants and trees that grow in the region of certain battles—information you will need in a later chapter of your historical novel. Print out that page or bookmark it so you can reference it later. A good researcher builds and maintains his own directory of significant sites. Collect those that relate to your current project.

Tips for Using Websites

Not all websites are straightforward and easy to use. In fact, some present quite a challenge. If you want to know more about the site and the people behind it, click on "About Us." This is also where you will sometimes find their contact information. The first place to look for contact information, however, is "Contact Us."

When you find a good site on your topic, study the articles and interviews posted there and check out the links they recommend. Some links will prove to be great resources for additional information.

Visit the media page to see if they have issued press releases on new findings, for example.

Note any books they have for sale on the subject.

Message Boards

Visit message boards and forums related to your book topic. It's a good way to meet people to interview for your book. You'll also learn about resources you might want to check out. If you're writing about parenting multiples, for example, get involved in an appropriate forum. This might be the Triplet Connection or Multiple Birth Parents. Maybe you are seeking material for a book on hoarders. Visit the Children of Hoarders Forum or HoardHouse. In order to gather perspective and information on Internet matchmaking, look into some of the many dating sites and message boards online.

To locate message boards on your topic, at Google, or the search engine of your choice, type in "message board" plus your topic or topic plus "message board." It works either way. For example, "message board Alzheimer's," "message board photography" or "pet message board."

Interview Techniques

If you hope to add interest and credibility to your nonfiction book, you will probably want to tap into the opinions and expertise of others. Let's say that you're writing about obesity in children. After you've given your views and you've reported on current findings, enhance your book by interviewing people in the know. Talk to the directors of innovative fitness programs in schools throughout the U.S., parents of obese children, and a couple of doctors who specialize in childhood obesity. You may be surprised at how the scope of your project will change when you start pulling in expert perspectives and quotes.

If you're timid about approaching experts or have trouble asking the right questions, here are some tips to help you conduct more successful interviews.

1. **Locate experts.** Start a search for professionals and other individuals who can add credibility and anecdotes to your book. Try to interview people from throughout the U.S. and sometimes the world for a more

diverse representation. There are many ways to find experts—here are a few:

- Study books on your topic.
- Engage a search engine to locate experts on the Internet.
- Find specialists listed in online and print articles related to your topic.
- Search university staff web pages to find a qualified authority.
- Visit organization pages to locate an appropriate professional.
- Discover author experts at amazon.com.
- Locate nonprofessional experts through message boards. (See above.)
- Peruse sites dedicated to expert sources such as: http://www.expertcentral.com and http://www.expertclick.com.

2. **Learn something about the interviewee.** Before contacting an individual for an interview, find out something about him. Study articles in which this person is quoted. If she's an author, read her bio on the book cover or on her page at amazon.com. If he's a business owner, professor, organization leader, or a politician, call his office and request an information packet.
3. **Write a list of questions.** Try to come up with less than ten specific questions. Four or five of those will usually require some discussion. Ask open-ended questions. Instead of, "Are you looking forward to retirement?" ask, "What will you miss most about working?" Instead of, "Were you sad when your kids all went away to college? Ask, "How did you feel when you watched your last child leave for college?" I always like to ask almost everyone I interview, "What would you advise others in this situation?" For example, "What would you advise those who want to retire early?" or "What would you like to say to someone who plans to live for a year on a remote island?"
4. **Make contact.** Call or email the interviewee and briefly introduce yourself. Explain a little about your project. If you have a publisher lined up, be sure to say so. Ask him or her if you can call within the next few days and conduct a telephone interview.

Sometimes the interviewee will suggest that you do the interview on the spot, so be prepared with your questions.

If the subject wants to schedule the interview for another day, let him know how much time you'll need—generally fifteen to twenty minutes. Before setting a time, find out which time zone he's in. And offer to email him the questions ahead of time so he can prepare.

5. **Suggest an email interview.** This is becoming a popular way to conduct interviews. There is no transcribing involved. And most people are willing to participate in an email interview because they can think about their responses and write them out at their leisure. There are still people who prefer speaking by phone, however. And there are some valid reasons for avoiding an email interview:

    - You get a greater sense of personality when you conduct an interview in person or by phone.
    - Some people will procrastinate right past your deadline if left to respond to questions via email.
    - You usually have to send some follow-up questions for clarity and depth.

6. **Ask for clarity.** It is easy for words and phrases to be misconstrued. When you aren't sure about one of your interviewee's responses, ask for clarification. Don't take anything for granted when you're quoting someone, especially when the subject matter is outside your realm of expertise.
7. **Encourage anecdotes.** Text is more interesting and points can be made more effectively when using anecdotes. When an individual spews an interesting statement or makes a provocative point, ask for examples. An artist might say, "I really prefer working outdoors." This is charming, but wouldn't it be even more charming if she painted a word picture? You might say, "Give me an example of pursuing your art out of doors." Follow up with something like, "And how does it make you feel to sit at your easel on that knoll overlooking the meadow?" "How does this site make a difference in the results of your art?" Can you see the colorful possibilities?
8. **Confirm personal information.** Always verify the spelling of the interviewee's name. Ask how he would like to be credited. An author may want his latest book mentioned. A public relations agent will ask you to include her business name. A professor might prefer having his college affiliation mentioned.

9. **Ask for more.** Before leaving an interview, always request more information. Say, "Can you recommend any additional material that might help me with this project?" or "Is there anyone else with whom I should speak on this subject?"
10. **Send a copy of the quoted passages to the participant.** Once you have finished the writing, send a copy of the sections where you mention or quote this individual and ask for permission to use it in your book. It is a good idea to save all interview tapes and transcripts in case there is ever a question about something that was said. Your publisher may request your tapes before proceeding with the project, particularly if it involves a sensitive topic.

Note the interviewees' contact information so you can let them know when the book is ready for purchase. I generally give one copy of the completed book to individuals who participated in a major way, along with an order form for additional copies. I send flyers and order forms to those I may have just mentioned in the book.

Do You Need an Editor?

In a word, YES. Most professional writers are naturally good with words, but few are English majors. Many of us have areas of grammar, punctuation, composition, and style that give us fits. And surprisingly, some people who just love to write just plain stink at it. I think that excellent writing is a mix of talent and skill. And I believe that we never stop learning. A writer must stay constantly in student mode. We must be observant, inquisitive, and always willing and eager to learn.

I hear inexperienced authors state, "My manuscript is almost ready—it needs a little editing—but I'm going to send it to the publisher, anyway. If he wants it, he'll edit it, right?" Not likely.

NEVER, NEVER send something that is less than your very best. If this means hiring an editor, then do it. Even the best writers turn their manuscripts over to editors before sending them off to publishers.

Why does every writer need an editor?

- When you become too close to your work, you tend to overlook things that could actually make or break your manuscript. There may be problems that either you haven't noticed or you feel you've fixed with some clever technique.

- A writer sometimes becomes attached to phrases that add nothing to his story or, in fact, that detract from it. A good editor can help save you from yourself.
- You may have a style of writing that isn't exactly easy to read or to comprehend. You understand what you're saying because you wrote it and because you have read it many times. It makes complete sense to you. But it may still be unclear to readers.

Tips for Choosing an Editor

Determine whether you need a copy editor or line editor. A copy editor edits for spelling, grammar, and punctuation errors. A line or content editor edits for clarity and flow as well as grammatical errors. I recommend a line or content editor for most projects. Choose an editor who:

- Has been recommended.
- Has experience editing books like yours.
- Knows something about your topic/genre.

Further I recommend that you:

- Read something she or he has edited.
- Check out the editor's track record. Has the work she edited been published?
- Ask the editor to demonstrate his or her editing style on a few pages of your project.

Expect to pay a copy editor around $30-$40 an hour. A content or line editor will require $50 or more per hour.

There are things that you can do before hiring an editor. For example,

- Read your manuscript as if you are someone from outer space. Does it still make absolute sense to you or are there areas that need more explanation or that could be simplified?
- Use spell-check.
- Check for inconsistencies in the story or information. (If you write that your main character is from Bolivia, don't inadvertently mention his hometown in India. If you change a character's name from Sylvia to Samantha in midstream, make sure you changed all instances of Sylvia.)

- Study the latest edition of *The Chicago Manual of Style* with regard to appropriate capitalization, use of numerals, punctuation questions, correct use of titles, etc.

One of the biggest problems I see with hopeful authors is a tendency toward muddy writing. My main work as an editor is cleaning up the mud—helping the author to clarify his/her material. Here's an example of what I call muddy writing.

> "This gives the information I found through my own extensive research and my observations involving young children as they pursued various media over an extensive period of time."

Instead, I suggested that my client try this:

> "This book is the result of five year's research which includes my observations involving the artistic pursuits of a dozen youngsters."

Here's another example,

> "Jeremy hoped beyond all hope for the potential success that would be his as he jumped into the air reaching for the glory of all players who dream of ultimately catching a ball like this."

Why not simply say this, instead:

> "Jeremy sprang into the air hoping to make the greatest catch of the season."

The second most common thing I do as an editor is to eliminate words. Example:

> "On that particular day—a Wednesday—John decided that he would walk over to the corner store."

Why not this:

> "On Wednesday, John walked to the corner store."

Remember, one of the most famous succinct, strong sentences ever written was "Jesus wept."

Introduction to Self-Editing

I suppose it is impossible to know when our writing stinks. With training and practice, however, I think we can definitely learn. The best way to perfect your writing skills is to read and to write. But don't just read the easy stuff. Challenge yourself with thought-provoking materials of excellent literary quality. And don't just write in the same lackadaisical manner.

Use your best grammar and punctuation skills each and every time you write whether it is an email to a friend or potentially the world's greatest novel. Once you decide to become a writer or an author, you owe it to our profession and to yourself to communicate as if you are an author. How often do you send out a quick email without using spell-check? Do you feel that most people are generally forgiving of spelling errors and grammatical oversights? I don't think so—not when you are trying to pass yourself off as a writer/author.

You wouldn't believe some of the mistakes in the emails I get from people claiming to be writers. Here are a couple of actual examples:

> "I am wrighting a book but i don't know ware to get it published after its done could you help me get my book pubished."

> "I would like you to look at my proposl but it is only half way complete and I have to finish it before you actuslly look at it. Or at leawst let me write a few chapters, I am almost done with one. Before you go ahead. Is thqt okay to wait until im done."

The next several pages are devoted to the most common errors I see in the course of my work.

New Punctuation

They say that there's nothing new under the sun, but I've learned a thing or two since the advent of the computer age. For example, did you know that the old rule you were taught in typing class in the '50s, '60s, '70s and even the '80s—two spaces after a period—is passé? Now, the rule is one space after a period, colon, question mark, etc. Why? Because we used to prepare typed material for typesetters. Now that we're using computers, we are typesetters. The letters on the keys of a typewriter all take up the same amount of space. We used an extra space between sentences in order to indicate a sentence break. The letters we type on the computer screen take up different amounts of space (example, "i" "m"), so there is no need to define the sentence break using an extra space.

The em dash is no longer left to dangle between words. According to *The Chicago Manual of Style*, it connects the two words. To form the em dash, type the first word. Without spacing, type two dashes. Without spacing, type the second word. When you hit the spacer bar after the second word, the em dash is formed.

Perhaps you've been confused about the placement of punctuation with relationship to quotation marks. You see punctuation both inside and outside quotation marks. With a few exceptions, punctuation inside quotation marks is correct here in the U.S. But, in other countries, commas, periods, question marks, etc., go outside quotation marks.

Those of us who cut our teeth on typewriters were taught to underline book titles and other words and phrases that needed to be italicized. You couldn't create italics when using a typewriter or when writing by hand. Underlining was a signal to the printer that a word should be put in italics. Now, if you use a computer, you can add italics yourself and you should. Underlining is no longer appropriate as a way of indicating italics.

Many writers seem confused when it comes to using the cute little apostrophe. Use the apostrophe to denote possessive and plural possessive. "The boy's boat" indicates that the boat belongs to the boy. "The boys' boat" shows that two or more boys own the boat.

Use an apostrophe to show personal ownership as well. For example, Patty's purse or Margaret's shawl, Dennis's book, Frances's guitar.

While it is correct to use an apostrophe when writing in single letters—he got all A's and B's or Mississippi sure has a lot of i's, it is incorrect to use an apostrophe when referring to a series of years. For example, 1920's is wrong. Write 1920s instead.

Editing Tips

The following is a basic guide to editing. Unless you are an English professor, you may notice at least a couple of familiar errors that you make from time to time. These are all things that you really must be aware of when writing a book, article, or anything else for publication. Be sure to:

- Write complete sentences.
- Eliminate unnecessary words.
- Use simple terms and words. If you try too hard to impress your readers with your vocabulary, you may succeed only in confusing them.
- Edit for words that are repeated/overused. Come up with several different words to use in place of something to which you'll be referring frequently throughout a paragraph. Instead of using the word *thought* fifty times in a chapter, substitute other words such as *idea, contemplation, notion, inspiration, concept, opinion,* and *philosophy*. If you're writing about a dog, call him by name, and use additional words such as, *pet, pooch, the animal, the furry critter, canine,* and *wooly guy* instead of continually referring to him as *dog*.
- Vary sentences. Intermingle sentences of all sizes and many styles throughout your book to make it easier and more enjoyable to read. Imagine reading a book with sentences all containing just five words. It might read like this: "Jack went to the track. He spent over five dollars. He bet on the bay. He really hoped to win." Booooorrrring!!!
- Know when to end it. Some writers try to say too much in a single sentence. They use commas where they should use periods. If you create an extraordinarily long sentence, examine it and see if you can successfully break it into two or three sentences. Often, there is a profound statement found among the clutter of a too-long sentence. Isolate it by creating a new sentence and that statement will surely stand out and make a greater impact on your readers.
- Avoid over explaining. Practice clarity without getting too involved in complicated explanations. Tell your story and share facts using succinct sentences and descriptive words. In fact, strive to show the action and activity in a story rather than simply telling it. This technique serves to move a story along in a more natural and interesting way.
- Use the active rather than the passive voice. Instead of, "It was her choice to opt for the blue coat." Say, "She chose the blue coat." Instead of "There were hundreds of birds flying in our direction." Try, "Hundreds of birds flew at us." One way to make sure you're not using the passive voice is to eliminate *it* and *there* at the beginning of sentences.

Another indicator that you're using a passive instead of active voice is the word "by."

> Passive: She was hit by the ball.
> Active: The ball came out of nowhere and hit her on the head.

- Be consistent. Keep to your choice of tense, for example. Don't change back and forth between past and present tense or first, second, and third person. By the way, first person is *I*, second person is *you*, and third person is *they* or *she*. Be consistent with commas, periods, indents, and your choice of words. Will you use "Web site," "web site," "website," or "Website," for example? Which do you prefer, "ebook," "eBook," or "e-book"? In situations where more than one usage is correct, make a choice and stick to it. (Note: *The Chicago Manual of Style* suggests "website" and "e-book.")
- Avoid clichés. I love clichés and I tend to overuse them in speech. I must consciously edit to eliminate them from my writing. A cliché is a trite, predictable and generally over-used saying such as: "You can bet your bottom dollar." "She laughed all the way to the bank." "Better late than never." "You can see the writing on the wall." Be creative—come up with new phrases to make your point.
- Avoid using what I call qualifiers. The words *very* and *really*, for example, often weaken a perfectly good sentence. Instead of "Jacob had a very good time," try "Jacob had a great time." Rather than "She is a really good friend." say, "She's my best friend." Or "She's a good friend."
- Catch spell-check errors—real words that can change the meaning of your sentence, but that are not picked up by spell-check. You might intend to write "no hurry," but accidentally type "now hurry." Big difference there. You might mean to type, "He does not wish to be disturbed" and write, instead, "He does now wish to be disturbed." Or you may want to say, "I don't eat worms." But you miss a word and it reads, "I eat worms." Other words that can trip you up are sign/sing, course/curse, plus/pus/pulse, about/abut, manger/manager, trick/thick, cove/cave. Don't get burned by your spell-check. Sometimes your computer will correct a word wrongly. You might want to write *definitely*. If you make a mistake while typing it, your computer may change it to *defiantly*. While writing the original edition of this book, I spotted a couple of spell-check mistakes. I meant

to type *willingness* and it came out *wiliness*, instead. In another instance, I meant to say that a colleague's sales *soared* and I (or my computer) inadvertently typed *soured*. Big difference.

- Use the right word. Some words sound-alike or look-alike such as presumption and assumption, assure and ensure, born and borne, breach and breech, appraise and apprise, breath and breathe, avenge and revenge.
- Watch out for redundant phrases or instances of unnecessary repetition. Here are a few: ISBN number, two twins, widow woman, unmarried old maid, autobiography of my life, unexpected surprise.

Use words correctly.

Understand the differences between common words that are similar and always use them correctly. Here are a few words that people have trouble with:

Whose and who's:

Who's is a contraction for who is. "Who's coming to dinner?" *Whose* is the possessive. "Whose horse won the race?"

Who and that:

Too often, we hear newscasters and others refer to a person as *that* instead of *who*.

You would say, "It was the storm that did the damage, but Lila is the woman who saved the day."

Then and than:

Then means at that time—"He was younger, then."
Than is used in comparisons—"Sharon is taller than Sam."

Your and you're:

Your means this belongs to you and *you're* is a contraction for *you are*.

There, their and they're:

There denotes a place. "Set the plant over there."
Their is the possessive of belonging to them. "It's their blanket."
They're is a contraction for they are. "They're coming home today."

To, too, two:

To indicates motion or action as in "I gave the blanket to him." Or "He is going to jail."

Too means also, in addition to, or in excess. For example, "He wants a blanket, too." "I think he is too greedy."

Two refers to the number 2.

By, bye, buy:

By is used in numerous ways. Here are a few examples: "The blanket is in the chair by the fireplace." "That book was written by Jonathan Robles." "I'd like to drive by that place again." "He should be finished by now."

Bye is short for good bye.

Buy means to purchase. "She said she would buy him a new blanket."

It, its, it's:

It refers to an object.

Its is the possessive form of it. "The bus seemed to lose its way." "The ant made its way along the cabinet."

It's is the contraction of it is or it has. "It's hot today." "It's never been hotter."

A and an:

There seems to be a lot of confusion about using the word *an* before a word beginning with an H. The rule relates not to the letter itself, but to the sound of the letter. If the H is silent as in the words, honor, hour and heir, the word *an* is correct. If the word has a hard H sound such as in hammer, horse, heaven, or head, use the word *a* before it.

Examples of H words used with a:

"Let's go to the library and check out a history book."

"I'd love to ride a horse."

"You have to wear a helmet if you plan to ride your bike."

Examples of H words used with an:

"You must wait for an hour after eating before you can go swimming."

"I am an heir to a small fortune."
"I'm going to ask for an hourly wage."

There is no excuse for turning out a manuscript riddled with poor grammar and spelling errors. If in doubt, refer to an online grammar site or a trusted style manual. *The Chicago Manual of Style* is recommended for book authors.

Edit, Edit, Edit

Once you've finished editing your manuscript, start looking at it from different angles:

- Print out the manuscript and put it in a three-ring binder.
- Proof it again and again, if necessary.
- Check facts and statistics.
- Make sure that the font, headings, subheadings, and so forth conform in size and style throughout.
- Do chapter titles and headings correspond with the table of contents?
- Start making a list of the words you plan to include in your index.
- Ask appropriate experts if you can send a chapter or two for them to review for accuracy.

Let's Become Familiar with the Parts of a Book

What will you include in your book? There's the text, of course. This comprises the story, information, instructions, and other material you've written and compiled for your readership. What else does your book need?

Fiction

A novel or children's book generally needs only a copyright page, title page, and the story. You could also include a table of contents (where appropriate), dedication page, and acknowledgements page if you want to. Some authors of fantasies, science fiction, and so forth, might include a chart listing characters. If this is book one of a trilogy, provide information about the other two stories. Of course, you can also add an about the author page, testimonials page, or any other inclusions you desire. It's your book, after all.

Nonfiction

A nonfiction book—that is a biography, memoir, how-to, self-help, or history, for example—needs a copyright page, title page, table of contents, and text. Depending on the subject matter and scope of the book, you might also decide to include a dedication page, about the author page, acknowledgements page, testimonials page, preface, foreword, introduction, glossary, and/or bibliography. If your book would make a good reference book, please compile an index.

Here are your options and a description of each:

FRONT MATTER

Title Page

This is the first page that appears in your book. It is a right-facing page and generally includes the book title, subtitle, author's name, the publishing company name, and contact information.

Copyright Page

This is usually a left-facing page where you post your copyright information, Publisher's-Cataloguing-in-Publication (PCIP) information, and ISBN (part of the PCIP block). You can also list your cover design and book design persons here, if you like.

Dedication Page

Here, you might want to acknowledge someone special in your life—a parent, spouse, child, friend, mentor, teacher . . . Generally, this is someone you would like to thank for standing by you while you toiled on this tome, who gave you the inspiration to write it, or who helped you to gain the skills to write it.

Table of Contents

A table of contents is your chapter outline designed for the reader's convenience. Start the table of contents on a right-facing page. Make it as detailed or as simple as you wish. Of course, you will list each chapter by name and give the starting page number. I usually list the major headings within each chapter of my nonfiction books, as well. You can include page numbers for these subheadings or not. A table of contents for fiction generally includes just chapter titles (for books that have them) and the starting page number for each.

Foreword
A foreword is written by someone other than the author—an expert in the area of your book topic, perhaps, or another author.

About the Author
Most readers are interested in who you are. Whether they're about to purchase or read a novel or a how-to book, they want to know who wrote it and what qualifies that person to write it. I believe that something about the author should be included in every book. But it doesn't have to be a long resume in the front matter of the book. It can be a blurb on the back cover with your photograph or an afterthought on the last page of the book.

Acknowledgements Page
Here is where you thank everyone who helped with your book, your mentor, your page and cover designers, the folks who provided information for the book, your editor, your agent—even your cat, if you wish.

Testimonials Page
By the time you are ready to reprint your book, you've probably accumulated many book reviews and testimonials. Consider publishing some of them in the front matter. You can also collect testimonials for your first edition by sending the manuscript out to key people prior to publication.

Preface
A preface generally contains a message from the author—what compelled him/her to write the book, how the research was conducted, what you hope this book will accomplish for your readers, etc.

Introduction
An introduction can be useful for nonfiction works. Some novelists like to use an introduction to set the scene for their stories. An introduction is generally written by the author.

Disclaimer
You might want to add a disclaimer to your book. Most authors who do this place the disclaimer just before the first chapter begins. You might state in your "Yoga for Beginners" book that, while the yoga moves you

suggest are safe for a healthy person, you recommend that each individual do the exercises only with a physician's approval.

Note: Every expert I consulted about the front matter listed these pages in a different order. Some suggested that an author could also include an errata, frontispiece, list of tables, list of projects, list of abbreviations, list of previously published books, and list of contributors to the front matter.

I recommend consulting books similar to the one you are producing and choose the front matter additions and order that is logical, practical, and appealing for your particular book.

BACK MATTER

Afterword or Epilogue

This material follows the main text and includes the author's final statement or conclusion.

Appendixes

An appendix might comprise additional explanations for aspects of a book. This is where you put material that you don't want to include in the text because it is cumbersome or it bogs down the story or the flow of the text. You might want to simply mention in the text that Jesse James was accused of stealing a horse. You can tell the rest of the story in an appendix, if you wish.

One of my clients has self-published a book featuring the story of her daughter's successes despite her struggles with a lifelong fatal illness. This author has ended the book quite appropriately, yet she wanted to add comments that some of her daughter's friends made after she died. The author planned to tack them on at the end of the story. I suggested, however, that she create an appendix in the back matter for these comments and letters. This way, the book ends as it should and readers won't be confused by the additional material. If they want to access it, it is in the appendix for their perusal.

Glossary

A glossary defines any industry-sensitive words the author uses throughout a book. Even though the uncommon words may have been defined within the text, a glossary provides a handy guide for folks who desire additional explanation or who want a quick reference to the words.

Bibliography

Generally this is a list of the books and other material you used in your research for a nonfiction book. A bibliography is helpful for students and others who need additional information on the topic of your book.

Subject Index

An effective subject index helps readers to quickly locate information contained in your book. I recommend studying indexes in other nonfiction books to help you design yours.

Other Matter

You might want to include a page listing photo credits or an advertisement for your services. It's all okay. If you are self-publishing, you are in charge. You can even sell advertising space in your book in order to finance publication, if you desire.

How to Finish a Book

Finishing a book is sometimes hard to do. Authors often fall so completely in love with their project that they look for any excuse to continue. By now, you've established a routine of writing that you enjoy. It's hard to think about giving it up. But, if you expect to see this book in print, you will have to finally end it.

How do you know when your book is finished? As a rule of thumb, if you can read all the way through your manuscript without making a change or bogging down in places—when you can feel good about it from start to finish—then you are ready to end it and turn it over to a good editor.

How Long Does It Take to Write a Book?

Generally, a book will take between three months to a year from the glimmer of the idea to the last page of the book. This depends on the amount of research necessary, of course, the size of the book, and the time you spend writing.

Surveys show that a typical nonfiction book takes 725 hours to write or 90 eight-hour days. That's approximately eighteen work weeks or four and a half months.

Counting Words

Determining word count is another question that will come up as you're working on your book—how does one determine word count and compute typewritten pages to finished book pages? While some people will advise against relying on your computer word count program, what other measurement do you have that even comes close?

A double-spaced manuscript page with 1 ¼ to 1 ½ inch margins typed using 12-point Times New Roman contains approximately 250 words. There are around 300 words on a typical printed book page. So for a 200-page book or approximately 61,000 words, you'll need to produce around 244 manuscript pages.

Criticism—Take It Like a Wo/Man

When you become a published author, no longer are you able to keep a low profile. The days of sitting quietly in your private space and relishing every word you pen may be over. Once you bring your writing to the surface—actually begin the process of publishing it—you are opening yourself up to opinion. Some of those opinions are positive and will feed your writer's soul. Others may come in the form of criticism. Showing your work to a publisher may be your first experience with both positive and negative feedback.

A publisher might suggest that you do more research, for example. That could hurt, especially if you feel that you've spent more than ample time studying your topic. She might tell you that your concept has been done hundreds of times and is old hat. "Ouch!!" And you thought you had a fresh idea. He might say that your manuscript needs editing.

Rather than arguing with a publisher, just take it. Do not say anything that you might later regret. If you think about it for a while, you may realize that the publisher is right. Once you have a good cry, punch the wall a few times, and eat a barrel of your favorite comfort food, spend some time pursuing the possibilities presented by this experienced professional. He may be wrong or he may have just given you the key to success.

Recommended Reading:

The Chicago Manual of Style, 16th Edition (The University of Chicago Press, 2010).

The Self-Publishing Option

More authors are choosing the self-publishing option and many are surprised to discover how much work it is. Self-publishing is a business and should not be taken on purely as a means to boost one's ego.

To be successful, you must enter into the world of self-publishing with a viable project, an open mind, creative ideas, lots of energy, a bank roll, and a willingness to work hard. You should view authorship as a business. But, when you are also the publisher, your business responsibilities multiply as do your opportunities for success. Of course, a large part of your job as a publisher is to choose projects with potential.

> Publishing is not an extension of your writing.

Why Self-Publish?

There are a variety of reasons why people choose to self-publish their books. Some authors love having total control over their projects. Others need to get a book out quickly. Some people simply dislike the politics and discrimination they feel is apparent in the publishing industry.

Some of us self-publish because it is more lucrative. Sure, you must foot the bill to publish your own book, but you get to keep all of the profits. When you go with a traditional royalty publisher, your take is generally somewhere between four and fifteen percent.

Let's say that your self-published book sells for $22.00. The costs for your first run come to around $3.00 per book. If you sell only 500 copies on your own, you've earned a profit of $9,500. If you're collecting even fifteen percent royalties on the retail price from a publisher for this book and together you sell as many as 1,500 copies, your profits are under $5,000.

If you work harder and sell 1,500 copies through your own publishing company, you've earned yourself $28,500. Self-publishing is beginning to look rather attractive, isn't it?

Is Self-Publishing for You?

Self-publishing can be daunting. It's easy to be overwhelmed in the process of setting up a publishing company, writing a book, and taking care of the business aspects of preparing that book. And then there's promotion.

Publishing is not for the faint of heart, the short-sighted, or the introvert. It's a commitment that demands courage, risk-taking, planning, energy, creativity, and assertiveness. Before entering into the realm of self-publishing, consider the following:

- Is there an audience for your book?
- Are you willing to take the steps necessary to establish and operate a publishing business?
- Do you have the funds available to pour into your publishing project?
- Do you have room to store boxes and boxes of books?
- Do you have the time and inclination to promote your book?

I'm often asked which is the best publishing method. I always say, "It depends on the book and it depends on the author."

Certainly, self-publishing is not for everyone. I know elderly people who want their memoirs published, but who do not relish the hassle of self-publishing—setting up a company; finding a cover designer, printer, and distributor; promoting the book; taking orders and shipping books, etc.

Someone with a full-time career and who writes a book as a sideline, probably doesn't want to get involved with operating a publishing business.

Anyone on a small income will find it difficult to finance a self-publishing venture.

I often coach authors in starting their own publishing companies and have observed about a fifty percent success ratio. Those who succeed have built a business around their projects and they take that business seriously. They have goals and they evaluate their goals regularly. They give their projects their full attention. If they lack skills in a particular area, they hire someone to take up the slack.

If you're not sure that you can handle or would enjoy the task of becoming a publisher, run a test product. Write a book or a booklet and test the waters. Produce the book on your home computer and have a local business center copy and bind it. Most business centers have the capacity to fold and saddle stitch (staple) a book or finish it with plastic comb binding. Or use a POD printing company (not a POD publisher) to produce your book in small quantities for consumer testing. While most will print as few as one to twenty-five books, I suggest a print run of at least 100.

Explore the Pros and Cons of Self-Publishing

What is a pro to one author, quite frankly, may be a con to another. Before deciding to self-publish, take into account your talents, skills, and abilities. It's important that you know the limitations, benefits, responsibilities, and costs of self-publishing.

According to first-time publisher Norma, "The process of self-publishing a book involves two tasks. First you give birth to the book, which is the easier part. If you're smart, you'll choose a subject that people want to know more about or that is *in*. The second and hardest part of publishing is the busy work that follows the writing—finding an editor, setting aside enough money to avoid debt in case book sales are sluggish, getting printer bids, designing the cover. The worst part of this business for the creative, right-brained types is marketing/promotion. Here you must become a pushy alien person making phone calls, writing letters, and surfing the Internet all the while in this ego-shattering rejection process trying not to become a sherry-guzzling, bewildered basket case."

Let's review the benefits of self-publishing:

- You'll definitely see your book in print.
- You can have a finished product within weeks instead of months or years.
- You have the potential to make more money.
- You have all of the control.
- There are tax breaks to owning your own business.

- You are the best possible marketing agent for your project.
- Your book will keep selling for as long as you are willing to market it.

Self-publishing can be a prelude to traditional publishing success. Richard Paul Evans self-published *The Christmas Box* because he couldn't find a publisher. Some say that he sent his manuscript to only six publishers before deciding to publish the book himself. Simon and Schuster eventually paid Evans a hefty advance and they took over publishing this New York Times Bestselling book. Richard Nelson Bolles initially self-published *What Color is Your Parachute*? John Grisham self-published his first novel. Ron L Hubbard self-published *Dianetics*.

Other famous self-published authors include Elizabeth Barrett Browning, Robert Bly, Zane Grey, Deepak Chopra, Edgar Allan Poe, and Ernest Hemingway.

Here are comments from two self-published authors whose books were ultimately picked up by major publishers:

Adam Shepard chose to self-publish *Scratch Beginnings*, his "rags to fancier rags" memoir. After selling 12,000 copies on his own, he managed to interest an agent in the book and the agent sold it to HarperCollins. Shepard says, "My publisher is fantastic, but I'm seeing lately that the playing field between being traditionally published and self-published is much more level than it used to be. I got the Today Show, CNN, 20/20, Fox News, NPR, and others. I discovered that they were much less concerned with the fact that I was self-published and more concerned with bringing a good segment to their viewers. HarperCollins saw what I could do on my own and knew they could use their resources to take my book to the next level. Their name and their network of contacts have really worked to my advantage."

Debbie Allen also did well with her self-published book, *Confessions of Shameless Self-Promoters*. She was a guest on the Howard Stern show, and the book made Amazon bestseller status. After selling 10,000 copies on her own, her agent (who had recently placed one of her more current books), took this book to McGraw-Hill. Within only a few months, they produced the updated edition. According to Allen, "Self publishing can get you only so far. I'm very good at marketing—that's why I did well—but most people are not good at marketing." Allen was ready to go with a traditional publisher because she wanted, as she puts it, "more bookstore exposure." She says, "When you are with a major publisher, you reach people you cannot reach on your own and that can lead to huge opportunities. The credibility from a major book publisher can take you from just anyone who can publish a book to a *real* published author."

What about the downside to self-publishing?

- Marketing a book is a full-time job.
- Self-publishing is costly.
- There's a lot of decision-making involved.
- Promoting a book is 100 times more difficult and time-consuming than writing it.
- Your book will keep selling for as long as you are willing to market it.

Self-Publishing Basics

If you're still interested in self-publishing, here are some of your options: You can have your book printed through a traditional printing company, take it to a print-on-demand (POD) company, print and bind it at home yourself, or produce an ebook.

The most cost effective way to produce a quality book is through a traditional printing company that uses the old ink on paper method. But the total output may be more because you have to order books in larger quantities. There are often differences in quality and price between printers. Ask half a dozen or so printers for price quotes, samples of their work, and references.

Printing will be your biggest production expense. Expect to pay anywhere from $1,500 to $20,000 for 1,000 to 5,000 copies of your book (depending, of course, on page number, quality of paper and cover stock, number and type of illustrations, amount of color used, binding style, and so forth).

Request for Price Quote

When requesting a price quote from printers, make sure that you are comparing oranges to oranges. Send the same information and specs to each printer that you contact. Under *specs*, tell the printer the number of books you hope to purchase. It is a good idea to ask for two or even three different quotes—under quantity you might type 1,000, 3,000, and 5,000. The printer will figure price quotes on each of these quantities.

Tell the printer your estimated number of pages. Don't worry if this ultimately changes. You may decide later to add a fifteen-page index. Your primary concern now is to get a ballpark idea of the cost you're facing, to compare costs between printers, and to examine some of their samples so you can decide which company you will want to work with. When the manuscript is finished, you can request an exact quote for your project.

Here's a guide for creating your own Request for Price Quote:

- Provide your book title, publishing company, and author's name.
- Quantity (ask for quotes on two or three quantities).
- Give your projected number of pages (for the book).
- What size book do you want (dimensions)?
- Give the number and type of illustrations.
- What weight paper and cover stock do you want?
- Ink (inside and out). Your choices are 1, 2, 3 or 4 color. You might want a 4-color (full color) cover with black ink only for inside text.
- What binding do you prefer? (Hardcover, perfect bound, saddle-stitched, or spiral bound?)

Design Your Book

Even if you are not technologically or creatively equipped to design your own book cover, it will behoove you to take some responsibility in the process. The cover is highly important. Study the design of popular books in your genre/topic. What makes these books stand out? Learn from the experts. Spend time at your local bookstore. Look at the books on the bestseller list. While in the bookstore, watch to see which books are being handled. What is it about the cover that attracts people?

Self-publishing guru, Dan Poynter has compiled statistics that say a bookstore browser typically spends eight seconds looking at your front cover and fifteen seconds on the back cover. That's how long book buyers generally take to decide whether or not to purchase a book. I heard him speak recently, however, and he is now saying that potential consumers spend something like one second on the front cover and five on the back.

I've watched thousands of book browsers at dozens of book festivals over the years and what Poynter says is true. I also notice that some books attract people and others do not. If a cover isn't interesting or attractive and the title isn't catchy or intriguing, the book is bypassed time and time again. People don't even bother to pick the book up.

Style and color are important factors in a good cover design. But so is ease of readability. A title should be easy to read at some distance. Unless you are Danielle Steele or James Patterson, the author's name is relatively insignificant. For the title, use bold lettering in an easy-to-read font and a color that makes the title stand out.

In most cases, you're going to hire someone to design your cover and you can expect to pay anywhere from $250 to $3,500—an expense that could make or break your book. Before hiring a cover designer, check his track record. Has he designed books before or is his expertise in another area of graphic work?

A designer may want to read a portion of your book to get ideas for your cover design. You've been working intimately with this book for several months and probably have some ideas of your own. Share them with your designer. Many a collaboration between author and artist has resulted in dynamite book covers.

You might also need to hire someone to design the interior of your book. Before hiring a page layout and design expert, study books similar to yours and determine the style you prefer. Will you produce a rather straightforward book using all text? Perhaps you'll want a lot of boxes, shading and bullets to break up the text. What font size and style do you prefer? Where do you want your page numbers—top? Bottom? Center? Right? Left? Will you include a quote or drawing at the beginning of each chapter or a recommendation at the end?

Your cover design person and your page layout person should have the expertise to work with the printer in transferring your files appropriately. This may sound elementary, but many a book has been destroyed by miscommunication at this crucial point. Many sloppily designed pay-to-publish books are the result of inexperienced page designers who didn't know how to accurately prepare files for the printer. A good printer will catch potential problems and work with your designer until there is a suitable resolution. But don't count on this. Always hedge your bet by working with experts.

Locate a page layout person and a cover designer (usually two different people) by talking to other independent publishers and authors. Ask for recommendations. When you find books in your home library or at a bookstore that you particularly like, check the copyright page or acknowledgements page for the name of the companies or individuals who designed them. You'll find numerous layout and design people listed on the Internet, advertised in writing/publishing magazines and newsletters, and even in your local Yellow Pages. Certainly, many of them are talented and reliable. To find out which ones are, ask for references and samples of their work.

Hire someone who is accustomed to producing books such as yours. A designer who has only designed brochures for corporations might not understand the mechanics and psychology of producing a book cover. If your page layout person hasn't worked with a saddle-stitched (stapled) book before, she might not know that she has to use a technique called *creeping* to keep text from being buried in the center fold of the finished book.

Locate a directory of over 11,000 cover designers here: http://www.guru.com. Click on "Graphic designers" then "Cover design." John Kremer lists cover designers at http://www.bookmarket.com/101des.htm.

Be Prepared for Promotion

A major part of self-publishing is promotion. A successful self-publisher must have a business head, ongoing enthusiasm for his project, and a bent for marketing. Some experts say you should set aside as much money for marketing the book as you paid to have it produced. But, there are also countless ways to promote your book for little or nothing other than your time.

Don't expect to produce a book, do a blast of marketing during the first few months, and then just sit back and collect money for evermore. Your book can live for as long as you are willing to promote it. Once you stop promoting, it will likely die.

How do you plan to market your book? Don't assume that major booksellers will clamor to get cases and cases of your book to stock on bookstore shelves. It's more and more difficult for an independent publisher to get shelf space in the big bookstores. One way to get the attention of these mega-bookstores is to publicize your book widely and strongly enough that customers start asking for it by name.

If you did the appropriate research before writing and publishing your book, you are prepared for the task of promotion. When you are prepared, willing, and able to aggressively promote your book, you will most likely succeed.

A publisher must wear many hats. He or she is responsible for specific tasks and the steps can be confusing. Here is a clear, concise guide that you will find most helpful for your current publishing project and all of those in your future.

Your Time-Line for Producing a Book

Before Writing Your Book

1. **Write a book proposal.** While a book proposal is generally thought of as your foot-in-the door to a publisher, there is an even greater purpose. As I pointed out in Chapter Four, a book proposal will tell you whether you have a book at all and, more importantly, an audience. Before sinking your life savings and a year or more of your life into this project, make sure you actually have something worth publishing. (Study Chapters Four through Seven for help in writing a book proposal.)
2. **Determine if publishing is for you.** Talk to others who have self-published to find out what it entails. Read about self-publishing. I recommend *The Self-Publishing Manual* by Dan Poynter. Take Patricia Fry's online self-publishing course (http://www.matilijapress.com/course_selfpub.htm) Study how a book is marketed. Preparing the book for market is a huge job, but marketing your book is ongoing. The amount of time you put into marketing will relate directly to how successful your book will become.

While Writing Your Book (Three to six months before completion.)

3. **Name your publishing company.** Be careful about using a name that reflects the nature of your book. You don't want to limit yourself. You may decide to publish books in different genres/subjects in the future.
4. **Apply for a Fictitious Business Name.** The form is available through your County Clerk. Have two or three names in mind in case your first choice is taken.
5. **Establish a business address.** If you're working out of your home, consider signing up for a post office box or one at a business center to use for business correspondence. If you get some major publicity, you don't want the world to know where you live.
6. **Order business stationery as well as mailing labels and supplies.** Keep it businesslike and simple. (Read more about shipping books in Chapter Fifteen.)
7. **Open a business checking account.** You will soon be receiving checks to your publishing company—you'd better have a place to deposit

them. It's wise to use this account for paying bills related to your business, too.

8. **Request a block of International Standard Book Numbers (ISBN).** Assign one number to each title you publish. (Obviously, you just need one number now.) This number identifies your publishing company and the book and is necessary for books sold in the retail market. Assign a new ISBN to each edition of your book. This means that whenever you revise it to any extent or change the title, for example, you will need to assign a new ISBN to it. R.R. Bowker is the U.S. agency for distributing ISBN. You can now purchase just one number. Order one ISBN through Bowker at http://isbn.org for $125. Pay $250 for a block of ten. You can also order blocks of one hundred or one thousand. Bowker now authorizes a few others as agents for single ISBNs. Publishers Services, at http://www.isbn-us.com, sells a single ISBN and a bar code for anywhere from $55 to $139. Important: Be sure that the ISBN you purchase is registered in *your* publishing company name.
9. **Fill out an Advance Book Information (ABI) form.** About six months before your book is finished, fill out the form at http://bowkerlink.com. This insures that your book will be listed in *Books in Print*—one of the industry's most important directories. There is no charge for the form or for the listing. According to R.R. Bowker, *Books in Print* data is used in major and independent bookstores and chains as well as libraries to locate books. So you definitely want to be listed. You will need to register online in order to access the ABI form.

Note: list the "publication date" for your book to coincide with the date you will use in your initial promotion and when sending books to prepublication reviewers. (See Number 22 in this list.)

10. **Request Copyright forms.** Contact the U.S. Copyright Office at Library of Congress, 101 Independence Ave., SE, Washington, DC 20559-6000 or http://www.copyright.gov. While it is okay to apply for a copyright before your book is completed, I generally wait until after I've finished the book. But don't wait for your proof of copyright to arrive before producing your book. It can take months to receive. As of August 1, 2009, the filing fee rose to $65. It's still $35 for those who file electronically.

11. **Contact your State Board of Equalization and request a resale permit.** See the state government pages in your telephone directory.
12. **Assign an ISBN to your book.** (See Number 8 above.)

While You're Doing the Final Editing (About two months before the book is published—four or five months prior to your official publication date.)

13. **Order your Publisher's Cataloguing in Publication information (P-CIP).** This information, which will be printed on your Copyright Page, is important for library use. It includes the Dewey Decimal and Library of Congress classification numbers. Contact Quality Books at 800-323-4241 or visit their website at http://www.quality-books.com/pcip.htm. They charge $100 for first editions. Or use the Donohue Group, Inc. Their fees are $78 and $110, depending on how fast you want to receive the PCIP block. They also issue bar codes. Call 860-683-1647 or visit their website at http://joomla.dgiinc.com.
14. **Search for a printer.** Send a Request for Price Quote to half a dozen printers. (See instructions for preparing a Request for Price Quote above.) Find printers listed in your local Yellow Pages, in *Literary Market Place* (in the reference section at your library), and ask for recommendations from other small publishers. Get a quote from Ron Pramschufer—a broker for printing companies—at http://www.selfpublishing.com/printing.
15. **Commission someone to design your cover.** Since a good cover design can sell books, it follows that it can turn the heads of reviewers, as well. You may want to have your cover design set before you send prepublication review copies. Perhaps your designer could print out a few copies of the cover to use in binding your review galleys or just enclose a sample of the cover with your galley. An excellent cover could make the difference between a review and no review. (More about the prepublication review process in Numbers 21 and 22 of this list.)

To locate a good cover designer, contact authors and small publishers to find out who designed covers for their most successful books. Locate graphic artists and illustrators through the Yellow Pages or a local arts directory. Locate a directory of over 11,000 cover designers here: http://www.guru.com. Click on "Graphic designers" then "Cover design." John Kremer lists cover designers: http://www.bookmarket.com/101des.htm.

When Your Manuscript Is Completed

16. **Hire a good book editor.**

After the Book Is Professionally Edited

17. **Prepare your book for the printer.** Either hire someone to do page layout for your book or do it yourself. Stay on top of quality control during this process. Watch that all margins conform, the font size is consistent (text 12-point, headings 14-point, chapter heads 16-point, for example), spacing remains constant, etc. Things can change when a manuscript is transformed into actual book pages. It is up to you to catch any problems that occur along the way.
18. **Set your book price.** There are a couple of ways to figure your price. Some experts suggest pricing your book at an amount eight times the cost per book. This means that if the total cost of producing each book is $5.00, you should charge $40 for the book. If you produce an 80-page book for around $1.50, you must charge $12. That's a little outrageous, don't you think? Other sources suggest setting your price at five times the production costs. Keep in mind that booksellers want a forty percent discount (some now ask for fifty percent) and distributors and online bookstores generally require fifty to fifty-five percent. I recommend that, along with your cost considerations, you compare the price of books similar to yours to help in determining your price.
19. **Order a barcode.** There are probably dozens of barcode distributors. The one that comes up most prominently in searches and the one that I use is Barcode Graphics, http://barcodegraphics.com. Before ordering your barcode, you will need to establish the price of the book and have assigned the ISBN. I generally pay around $30 for a barcode.

When the Page Layout and Cover Design Are Finished

20. **Choose a printing method and a printer.** Find out how they want you to deliver the book and cover design. (If you have hired experts to help

with these aspects of your book, they should be well-qualified to work with your choice of printers.)

21. **Order galleys for prepublication reviewers.** If your book qualifies—not all books do—have your printer (or a local business center) print and bind five to twenty or so copies of your almost completed book.
22. **Send prepublication review copies.** While some experts are now suggesting that the small publisher doesn't have a chance for a review by one of the important prepublication reviewers, others recommend submitting your manuscript. If you get a review, this could jumpstart your book sales in a big way. Some prepublication reviewers are opening up review possibilities for self-published and POD published authors FOR A FEE.

I know self-published authors who have had marvelous reviews in these major review publications without paying a fee, however.

Prepublication reviews appear in journals that are read by the book industry: bookstore and library buyers. And these particular reviewers want to see the book before it's published. While you can send your manuscript, you'll make a better presentation if you have it bound as a book. (But DO NOT wait until your book is published to send it to the prepublication reviewers. They will not review published books.)

Enclose a cover letter with your book that includes the title, author's name, publication date, ISBN, name of publishing company, price, and contact information. If you have a distributor or wholesaler lined up, list their contact information, as well.

Since prepublication reviewers want to see your book three to five months before publication, you'll set your official publication date accordingly. Your "publication date" does not actually reflect the date your book arrives from the printer. The publication date is the date you set in the future to give your marketing efforts a chance to kick in before your book is considered old news. You can still sell copies of your book during the period between your first print run and your official publication date. How far ahead should you set your publication date? Generally, four to six months in the future. If your book is scheduled to go to the printer in June, you might set your official publication date for sometime in October or November.

This information is basic, read each reviewer's submission guidelines before submitting, and follow them.

Here's a list of the major prepublication reviewers. For information about general reviewers for published books see Chapter Twelve.

Publishers Weekly
71 West 23rd St. #1608
New York, NY 11010
http://www.publishersweekly.com (for submission guidelines)

Library Journal
160 Varick St., 11th Floor
New York, NY 10013
http://www.libraryjournal.com

American Library Association Booklist
50 Huron St.
Chicago, IL 60611
http://www.ala.org/booklist
Click on "Inside Booklist" and then "Submissions."

Foreword Magazine
129 ½ E. Front Street
Traverse City, MI 49684
http://www.forewordmagazine.com

Kirkus Reviews
http://www.kirkusreviews.com

Kirkus Reviews has been doing traditional prepublication book reviews for over seventy years. They now also review self-published, e-published, and pay-to-publish authors through Kirkus Discoveries. They charge $425 for their standard review services. To learn more, visit their website at: http://www.kirkusreviews.com/discoveries.

While the Book is at the Printer (Approximately two to six weeks prior to receiving the finished book)

23. **Solicit prepublication orders.** Send announcements to your mailing list which should include everyone who has expressed an interest in your book, as well as friends, family, neighbors, co-workers, and acquaintances. Tell those to whom you plan to give complimentary copies that they have one coming and that if they'd like to order additional copies, they may do so.

Mail notices to local libraries, bookstores, and anyone else who may be interested in the topic. Promote a book on pet photography to pet stores, photography and camera shops, photographers, camera clubs, animal trainers, and veterinarians. A book on childhood obesity might be promoted to doctors, family therapists, schools, and parents' groups.

Make it easy for people to order books and you will receive orders. By this I mean design an easy-to-use form. Allow payment by check, credit card, or PayPal and consider offering a discount for orders placed by a certain date.

Don't cash checks until the books have been delivered/shipped.

24. **Fill out and send the copyright form.** There's a $65 filing fee (or $35 if you file online).
25. **Create a list of post-publication reviewers.** This might include book reviewers for magazines, newsletters, and websites on the topic/genre of your book as well as general book reviewers. (Check out the collection of ideas in Chapter Twelve.)
26. **List those to whom you wish to send complimentary copies.** This might include those involved in helping to create the book: cover designer, typesetter, and anyone else who contributed in a major way. Address mailers for key book reviewers and in preparation for your first shipment of complimentary copies.
27. **Start planning your promotional program.** (Read Chapters Twelve through Fourteen.)

After Receiving the Book from the Printer

28. **Ship and deliver review copies, complimentary copies, and prepublication orders.**
29. **Send two copies of the book to the Copyright Office** (address on Copyright form)
30. **Send three copies of the book to the Library of Congress** (address on Copyright form)
31. **Fill out paperwork for the State Board of Equalization.**
32. **Apply for a business license.** Check into your city/county requirements for the necessity of a business license.
33. **Send copies of your book to your choice of distributors and wholesalers.** Find listings in *Literary Market Place* and at http://www.bookmarket.com/distributors.htm and http://www.publishersglobal.com. (Read about working with wholesalers and distributors in Chapter Twelve.)
34. **Put your promotional plan into action.**

Recommended Reading:
The Self-Publishing Manual by Dan Poynter (Para Publishing, 15th printing, revised, 2007).

Book Promotion Basics for the Bold and the Bashful

People are not going to swarm to purchase your book just because it exists. In most cases, it takes a lot of thought, preparation, planning, work, and compromise in order to break even let alone profit as an author. And the work is ongoing for as long as you want that book to sell. Just as you were consumed with the process of writing the book, now you will need to totally immerse yourself in the gigantic task of promoting it.

Writers are notoriously reclusive. Most of us work in solitary confinement and we like it that way. When we become authors, we hope to see our books hit the bestseller list, but we'd rather not get involved with making that happen. What we want is to continue writing, right?

Unfortunately, this concept is not realistic. In order to entice readers for your book, you must promote it. And this is true whether you are self published, have a traditional publisher, or have gone the pay-to-publish route.

Sure, you can hire a publicist to jumpstart your book sales. But even this won't absolve you from the promotional process. Even though she landed a traditional publisher, Debbie Puente solicited the assistance of a publicist to boost sales for her little gift book, *Elegantly Easy Crème Brulee and Other Custard Desserts*. Upon publication of her book, she launched a promotional campaign and sold thousands of copies of her book on her own. When she felt as though she'd run out of ideas and connections, she hired a publicist. But she still didn't get any rest. She said at the time, "I've never been so busy." If you hire a good publicist, be prepared to travel all over the country making personal appearances possibly even giving radio and TV interviews. Puente found herself guesting on some popular daytime television shows quite frequently. Did these appearances boost sales? Absolutely!

Most publishers today do little or nothing to promote your book. They rely on the author to get the word out and to make those sales. And who better to promote than the author. You know your book better than anyone else does and you care about it more. Promotion is a whole different activity than writing, however.

Children's book author Sandra Cropsey says, "Had anyone explained to me the ins and outs, the ups and downs of marketing, I'm not sure I would have ever published. Marketing is so far removed from the experience of writing that it is like this constant stranger who speaks a different language with which I am neither equipped nor have the ability or even the desire to understand. If someone would lock me in a room, tie me to a chair, and maybe threaten me with bodily harm, I might be enticed to market. Most days, however, I would prefer to just have my teeth ground down. Success for me will be selling all the books and repaying the loans."

Set Reasonable Goals and Keep Raising the Bar

No matter how distasteful the concept of promotion seems to you, if you want to sell books, it's necessary. The greater understanding you have of this process before you become a published author, the better.

I had an interesting email conversation with a relatively new author last year. He said that he has sold "only" 50,000 copies of his book. I told him that was a very good number. He said, "Not according to my expectations." We talked about expectations earlier in this book. I warned you against having unreasonable expectations, but encouraged you to have meaningful goals. This author reminded me that there is sometimes a fine line between unreasonable expectations and lofty goals.

Lofty goals become unreasonable expectations when one is ill-informed and ill-prepared. In order to meet goals, one must recognize potential obstacles and be willing to work around them. He must become aware of the opportunities and take advantage of them.

Publisher/author, Elizabeth Burton says, "I see far too many aspiring writers with unrealistic expectations who simply won't accept that they aren't going to become the next Stephen King or Annie Proulx the minute their book comes out. So after the first five or ten times they try to promote to a bookstore and get turned down, they give up instead of looking for alternatives."

The only way that anyone can fail is to quit. So how did this young man sell 50,000 books? He had an article published in *Playboy Magazine* (3,200,000 circulation) and this led to an interview on a prestigious TV show. He said that now sales are strictly word of mouth and he spends most of his time working on his next book. Must be nice, eh?

Speaking of lucky breaks or being in the right place at the right time, Barbara Saltzman, who self-published a children's book written by her son who died of Hodgkin's disease at the age of twenty-two, got a jump-start on sales when the *Los Angeles Times* ran a review. She didn't rest on those laurels, however—she kept promoting. She traveled to libraries across the states and read *The Jester Who Lost His Jingle* to groups of children. She has since established a nonprofit organization around the book and accompanying dolls, and there are currently over 325,000 copies of the book in circulation.

This could be you. All it takes is a well-written book on a timely topic for which there is a large audience and your ability and willingness to vigorously promote to that audience. Before ever writing the book, you should be thinking about promotion.

One author told me recently, "My expectations were definitely not met because I failed so miserably in the marketing of the book. I was just unable to find a way to reach the audience that I needed to target and then I ran out of funds to have the book included in the mass mailing offered by PMA (now IBPA). There are thousands of people out there who would benefit from this book if only they knew about it."

I'm pretty sure that the mass mailing would not have pulled this author out of the quagmire. The "masses" were not her audience. Hers was a book useful only to a small segment of people utilizing a specific type of medical procedure. Her audience would be found through physicians' offices, medical centers, hospital gift shops, pharmacies, medical/health magazines, and websites and targeted mailing lists.

So how does one approach the sometimes daunting task of promotion? In a nutshell, set reachable goals. When you meet a goal, consider yourself successful and set a new one.

What You Must Do to Promote

Start by building promotion into your book. As I suggested in Chapter Six, involve a lot of people in your book, connect it to an organization or industry that might help with the promotion and sales, and make sure that the book has everything it needs in order to be sold through traditional means.

An author came to me a few years ago asking for help promoting his book. He was frustrated because he couldn't get it into bookstores and other retail outlets. I agreed to take a look at his book and discovered several problems right away. First, his subject matter was not conducive to a mainstream audience, so traditional bookstores were probably not his venue. He had self-published this book and had not bothered to identify it via an ISBN. The book did not have a barcode nor did he get the Library of Congress block.

All I could suggest to this man was that he promote and sell his book via the Internet and maybe through catalog sales and back of the room sales at civic group meetings.

He had another option. He could order an ISBN and have a barcode printed on stickers to be placed on each book. He still may not be invited to sell his book through bookstores. But, if he had the opportunity, he would be prepared.

Books in Print

Make sure that your book is listed in *Books in Print*. Your traditional royalty publisher will arrange for this. If you are self-publishing, it is your responsibility to fill out the Advance Book Information Form (ABI). If you go through a pay-to-publish company, be certain that they are taking care of this detail for you. If not, you get the forms and do it. (Refer to Chapter Eleven.)

Books in Print is the primary resource list of books published in U.S. Bookstores use this system to locate books requested by customers. If you are not listed in *Books in Print*, you could be missing out on sales.

Bookstore Sales

It might help you to know that even established publishers have trouble getting their books on bookstore shelves. There are just too many books. And as with everyone else in business, the dollar rules the bookstore owners' and managers' decisions. The books that are selling get space, those that aren't, are returned. Also, it is my understanding that large book publishers get preferential treatment because they purchase shelf space in major bookstores.

This is not to discourage you from ever entering a bookstore with your book. On the contrary, many self-published authors enjoy numerous book sales through bookstores. How can you make this happen? Visit independent bookstores and pitch your book locally and while traveling. When you're interviewed for a radio show or make an appearance at a conference in another city, alert the local newspapers and a couple of independent bookstores. The bookstore managers will typically order a few copies of the book in preparation for any resulting sales. If the books sell, they order more. It is up to you to keep customers coming in, so your next logical step would be to send press releases to the local newspapers and write articles for their regional publications.

You may receive purchase orders from bookstores when customers order copies of your books. These customers might have seen one of your books mentioned in your bio at the end of an article published in a national magazine, noticed your book in the library, or learned about it when you were speaking to a group.

The primary way to get into bookstores is through your track record. You must do something to generate sales: Send press releases, do speaking engagements, write articles, do radio shows, and solicit book reviews, for example. The key is to get word out about your book. When customers keep asking for the book, bookstores will start carrying it. But forget about trying to manipulate sales through bookstores by sending friends in to purchase your book. A flurry of fake sales will not convince booksellers to stock your book.

Consider selling books through specialty bookstores. Did you know that there are bookstores that specialize in books related to cats, cooking, metaphysics/spirituality, ethnic topics, women's issues, children, art, science, home and garden, travel, photography, and mysteries, for example? Shining Lotus Bookstore in Denver, Vision Quest in Arizona, and Mystical World in New Jersey all focus on spiritual and metaphysical books. Books for Cooks in Maryland specializes just in cookbooks. Jennie's Garden Books in British Columbia sells only books related to gardens and gardening. Children's Book World in Los Angeles and Chicago Kids Bookstore both cater only to children.

Standard bookstores are generally the first and sometimes the only place some new authors think of for selling their books. But it may be the last place you'll want to pursue. Why? The reality is that bookstores account for less than fifty percent of book sales. Some say that the major bookstores get only a quarter of all book sales.

Even if you do get your book on the shelf, it doesn't guarantee sales. And without sales, your book won't last long there.

Do you really want to be in bookstores? It's easy to get lost among all of the other thousands and thousands of books. If so, here's an opportunity for those who don't have a publisher getting this done for you.

Barnes and Noble has a warehouse program for qualifying self-published and pay-to-publish books. Learn more about this opportunity at http://www.barnesandnobleinc.com. Click on "For Authors." Go to the bottom of this page and click on "Getting your book in Barnes and Noble."

The Small Press Department
Barnes and Noble
122 Fifth Ave
New York, NY 10011

This company will consider books based on salability which means: a book with all of the appropriate amenities on a topic that people are actually interested in.

How to Work with Booksellers

I may seem a little negative about bookstores. So let me take a few steps back. Bookstores are definitely one avenue for book sales, and you should not exclude them from your promotions plan. I suggest, however, that you consider bookstores as only one facet of your marketing program. Here's how to work with bookstores.

Bookstore buyers purchase books from publishers in one of two ways. Generally, when a customer orders a book, the buyer issues a purchase order (PO) for one book, and you ship the book along with an invoice for the amount less the bookstore discount (usually forty percent), plus shipping. It is not unusual to receive payment as many as ninety days or even 120 days later. I've had problems with some bookstores paying me at all. My few business losses have not come from individual customers, but bookstores. More and more bookstore owners are issuing credit card numbers so you can charge for the book prior to shipping. This works for me.

Some independent publishers I know adjust their bookseller discount according to the quantity ordered. They might give thirty-five percent for sales under twenty books and forty percent for sales of twenty to 100 copies.

Sometimes, you can negotiate a consignment agreement with a bookstore. The bookstore orders several copies of your book to carry in the store. You invoice them at the time of delivery/shipment and they pay you either by the end of that month or as the books are sold. If a bookseller that I'm dealing with has a habit of paying late, I will collect for the previous shipment of books before delivering/shipping more.

I also offer booksellers a return policy. I tell them that if the books don't sell, I'll pick up those that are still in good shape and refund their money (or deduct what they owe me). This gives the bookseller more incentive to carry the books—no risk involved. If I do my job as promoter, there is no risk to me, either.

While I was in the process of revising this book, I asked colleagues, clients, and customers what they would like to see added. One independent publisher said that she'd like to see more written about bookstore consignment agreements. Both this publisher and I have seen bookstores close and the proprietors disappear into thin air with supplies of our books. There's also the not so rare situation where you deliver a dozen books and the bookseller claims you only left ten. I don't know how one could prevent this from happening, other than to stay in close and constant contact with booksellers, which I recommend, in any case.

Use duplicate invoices each and every time you deliver or ship books to booksellers. I also recommend devising a consignment agreement. Here's a book that might be useful to independent publishers: Tad Crawford's *Business and Legal Forms for Authors and Self-publishers*, third edition (Allworth Press, 2005).

Book Signings

While I recommend book signings, I have to warn you that this probably isn't the best way for the average author to sell a lot of books. First of all, you don't have a name that will draw a crowd. Sure, your friends and relatives will come out to support you, but they've already bought your book or you've given them copies. Without celebrity status, it takes a provocative subject and/or a great deal of promotion to get more than a few token attendees at a book signing.

Am I trying to discourage you? Not necessarily. But from the onset of planning a book signing, I want you to be thinking about something other than sales—think exposure. Marketing experts say that a customer needs to see something or hear about it a total of seven or eight times before he is likely to buy it. Without exposure, just think of the customers you would never get.

Book promotion takes repetition. You may spend all day at a book festival or plan all month for a book signing and sell only a few copies of your book. It's disappointing. But try not to be so attached to big sales that you miss opportunities to create bridges to future sales.

> Promotion is not necessarily sales, but it is the public relations essential toward growing sales.

Think about it, if you're a mystery buff and you hear about a mystery by a new author, you may not respond because, after all, you don't know this author. You hear the book mentioned again on the radio. You sort of half listen, but still don't rush out to buy it. Later, a friend tells you that he has read the book—hmmm, you begin to get interested. You notice the book while shopping for a Father's day gift and still don't buy it. Finally you see it listed on a mystery book website and you decide to order it. Don't say that you haven't done this. We all have. The point is, when you think marketing, avoid focusing only on sales. Consider exposure, as well.

You may be surprised at some of the people who purchase your book. This might include your neighbor who seemed uninterested in your dog grooming book and who doesn't even own a dog. Yet, she pops in and orders three copies as Easter gifts for her pet-owning daughters. The checker at the grocery store may recognize you from a flyer she saw posted and ask about purchasing your local history book for a newcomer to the area.

Your cousin who lives in another state may respond to your Christmas card book announcement and order a few copies. Just remember, the fastest and most surefire way to have a book fail is to stop promoting it.

Even though book signings generally don't generate a lot of sales, I recommend that you do some. As I said, it is great exposure and, who knows, you might get lucky. One of my clients sold fifty copies of his true crime book at a local signing. He drew about 150 people to the small independent bookstore that evening. How did he do this? He followed the guidelines outlined below:

Book Signing Tips for Authors

1. Don't wait for an invitation. Take the initiative and approach the managers of businesses related to your book topic and local bookstores. Offer to give a presentation or to sign books for their customers.

2 ½ weeks before the event:

2. Send press releases with a photograph of yourself or your book cover to all newspapers within a forty-mile radius. Tell about your book, yourself, and what your presentation will consist of. Include your phone number and email address. An editor may want to contact you for more information.

Note: If your book is conducive to a demonstration or presentation, create one that is highly entertaining or interesting. Presentations often attract more people than a straight book signing does.

3. Make calls and send post cards and emails to friends, acquaintances, business associates, club affiliates, and others who might be interested in attending your presentation or signing.

10 days in advance of the event:

4. Find out if the store plans to design posters and flyers to advertise your signing. If not, do this yourself and deliver them to the store a week in advance of the event.

5. Offer to design a store display of your books.

One week in advance of the event:

6. Know ahead of time what to expect: Will you have a microphone? Lectern? Table at which to sit for signing? Or will you have to arrange for these things yourself?
7. Check the store stock. Will you need to bring additional books to sell? (If you're relying on a publisher to get books to you, order them several weeks in advance.)

The day of the event:

8. Dress to stand out in a crowd, but not so dramatically as to distract from your presentation.
9. Be prompt. Arrive a little early and take time to settle in.
10. Bring handouts such as a related article, report, or a sample chapter.
11. Reach out to people—don't wait for them to come to you. Hand copies of your book to folks in the audience or those who visit your signing table. Walk around the store and hand them to customers. It is easier to sell a product to someone who holds it in his/her hands.
12. Keep track of the number of books you autograph in case there is a discrepancy.

After the event:

13. Send a note of thanks to the store manager and staff.
14. Attend other signings and note what works and what doesn't.
15. Realize that signings and presentations will rarely exceed your expectations and hardly ever meet your highest goals. But *any time* you are given the opportunity to have this sort of free publicity, you are making headway in your promotional effort.

Many authors sell books while traveling and some plan book tours. Clair Button currently works as a botanist in Oregon and is the author of *Cow Cookies*, a modern western mystery novel. He spends his vacations promoting his book. He says, "Before the trip, I attempt to find and evaluate whatever bookstores are in the towns we will visit. I stop in and introduce myself and my book to the owner or book buyer. Each visit takes from ten to thirty minutes. I try to negotiate a discount sale or consignment. My goal is to sell them at least one book to evaluate." He says, "I let them know when I'll be passing through town and offer to meet with them to do a signing or a reading."

Some authors have successfully solicited commercial sponsors for book tours. If your book relates to business, a corporate leader may agree to sponsor your tour. A book for families of Alzheimer's patients might find a sponsor among appropriate organizations.

Specialty Stores

Specialty stores are often overlooked as outlets for books. But think about how many stores carry books. Dan Poynter was among the first to point out to authors and independent publishers the concept of thinking outside of the bookstore. One of his early books was on parachuting. Like most of us when we start out, he expected to sell this book through bookstores. His diligence led him to discover, however, that a better place to sell that book was through stores that sell things related to parachutes and parachuting.

I know an author who sells her local hiking book through sporting goods stores, the local visitor center, and a busy surplus store. A joke book related to cars might do well in automotive shops or parts stores. Pitch your book of hors d'oeuvres to wine bars and a book about knitting scarves to craft stores. You should be able to sell your history book through museum gift shops, your sweet gift book through hospital gift shops and stationery stores, your book on living with diabetes through pharmacies, and your kids' nature studies book through toy stores and museums.

Choose your venue carefully. I've had a few retail agreements from hell. Several years ago, there was a popular yogurt shop downtown. Knowing that they had quite a large volume of foot traffic, I asked if they would like to carry my Ojai Valley history book.

It wasn't long before the proprietor called asking me to replace a couple of books because his display copies were now soiled and tattered. It seems that even adults have no qualms about enjoying a good book while licking a dripping yogurt cone.

I suggested that we put just one book on display to be used and abused and store new books for purchase behind the counter. That wasn't completely satisfactory, either, because I didn't feel it was good business to have a less than perfect book on display.

Later, when major bookstores began serving fancy coffee, I wondered about their rate of returns because of sticky pages.

Tips for Getting Book Reviews

Book reviews sell books. Most people, when they think of having their books reviewed, consider only the prestigious prepublication reviewers: *Kirkus Reviews, Library Journal, Publishers Weekly*, and so forth. Rarely does a self-published or pay-to-publish book or even a book produced by a small traditional royalty publisher make one of these lists. This is primarily because of sheer volume. There are just a handful of these influential publications and thousands upon thousands of books coming out each year. The staff at *Foreword Magazine* receives around a thousand books per month and they review only eight percent of them. *Kirkus Reviews* receives 4,500 titles per year, and they review only 200.

I know one author who had her self-published book accepted for review by *Library Journal*, and sales soared. So while it is extremely difficult to land a review with these particular prepublication reviewers, it is certainly not impossible. You may just have the right book and present it at the right time. With a little luck sitting on your shoulder, a review could happen.

In the meantime, while you're waiting to find that four leaf clover, why not solicit the hundreds of other book reviewers who are willing and eager to share their opinion of your book? Who are these reviewers? They are editors of appropriately targeted magazines and newsletters, bloggers, and website managers.

Book reviewers work in a couple of different ways. While most publications and websites that use book reviews actually have reviewers on staff (or volunteers who do book reviews), others will publish your review—a review that you submit. You can submit reviews that other reviewers have done (with their permission) or you can pay a friend or colleague to review your book and to write a review.

But I would steer clear of agencies that charge large fees for review services. There are too many people jumping on the publishing bandwagon these days and charging for services that you don't need to pay for.

Before sending your book for review, make sure that your book topic is right for the publication. There are magazines, websites, and newsletters representing practically every subject and concept on earth. And then there are sites and publications dedicated specifically to books. Your novel will probably have the best chance of being reviewed in the latter. Your children's book would surely be selected for review at any number of children-related websites and publications. *Christian Home and School Magazine* publishes reviews for children's books, for example. *BookPage* posts reviews for books on many subjects. Have your fantasy or comic book reviewed at *Seized by the Tale* website.

A book review is an excellent way to promote your book for free. In fact, there are countless opportunities out there for getting your new and even your older books reviewed. It's just a matter of diligent research.

My writing/publishing books have been reviewed in over 100 writing/publishing-related magazines, newsletters, websites, and newspaper columns. *The Mainland Luau* was reviewed in dozens of cooking/foods/Hawaiian magazines, newsletters, newspaper columns, and websites.

While some of the reviews were through invitation, most of them occurred because I was out there making it happen. I located appropriate reviewers, I contacted them, and I followed up with them. How does an author go about finding reviewers for his/her book? Here are some guidelines:

1. Have clarity about your topic/genre. Let's say that your nonfiction book features techniques for dealing with depression. You could conceivably get this book reviewed in the health section of newspapers throughout the United States as well as websites, magazines, blog sites, and newsletters related to depression and other health issues. This is such a widespread topic that it would be appropriate for women's magazines as well as men's, teen, religious, and many general magazines. Try soliciting rural magazines (pointing out the problems with depression for people who are isolated) or regional magazines (perhaps one of your major contributing professionals is affiliated with a university in Texas, you referenced a research agency

in Virginia, and you wrote of the difficulty with depression for folks living in New York City). Can you see the possibilities? You could solicit reviews in Texas-based, Virginia-based, and New York-based publications.

2. Research newspaper columns, magazines, blog sites, websites, and newsletters. You probably have a file full of resources. Use them, but also locate additional review possibilities. Do an Internet search to find appropriate review opportunities. Refer to *Writer's Market* for magazine listings. Study *Gales Directory of Publications* for newsletters on your topic. (Locate *Gales Directories* in the reference section at your public library or online—probably for a fee.) You'll find directories of newspapers at http://www.newspaperlinks.com and http://www.newspapers.com.
3. Introduce your book through a letter to the webmaster, editor, or columnist and offer to send them a review copy. When you get the okay, send your book with a cover letter reminding the editor that they requested the book. Include copies of a few former reviews, your contact information, and a press release. Unless there is a deadline or another reason for urgency, I always send review copies via media mail. The savings can be $1.00 or more per book. Be sure to log the books that you send for inventory and tracking purposes. (Note: More and more reviewers are accepting ebook review copies.)
4. Follow up with an email, phone call, or letter to make sure the book was received and to ask when the review is scheduled. You may have to follow-up more than once. Unfortunately, not every reviewer who receives it will review your book.
5. Thank the reviewer once the review appears. Ask him or her to post their review at your amazon.com book page. (If your book is listed at amazon.com, readers and reviewers can easily post their reviews and comments there.)

If you will dedicate just thirty days to soliciting book reviews—contacting a dozen editors/webmasters each day—you could conceivably land as many as 200 reviews by the end of the month. How many sales would that generate? If your book is on amazon.com, if you have a website, and if Baker and Taylor or Ingram is distributing your title, book sales could increase considerably. If even five people are inspired by each review to purchase your book, that's 1,000 books sold and anywhere from $2,000 to $10,000 or more in profits.

Magazines That Review Books

Here are a dozen magazines with book review columns:

The Iconoclast editors review books in the fiction and poetry genre. They want to receive reviews of 250 to 500 words. But they may also agree to review your book and write the review themselves. Contact Phil Wagner at 1675 Amazon Rd. Mohegan Lake, NY 10547-1804.

Bibliophilos publishes 1,000- to 1,500-word reviews of books present or past. Request their guidelines by writing to: 200 Security Building, Fairmont, WV 26554. Contact Dr. Gerald J. Bobango.

The editors at *January Magazine* review books of all types. They also publish stories about authors and others involved in the publishing process. Book topics of interest to the *January Magazine* staff range from children's to true crime and cookbooks to mystery. For more information about submitting your book for review contact Linda Richards at Linda@januarymagazine.com.

Mothering Magazine will publish reviews of books featuring the natural family—alternative sources to mainstream family living and health issues, for example. Contact Ashisha at POB 1690, Santa Fe, NM 87504. http://www.mothering.com.

Grandparents Magazine publishes book reviews of interest to our baby boomers and older generation. Learn more by writing to 281 Rosedale Ave., Wayne, PA 19087.

The First Line publishes reviews of books with an interesting first line. They don't pay much and their circulation is small, but if your book has an interesting first line, why not consider offering a book review to them—that's 250 more readers who will be aware of your great work. Contact David LaBounty, POB 250382, Plano, TX 750250382. Website: http://the firstline.com

The editors at *Spirituality and Health Magaz*ine review books in the spiritual and health realm. Contact Heather Shaw at editors@spirituality health.com. http://www.spiritualityhealth.com.

Ask for permission to send your historical novel to the Historical Novel Society for review in their magazine. Go to http://www.historicalnovelsociety.org/hnr-online-guidelines.htm or http://www.historicalnovelsociety.org/the-review.htm.

Get your romance novel reviewed in *Romantic Times Book Review*. Call 718-237-1097 ext. 23 or email Giselle@romantictimes.com.

Reviewers at *Midwest Book Review* review a variety of types of books and give primary consideration to small publishing companies and self-published authors. Contact James A. Cox, 278 Orchard Dr., Oregon, WI 53575. http://midwestbookreview.com.

The editors at *A New Heart*, a magazine for Christian healthcare workers and others, review books on medical and religious themes. http://www.hcfusa.com.

Note: Visit other authors' sites and their book pages at Amazon to find out who is reviewing their books. Contact those reviewers.

Online Book Review Sites

Here are a few of the many book review sites you might want to check out. http:/www.allreaders.com, http://www.bookpage.com and http://www.reviewsofbooks.com. Also check out http://www.suite101.com/writingandpublishing. Use the search function to find book reviewer recommendations. Do an Internet search to find additional book review sites.

Blog Sites for Book Reviews

For general fiction

http://blbooks.blogspot.com
http://heylady.net
http://booksonthenightstand.com

For historical fiction and other genres

http://bookfoolery.blogspot.com

For romance

http://www.smartbitchestrashybooks.com

For nonfiction

http://www.rainboreviews.com/nonfict.htm

Don't Overlook the Library Market

Libraries purchase numbers of books every year. Contrary to what you may hear about your own community library system, libraries do have budgets. Even in lean economic times, they buy books. And if you can get them to purchase books from you, they will generally pay full price. Most library buyers prefer to do business with library wholesalers, however. Why? Wholesalers give them a discount and, like booksellers, librarians find it easier and more cost effective to work with a handful of wholesalers rather than hundreds of small publishers and authors.

Before signing with a library wholesaler, you might try to make some sales directly, especially if your book is suited to some of this nation's specialty libraries. If your book is historical in nature and/or profiles early pioneers, contact genealogy libraries such as the major one in Salt Lake City, Utah. There are also military libraries and those related to science, academics, aviation, architecture, and law. According to the American Library Association, there are over 15,000 public libraries in the United States alone. Add to that, school, university, and specialty libraries and the number reaches over 100,000.

Locate public libraries here: http://www.publiclibraries.com. To locate libraries related to your topic, visit http://lists.webjunction.org/libweb.

While library personnel order books almost year round, their main ordering periods are in late December and late June. Make friends with local librarians by donating copies of your book. Offer to give readings at libraries. Donate a percentage of sales to the library fund. Libraries can be repeat customers. Books, especially paperbacks, take a beating when they're in the library system. The more they're circulated, the more wear and tear they endure. Librarians are eager to replace those books that get a lot of patron attention.

What type of books are library acquisitions managers likely to reject? They typically turn away those with spiral, plastic comb, or saddle-stitched binding. They also don't generally purchase workbooks. They require books with spines—it's best to have your title printed on the spine, as well. Librarians especially like reference books and those that are informative. Hardcover books last longer in library use. Books must have a Library of Congress Cataloguing-in-Publication block (your publisher provides this) or Publisher's Cataloguing-in-Publication block (provided by Quality Books or Donohue Group during the self-publishing process).

Librarians and bookstore managers also like to see a key on the upper left back cover indicating the type of book this is and the topic: reference/book publishing, writing/reference, history, autobiography, fiction/young adult fantasy, science fiction, parenting, etc.

Baker and Taylor is the major library book wholesaler. Others include Quality Books, Unique Books, Ambassador, Midwest, and Brodart. There is a procedure to follow in being accepted by these wholesalers. Be sure to check their individual guidelines.

You generally pay a library wholesaler around fifty-five percent on sales. And you can expect to wait as long as ninety days for payment. Some wholesalers will make payments earlier if you give them a larger percentage.

How to Work with Wholesalers

At some point on your promotional path, you will wonder: What is a wholesaler? Do I need one? It is most common today for publishers to use wholesalers to fill orders to bookstores, libraries, and other wholesale customers. And this is especially true for independent publishers. Bookstore managers, like librarians, prefer to order merchandise from a dozen or so distributors and wholesalers rather than hundreds of publishers.

Of course, if you can make the sale directly, you get to keep more of the profit. But you'll probably get more total sales if you partner with a wholesaler.

What's the difference between a wholesaler and a distributor? A wholesaler makes your book available to retail stores and libraries. There are two major wholesalers of books in the United States: Baker and Taylor and Ingram and about a dozen additional wholesalers that specialize. It is up to you to initiate an interest in your book. Once the bookseller knows about it and has customers asking for it, he will place an order through one of the wholesalers.

Distributors generally have sales reps out there showing your book around to booksellers. Most distributors either specialize in certain topics or genres or they are regional—they distribute books just in specific geographic areas.

While some self-published authors are reluctant to give up such a large percentage to wholesalers, distributors, and online booksellers, I recommend that you do so in order to reach more customers. It is a stubborn, short-sighted author who keeps all of his eggs in one tiny basket.

Baker and Taylor: http://www.btol.com.

Ingram Book Company: http://www.ingrambook.com.

How to Work with Distributors

Many authors have been led to believe that a distributor is the answer to all of their promotional prayers. In today's fiercely competitive publishing climate, a connection to a good distributor is definitely a plus, but it's only a piece of the promotional puzzle.

Choose one or more distributors related to the subject/genre of your book. Then create a demand for your book and the distributors can more easily place it in bookstores, libraries, and beyond.

A distributor wants to know your promotional plans. They like authors with more than one book in the pipeline. The reasons why they will reject your book are similar to the reasons a bookstore manager might give—it has the wrong binding, you have no promotional plans, or the subject matter is inappropriate.

The Independent Book Publishers Association (IBPA) has an online directory of distributors and wholesalers. Go to http://www.ibpa-online.org/pubresources/distribute.aspx. You'll also find distributor/wholesaler lists at http://www.parapublishing.com and http://www.bookmarket.com/distributors.htm. Here are a few distributors and wholesalers:

General Distributors

Publishers Group West. They are interested in good fiction and nonfiction titles. Contact them at PGW, 1700 Fourth St., Berkeley, CA 94710. Or visit http://www.pgw.com.

Independent Publishers Group, 814 N. Franklin St., Chicago, IL 60610. http://www.ipgbook.com.

Regional Distributors

Sunbelt Publications distributes books on California subjects including regional travel and reference books, guidebooks, and outdoor adventure books. Contact them at 1250 Fayette St., El Cajon, CA 92020 or http://www.sunbeltbook.com.

Heritage Group Distribution is a Canadian distributor. http://www.hgdistribution.ca.

Specialty Distributors

Rittenhouse Books distributes medical and healthcare books. Contact them at 511 Feheley Dr., King of Prussia, PA 19406. http://www.rittenhouse.com

STL Distribution Services distributes to the Christian marketplace. Darren Henry, Director of General Trade, 522 Princeton Drive, Johnson City, TN 37601. http://www.stl-distribution.com

You can expect to give a wholesaler around fifty-five percent of the retail price of your book and distributors take anywhere from sixty-five to seventy percent.

Amazon.com

In order to submit your titles for sale at amazon.com, go to http://www.amazon.com and scroll down to the bottom of the page. Click on "sell items." At the next page, choose "Advantage." The directions for signing up are there. Basically, you'll pay an annual membership fee of $29.95 no matter how many titles you list and fifty-five percent per book sold.

Amazon.com will order books via email. They ask you to send just the number they request and to include one copy of the purchase order with your shipment. In the advantage program, amazon.com will order at least a few books to keep in stock.

If you have a link to amazon.com from your website, Amazon will pay you a referral fee for books ordered by customers who use that link. For additional information, go to http://www.amazon.com/advantage and click on "Associates Central."

Another option is to link with CreateSpace. They will print your book or prepare it for Kindle and fill Amazon orders, affording you a larger percentage of the profits and no shipping cost. http://www.createspace.com.

Recommended Reading:

Promote Your Book: Over 250 Proven, Low-Cost Tips and Techniques for the Enterprising Author, by Patricia Fry (Allworth Press, 2011).

Reach Out Beyond the Bookstore

One of the biggest mistakes you can make as an author is expecting others to promote your book. It is your job to get the word out. No one knows your book as well as you do and no one loves it as much as you do. Not only are you the best person to promote your book— you, personally, are responsible for its success or failure.

While you may have an idea or two for promoting your book, I urge you to explore a variety of promotional activities. Pursue primary ones as well as some that may not seem so obvious. Chapters Thirteen and Fourteen are designed to prime your promotions pump and fill your head with new ideas you can use.

It's not a matter of finding the time to promote your book, it's a matter of making the time. Some experts suggest that you commit to at least four hours every week spent promoting or as John Kremer, author of *1001 Ways to Market Your Books* says, "Do five promotions each and every day."

Following, you'll find several promotional ideas that are recommended for most authors/independent publishers.

Create Your Own Website

It's important to embrace the technology age. I know that some of you aren't quite there. Some don't want to go there. And others may use a computer, but just haven't gotten around to delving into the world of websites and the Internet. It will behoove you, professionally, to take the plunge.

A website can provide an amazing showcase for your book(s). It's a magnificent marketing tool. You can send potential customers to your website to get information about your book(s). You can advertise your website on your letterhead, business cards, brochure, handouts, and other promotional material. People that you don't even know will find their way to your well-publicized website. In fact, having a website is like owning your own bookstore.

But not every website is successful. Following are some ideas for building and maintaining one that is.

- Create a website that's easy to navigate. Your book should take center stage. Post an excellent image of the book cover and a concise description. Give ordering information or provide clear links to your ordering page.
- Some authors give their story or the topic of the book priority on their websites and the book secondary. For example, greet site visitors with a book trailer (an enticing video) that expands on the story or theme of your book. Show the book on the left of the homepage and reveal the book introduction or first chapter to the right. Show photos, illustrations, or newspaper clips depicting the theme of your story or nonfiction book.
- Set up a merchant account system so people can order your book at your website. You might also establish a PayPal account for customers who prefer paying through this system.
- Link your ordering page to amazon.com for added customer convenience.
- Make it easy for potential customers to reach you. Post your complete contact information at your website. I don't advise publishing your home address or phone number at your site. Consider using a business center for receiving business mail. A mailbox at a local business center could run you anywhere from $85 to $185/year.
- Include your email link on every page in case a customer has a question or wants to talk about ordering quantities of books.
- Use colors that are easy on the eyes. A black background with light red lettering or yellow lettering on a light background is hard to see.
- Avoid using so much animation and other distracting techniques as to slow your website down and cause visitors to surf and shop elsewhere.
- Visit several websites of different kinds to help you make the decisions related to yours. Do you want a link bar across the top, along the side or links listed at the bottom of the page, for example?
- Create a theme website. Along with your book descriptions, post articles and resources related to your topic and link to appropriate sites. I've

seen theme sites related to cats, specific breeds of dogs, cycling, traveling, World War I, writing/publishing, architecture, and depression.

- Provide a sample chapter of your book for folks to read for free.
- Establish a testimonials page where you post reviews and comments from customers.
- A media page will also help potential customers learn more about you and your book through the media coverage you are generating.
- Consider communicating with potential customers and others who are interested in your topic through a web log or blog. Your webmaster can set up a blog for you. Or purchase appropriate software and do it yourself. There are many companies that offer blog programs and some of them are free. Here are a few that experts recommend: bBlog, Blosxom, Nucleus, Movable Type, and WordPress.

It can cost anywhere from $200 to $4,000 to have a simple or fairly basic website designed. But you may be able to get one for free. How? Ask a web design student to build one for you. That's actually how I got my first website. A friend needed a project for her web design class and I needed a website.

If you aren't interested in learning how to maintain your site, you will also need to hire someone reliable to update it and keep it operating smoothly. Make sure that this is someone who knows how to get you connected to the major search engines. This could be the same person who designed your site or someone else. Expect to pay anywhere from $25 to $100 per hour for web maintenance services.

Once you have a website, promote, promote, promote. Don't take the "build it and they will come" attitude. Promote it and they will come.

You Must Have a Merchant Account

Provide a buy button so customers can use credit cards to purchase your books.

Check with your local banker about their merchant account fees. Most likely, you'll want to choose a merchant account company that specializes in website accounts such as Intuit http://intuitpayments.com, USA Merchant Account at http://usa-merchantaccount.com, or Total Merchant Services, http://merchant-account-4u.com.

Make it easy for someone to buy your book. Each of us has our favorite way of purchasing books. While some prefer to pay by check, others will only make credit card purchases. Some customers like using PayPal. There are consumers who love buying their books through Amazon and others who will only purchase a book at a brick and mortar bookstore—even if it has to be ordered. It is good business to offer all of these options for your customers.

Blog for Exposure and Sales

Blogging is a popular way to keep your name in front of your audience, to attract new readers, to build your credibility and/or visibility in your field/genre and to give something of value to your potential and actual customers. Webmasters and marketing agents everywhere are encouraging their clients to start blogs. But it isn't enough to just start one. In order for it to be effective, you have to use it. Here are my tips for maintaining an effective blog site:

- Add new blog entries regularly—at least twice a week. Daily is even better.
- Provide something of value to your readers. Offer information, resources, and your perspective on issues pertinent to your field, topic, or genre.
- Note where you'll be speaking or signing next, online classes you'll be teaching, and publications where your book has been reviewed, etc.
- Promote your book in each and every blog entry, even if it's just a brief reminder, and give ordering information.
- Encourage dialogue. If you decide to turn off the "comments" feature of your blog site (which some people do because of spam), give your email address in each post.
- Advertise your blog. Occasionally send out emails to appropriate people in your addressbook and invite them to view a particular post you think would interest them. Include your blog address on business cards, brochures, etc. Use your Twitter and Facebook accounts to "advertise" specific blog topics. Post a link to your blog in your email signature and in your bio at the end of your published articles or stories.

Promote through Social Media Sites

Everyone is all a twitter about Twitter, Facebook, LinkedIn, and other social media sites. Most experts advise authors to have accounts at all appropriate sites. Use them to announce a new book, to attract visitors to your website and your blog site, to publicize a speaking or signing event, to offer a freeby, to provide a new resource, or to share breaking news on your topic, etc.

For more about how to promote your book through social media read Penny Sansevieri's book, *Red Hot Internet Publicity* (Cosimo Books, 2009) and Steve Weber's *Plug Your Book, Online Book Marketing for Authors* (Weber Books, 2007).

Launch a Virtual Book Tour

A virtual book tour is the same concept as an author tour, only a virtual book tour is online. Instead of making personal appearances with your book in real time all around your town or state, you schedule online activities around your book. You can plan as few or as many as you wish. Here are some ideas for virtual book tour activities: (Note: these are promotional activities you should be pursuing anyway, only you'll intensify the number and frequency of them for your virtual book tour.)

- Arrange to be guest blogger at several appropriate blog sites.
- Schedule a podcast or webinar at your site and/or other sites.
- Write articles for key websites and web-zines.
- Organize contests offering your book as a prize.
- Set up interviews on related blog sites and enewsletters.
- Contact online radio show hosts and ask for interviews.
- Launch a book trailer at your website.
- Offer something free from your website—a free ebooklet related to your initial book, for example. This is a great opportunity to collect the names and email addresses of potential customers.
- Advertise your virtual book tour far and wide: in your association newsletters, to your mailing list, to your blog followers, at your social media sites, through message boards and online discussion groups, and so forth.

Plan ahead for your virtual book tour. If you haven't done so as part of your promotions plan, spend a few months becoming acquainted with bloggers and site owners who cater to your audience. With the assistance of those you'll be contacting to participate in your book tour, create a workable schedule and make sure you meet all of your deadlines. You'll want your articles to appear during the same day (or week) as your podcast goes live, your book reviews are posted and your guest blogs are published, for example.

Keep your blog and Twitter followers apprised of your schedule during the tour so they can keep up with your activities.

There are companies that will set up your virtual book tour or you can do it yourself. Here are a few:

http://www.virtualbooktourexpert.com/
http://virtualbooktoursforauthors.blogspot.com/
http://tlcbooktours.com/

What makes for a successful virtual book tour?

- An understanding of book promotion.
- Diligent and thorough research into appropriate participants.
- Meticulous organization.
- Precision timing.
- Excellent sense of follow-through.

Promote through Fantastic Handouts

Always have something at the ready to hand out to individuals that you meet, to folks at book festivals and book signings, and to send in the mail. I like to use the cover art of a book on a bookmark or postcard size promo piece with ordering information on the back. Choose a size that is convenient to mail and that fits easily into a pocket or purse.

Your handout should be every bit as professional and appealing as your book is. I've seen a wide variety of promotional pieces. While some seem like an afterthought, others are so attractive that I can't bring myself to discard them once I get home from an event and empty my pockets.

What is the function of a promotional piece? It's a reminder, it's a sales pitch, and it provides ordering information. A good promotional piece should reflect the tone and appearance of your book.

Press Releases, Media Kits, and Sales Sheets

Press Release

A press release is an announcement you'd like to make or information you want to share with a readership, generally through newspapers. You can send press releases to newspapers nationwide or just to those in a certain region. There are services that will send your press release for a fee. I generally advise authors against paying a service to handle tasks they can easily manage themselves.

While a poor service can be next to worthless, a good one can be well worth the price. What you, as an author, want to strive for is a well-written, personal (non-generic) press release that is distributed to an appropriately targeted audience. If you are considering working with a press release service, make sure that you ask all of the right questions and get references. In most cases, the author should write his or her own press release.

First determine what you want to accomplish with your press release. Is your objective publicity for your book? Then your job is to come up with a reason why a newspaper or a magazine editor would want to run your story or interview you. What sort of information or intrigue can you offer—something controversial, a solution to a common societal problem, a human interest story, or something important or entertaining with a local slant, perhaps?

Answer the newspaper editor's burning question, "So What?" Tell him, through your press release, what is unique about your story or your book and how what you have to share is beneficial and to whom. Don't be afraid to weave in a little humor if it's fitting to your topic. And if you can tie your book topic to a holiday or a world news situation, all the better. Most author press releases are designed to announce a new book or an event related to a new book. Unfortunately for authors, book launches and book signings are commonplace these days. Consequently, we must be even more creative and clever when it comes to writing a news release.

Start by coming up with a title that reaches out and grabs the editor's attention. Let's say that you are pitching a book featuring how to fix up your home to sell. How about this, "New Book Helps Homeowners Get More Cash For Their Homes."

For a book on doggie dress-up, you might address the *Pet Corner* or *Patter on Pets* column in newspapers nationwide with this lead, "Dogs Are Leading the Fashion Parade" or "Is Your Dog Making a Fashion Statement This Spring?"

A press release is not a one-size fits all letter. You may have to write several versions of your press release to attract different types of editors. As an example, perhaps you have written a book on collecting gumball machines and other candy dispensers. You may focus your press release on the largest collection of Pez dispensers in a certain city for a local newspaper. You might reminisce about the manufacturing of early gumball machines for the senior section in various newspapers throughout the states. Or create a press release for the entertainment section of newspapers nationwide featuring a few celebrities who collect candy dispensers.

When writing your marvelous press release, think benefits not features. A feature is a selling point that describes the book; a benefit tells readers how the book will help them in some way. They want to know, "What's in it for me?"

Stay abreast of trends and fashion your press release to conform. For example, you may notice that the waistbands on jeans are coming back up to the waist. This would be a good time to distribute press releases promoting your book featuring fashion belts and other handmade accessories.

You may notice a lot of articles and commentary lately in newspapers everywhere focusing on the economy. What better time than now to introduce your new (or even older) book, *Money Matters; Budgeting Techniques for Today's Family.*

A press release is not an advertisement and it should not read like one. A press release should be newsworthy. Avoid pitching a product. Pitch a story, instead. Point out a need and show how your book can fill it.

Sometimes it's difficult to come up with fresh ideas for a press release or a promotional brochure. This is why I suggest soliciting customer feedback. Others may describe your book in an entirely different way than you typically do. Listen to your readers. Glom onto their words and use them to sell books.

Approach the right person with your excellent press release. Do your homework and find out the name of the appropriate editor and how that particular publication prefers to receive the press release and when. Some editors will request a press release be sent by mail two weeks before an event, for example.

Include your contact information in case the editor has additional questions and make sure it is imbedded within the press release so folks reading it will know how to reach you. Also provide a photograph of yourself and the cover of your book.

Note: Keep your press release to one page.

What can you expect when you submit a press release?

- It may be published as is.
- The editor may call you with additional questions.
- A reporter might call and ask for an in depth interview and ultimately write an article about you and your book.

Of course, there's always the off chance that the press release will be ignored. It's common to fall between the cracks in this age of great communication. So be sure to follow up with an email or phone call if you haven't heard from the editor within three or four weeks (one week for time-sensitive material).

Sample Press Releases

This is an example of a press release announcing an event.

Contact: James Johnson—xxx-xxx-xxxx

For publication between June 10 and June 14

Subject: Book Signing for *Robin's Robins*, a children's book
Popular teacher/author James Johnson to sign his children's book, *Robin's Robins* at:
Greta's Book House
1314 Sunset Lane
Chandler, WY
Saturday, June 15
2-4 p.m.
Reading at 3:00 sharp

Robin's Robins is the charming, adventure-packed story of a lonely little girl who befriends a pair of abandoned robins who ultimately bring her out of her shell. It's a toss up as to whether Robin or the robins instigate the exploits that take the trio to places formerly unknown to Robin or to any of the other neighborhood children. Join in as Robin and the robins make new friends through several altruistic activities. Children will delight in the story of how the unusual group rescues Mr. Farley's goose,

helps an injured kitten, replaces a nest of misplaced eggs, and befriends the most terrifying creature in the woods. Age appropriate for children 8 to 10 years old.
Bring your children, grandchildren, nieces, nephews, and neighborhood children of all ages. Free gifts for every child.

This is an example of a new book announcement.

For immediate release
Students Inspire Teacher's New Children's Book
After working with dozens of at-risk children during his thirty-year tenure as an educator and counselor, James Johnson has written a book of hope for all kids. "*Robin's Robins* focuses on the message we attempted to share in the classroom each and every day of the school year," says Johnson, "the joy of giving."

Johnson believes that altruism isn't something you can command or even expect from 3rd, 4th, and 5th graders. It has to be taught. And teach it, he did, every chance he got. What's in it for the kids? According to Johnson, "A child who learns how to give—who is rewarded by that great feeling we get when we've made someone else's life sunnier—is a child who develops a greater sense of self. This is one major way children gain confidence. My students taught me this."

Robin's Robins is the charming adventure story featuring a little girl who, like so many of our young people, has not had a chance to experience confidence-boosting activities until she meets up with two orphaned robins. As with any good suspense tale, the trio happen upon several opportunities to give something of themselves. And each time they do, they experience greater happiness. Good things begin to happen in their lives.

Johnson recommends this book for children ages 8 through 10. It can be purchased at Greta's Book House and at his website, XXX.XXXXX.com. He'll be doing readings at the downtown library every 4th Saturday of the month at 3 p.m.

Media Kit

Send or hand a media kit to a book reviewer, a journalist, or a magazine editor who might be interested in reviewing your book or interviewing you. A media kit usually includes:

- A review copy of your book, (or a description of the book, including ISBN, price, publisher).
- Your bio.
- A few of your published articles related to the subject of your book.
- Book reviews.
- Endorsements and testimonials.
- A list of awards your book has generated.
- Book tour dates that are scheduled.
- A list of scheduled media appearances.
- Your photograph.
- Examples of questions the journalist can ask you during an interview.
- Contact information.

If you are sending out quite a few media kits, you may not want to include a book in each one. Include, instead, a press release, your promotion piece/brochure, and your table of contents.

Locate newspaper directories here:
http://www.newspapers.com
http://www.newspaperlinks.com
http://www.onlinenewspapers.com
http://www.thepaperboy.com

Use the *Writer's Market* to locate appropriate magazines to approach. http://www.writersdigestshop.com.

Sell Sheet

A sell sheet is a relatively new concept for book promotion. I consider it a one-page media kit as it encompasses practically everything you've included in your media kit on just one page. Here's what to include:

- Title of your book.
- A small photo of the book.

- Contact information.
- A description of the book (including the ISBN, size, format, and category).
- A brief synopsis.
- The price of the book.
- The name of your publisher.
- A few endorsements (if there's room).

Include the sell sheet in your media kit or send it independently to bookstores, specialty stores related to your book topic, retail stores (such as Wal-Mart), and so forth.

Make News

I've suggested that you take advantage of trends and news to promote your book. If you can't find news that relates to your book, make news. If you wrote a novel about a homeless family, for example, you could make news, thus get exposure for your book, by spearheading an effort to find housing for a local homeless family, help homeless people get jobs, or start a free laundry service or clothing exchange program for the homeless. When this story appears in a newspaper or on a TV station, your book will surely be mentioned.

With the help of a few friends, I once presented a full-blown luau for 100 people and invited the press. This was a heck of a lot of work, but it resulted in a photo story on the front page of the Living section in our county newspaper, which mentioned my book—*The Mainland Luau.* The story of this outlandish, exaggerated promotional ploy was so unique that it rated a chapter in Debbie Allen's book, *Confessions of Shameless Self Promoters.*

Additional ways to make news might be to start a charity, launch a contest for your particular audience, or volunteer, for example. Start a clean-up project in your county or initiate a tree-planting activity in a burn area in order to bring attention to your book on green living. Establish a group hike for seniors to plug your novel featuring members of a champion senior softball team.

Solicit Free Advertising

What is promotion, anyway? It's considered promotion anytime your book is publicly mentioned. And promotion doesn't have to cost you a cent. In fact, with so many opportunities for free advertising, why pay for it? As we've discussed above, you can present your "ad" as news. All you have to do is tweak it. You can also promote your book through magazines, newsletters, and websites. (Read more about promoting through periodicals in Chapter Fourteen.)

Become familiar with newsletters, magazines, and websites in your area of interest or expertise. Most of them have sections where people can make announcements or provide news bites. Announce your book signings, the free things you offer through your website, or a fundraiser you're running related to the theme of your book, for example.

Write letters to the editor on topics related to your book and send it along with your bio which, of course, mentions your book. Participate in online discussion groups on the theme of your book—parenting, arthritis, scrapbooking, fishing, or woodworking, for example. Don't sit back and wait for an invitation to promote your book. Seek out opportunities for free publicity and take advantage of them.

How to Make Sales Using Your Mailing List

A mailing list can be one of an author's best promotional resources. Start one the minute you decide to write a book and keep adding to it. Include friends, family, neighbors, coworkers, clients, your kids' teachers, members of your gym, former classmates, people with whom you serve on committees, folks you meet online, and every person who expresses an interest in your book. Maintain this list and keep updating it.

Use your email and snail mail lists to announce a new book or to remind folks of a book you published last year. Send a promo piece with your Christmas cards. In fact, send your cards early so friends and family have time to order copies of your book for Christmas giving. Send a spring mailing with a charming card related to the changing of the seasons. Include information about your book and suggest that people order a copy to read during their spring or summer vacations.

Treasure your mailing list for it is one of the most valuable tools in your promotional tool belt. And the value isn't just in immediate sales. You never know when a distant relative will respond to your mailing with an invitation to be a guest on a TV talk show he produces. A former client might come from nowhere and offer to purchase a thousand books to use as an employee incentive within his corporation.

I once got a call from a woman on my mailing list whose daughter was the chairperson for a huge fundraiser in Florida that year. She needed authors to participate. This turned out to be an all expenses paid gig that resulted in multiple book sales and important connections for me.

Produce a Newsletter

Some authors produce newsletters in order to promote their books. A couple of years ago, Karen Lee Stevens launched an enewsletter to support her organization, All For Animals. Her book, *All For Animals*, followed. Stevens's desire is to motivate and inspire people to express more compassion toward all animals. Not only does her newsletter help in this mission, it gives her a venue for promoting her book. And it puts her in touch with people who have compassionate animal stories for her next book.

For more about how to create an enewsletter read Christopher Heng's article at http://www.thesitewizard.com/archive/newsletter.shtml. Learn more about the software you'll need to create and distribute an email newsletter at http://enewsletterpro.com, http://newslettersoftware.net or any number of similar websites. To locate others, do a Google search using the keywords, "enewsletter," "ezine," "how to start a newsletter (or ezine)," or "ezine/newsletter software."

If you are the author of a nonfiction book, when starting a newsletter or enewsletter, think "service." Rather than planning strategies designed to sell books, consider what you can offer that will help your subscribers. Provide useful information, resources, benefits to your readers and they will begin to trust you. Trust can go a long way toward selling a nonfiction book. Sure you should promote your book in each newsletter, but just as a reminder to subscribers. Avoid the hard-sell approach. Let your obvious knowledge and helpful nature lead to book sales.

Network, Network, Network

Networking is the coming together of people for the purpose of sharing information. When you discuss your project or publishing in general with other authors at a writers' conference, you are networking. When you tell a colleague about your latest book or you ask her who her publicist is, you're networking. Networking is a natural way to promote books. But it takes concentrated effort and a measure of protocol.

You must be willing to put yourself out there—to mingle, participate in small talk, and even schmooze. Networking is a two-way connection. Sometimes you're on the giving end and sometimes you are the receiver. Good networkers do both well and find both equally important and satisfying.

Where does one network? Join networking organizations and attend writing club meetings, conferences, and book festivals in order to network with other authors. Ask them how they sell books. Participate in activities and meetings associated with your topic in order to meet potential customers. But don't limit your networking efforts to certain venues. Talk about your book everywhere you go.

Network through online discussion groups and bulletin boards. It's amazing what you can learn by taking advantage of appropriate online opportunities. But don't take everything you read about publishers, book publicists, and others within the publishing/book promotion realm to heart. Consider those bits of wisdom and advice that resonate with you, but always check on their validity before investing. Whenever you are in doubt about a particular company, agency, or individual, check them out by doing thorough Internet research and be sure to see if they're listed at any of the most popular writer's/author's warning sites.

http://www.todayswriting.com/poetry-scams.html

http://writersweekly.com/whispers_and_warnings.php

http://www.sfwa.org/for-authors/writer-beware

For additional networking tips read the article, *Networking Tips for Authors* at http://spawn.org/editing/networking.htm.

Get on Radio and TV

Many radio and TV stations feature talk shows whose hosts are always seeking interesting guest experts and authors to interview. You are, after all, considered an expert in the field related to your book. Start with your local TV or radio station. Find out what shows are aired and know ahead of time where your book topic would fit in.

Check the phone book Yellow Pages, the station's website, or call the station to find out the name of the program manager or producer. Once you have located the contact person, either call and introduce yourself and your book or send a copy of your book (or a synopsis) and a photograph of yourself (for television). Tell the producer that you would like to be interviewed on MayBell White's Cooking Show or Doug Mabry's Anything Goes Show. Follow through and follow up and chances are, you will be invited to appear.

Before your appearance is scheduled, however, the program manager will probably want to speak with you by phone. He or she is interested in hearing the quality of your voice, your speaking abilities, and your level of enthusiasm for your project.

There are reportedly over 700 talk radio programs nationwide that feature interesting, intriguing, entertaining, and controversial guests. To locate appropriate radio and television stations throughout the nation, refer to *Literary Market Place*, *Gale's Directory of Publications and Broadcast Media,* or *The Business Phone Book U.S.A*—available in the reference section of your public library. You can do your own search or you can pay someone anywhere from $200 to $700 to position you for radio and TV appearances. Buy an ad in *Radio-TV Interview Report* (http://www.rtir.com or 215-259-1070) or sign up at GuestFinder (http://www.guestfinder.com). Fran Silverman has produced a useful book for authors in search of opportunities to promote their books on radio. *Talk Radio Wants You, An Intimate Guide to 700 Shows and How to Get Invited* by Fran Silverman (Amazon.com).

Watch for opportunities. If your book relates to global warming or the weather in general, start contacting radio and TV program directors as soon as you hear about an unusual weather condition somewhere in the world, or some typical symptom of global warming. Maybe your book is a novel focusing on the Reagan era. When something pertaining to Reagan hits the news wires, you should be approaching radio and TV hosts offering to be interviewed. Recently, there have been more school shootings in California. This would be a good time for authors with books related to this topic—gun control, parenting, the condition of our school system, or school bullies—to come forward with ideas for radio show topics.

Some radio stations now charge guests—making it seem more like an infomercial than a guest appearance. Most of my colleagues, however, advise against paying for air space at least until you've exhausted all free opportunities.

While you must dress and travel to appear on TV, you can conceivably do a radio interview by phone in your robe and bunny slippers. I recommend dressing for the occasion, however. Sit up straight in your chair and smile and you will come across sounding more alert and friendly. This is true. Record your voice speaking while wearing sweats and sitting slumped down in a chair. Then record the same words while dressed up, sitting up, and smiling. You may be surprised at the difference.

Beware! Radio personalities hate dead air—that silence that occurs when no one is saying anything. While planned pauses can add to a live talk, silence can damage a radio show. When the host asks you a question, he or she generally hopes you will respond with more than a monotone word. Be ready with explanations, anecdotes, and interesting information.

Express emotion, where appropriate—let your passion show. Enthusiasm, as you know, is contagious. If you aren't excited about your book, no one else will be.

Don't be afraid to give. Let's say that you're talking about your book, *Teaching Old Dogs New Tricks*. Share stories from your book. Give some nifty tips for handling a certain behavioral problem. But let listeners know that there are many additional anecdotes and training techniques in the book. Give enough and you will spark customer interest. Withhold and you may lose those potential customers.

Here is a publicist who specializes in helping you prepare for radio and TV appearances: http://kimfromla.com/

Hone Your Speaking Skills

An author can't sell books that no one knows about. One way to spread the word about your book is to go out and talk about it.

Aggressive promoter, Debbie Puente urges authors to talk about their books wherever they go. She says, "I sell books at the ballpark, the grocery store—everywhere I go, I sell books." But you must be a good conversationalist and have good speaking skills.

Speaking skills are also important for pitching publishers personally at conferences and on the phone.

Here are some suggestions. Please, don't just gloss over these important tips. Read them, study them, and put them into practice. When standing before an audience:

- Speak with a strong voice. Don't mumble or cover your mouth when speaking. Stand tall, speak to be heard, and enunciate clearly. If you lack confidence because of a dental, skin, or weight problem, for example, this is a good time to get those things taken care of.

- Use vocal variety. Vary the tone of your voice. Create high tones and low ones. Practice reading children's stories out loud to get a feel for vocal variety.
- Eliminate filler words. *Ah*, *um*, and *er* are filler words. So are *so* and *and* when used to connect sentence after sentence.
- Banish from your vocabulary repetitive phrases that have become a habit—terms such as *you know* and *know what I mean*? and *clearly*, for example. Pause, instead. Practice omitting filler words and words of habit in all of your speaking opportunities, whether during conversation or on stage at the microphone. Believe me, this does take practice!
- Use good grammar. Slang is pretty much accepted at many levels of intelligence and education these days. It's usually okay to use a bit for drama or to make a point. But avoid sloppy communication. Make proper grammar your rule.
- Make eye contact whether you're speaking with an individual or an audience. When speaking before a group, move your gaze around the room letting your eyes rest on each individual for a few moments or so. This is how you make everyone feel included.
- Don't apologize—it damages your credibility as a speaker. Don't say, for example, "Bear with me, I tend to drop my voice toward the end of a sentence." Instead, work hard to change that habit. Avoid stating, "Please forgive me for using notes—I didn't have time to prepare." Just do your best to handle the notes professionally and non-obtrusively.
- Practice using props so that your movements are smooth and your timing is precise.
- Repeat audience questions for all to hear. Don't you hate it when you are in the audience and the speaker responds to a question that you didn't hear? Involve the entire audience by repeating the question before you respond. It is your job as the speaker to make sure that everyone is on the same page and no one feels left out.
- Be well prepared. Practice your speech and then practice it some more. Avoid memorizing your speech as it may sound canned. But certainly have a plan and a direction. I've been known to toss out a perfectly planned speech and wing it, instead. I can do that successfully when I'm highly familiar with the material I'll be presenting.

- Learn to speak within a projected time limit. Often, you will be given a time slot during which to speak. It is imperative that you know how to comply. It takes practice to deliver a speech within a time frame. But the alternative isn't pleasant. How would you like to be interrupted before you get to the most important part of your talk? Worse yet, what if the speaker in front of you runs over and uses half of your allotted time? I've had this happen to me a couple of times. Now, I always check with the program organizer and those who are on the schedule ahead of me to make sure that everyone is in agreement as to the time segments. If I'm concerned that the speaker ahead of me will disregard the time element, I'll offer to signal him when his time is almost up.
- Know your audience and prepare your speech accordingly. If you aren't sure where your audience stands or what their interests are, ask. Say, for example, "How many of you own dogs?" "How many find grooming a chore?"
- Join a Toastmasters Club. Toastmasters is a self-help club for folks who want to improve their communication and public speaking skills. Toastmasters clubs offer a venue for practicing public speaking and receiving valuable feedback. And it offers an environment where you will gain self-confidence. Find a Toastmasters Club near you by visiting http://www.toastmasters.org. Or write to Toastmasters International, POB 9052, Mission Viejo, CA 92690.
- Attend presentations in a variety of venues and pay close attention. Learn from the skills and the mistakes of other speakers.

How to Locate Speaking Opportunities

Once you feel confident with your public speaking skills, begin setting up speaking engagements locally. Find service organizations listed in the city pages of your local telephone book or on the calendar pages in your newspaper. Ask your local Chamber of Commerce or City Hall for a list of service and specialty organizations. Organizations and associations are always seeking good programs for their weekly or monthly meetings.

If your book focuses on a specific theme, look for organizations related to this topic. For a book on gardening, contact garden clubs, the orchid society, the African violet society, and the organizers of the annual lavender festival. If your book features true Christian stories, contact the usual service organizations, but also get in touch with local churches, Christian youth groups, senior centers, Christian schools, and the ministerial association.

There you have it—this chapter alone gives you around three dozen ideas for promoting your book plus explicit details for accomplishing some of these ideas. And it's just a start. Read on to discover some of the more creative promotional ideas.

Recommended Reading:
Confessions of Shameless Self-Promoters by Debbie Allen (McGraw-Hill, 2005).

Creative Bookselling for the Enterprising Author

You're probably beginning to understand why not every promotional activity is going to be successful for every book or every author.

Study the promotion basics in Chapters Twelve and Thirteen and the creative marketing ideas in this chapter and begin to build your personal promotions plan. I suggest choosing half a dozen major promotional ideas (sign with Amazon; have a website built; send press releases to appropriate websites, magazines and newsletters; create a blog; establish appropriate social media accounts; solicit book reviews; do a few book signings; and write articles for magazines, for example). But also plan a few minor promotional activities to try throughout the year. You might send a couple of targeted mailings, rent a booth at a book festival, speak on a few occasions, and do some seasonal promotion.

Keep a Hot File

When I hear or read about a potential market for one of my books, I make a note and slip it into my promotional hot file. One day a week (usually on Sunday) I address these ideas. That's the day when I might send press releases using a fresh promotional angle to a new list of appropriate newsletters or to newspapers in a specific region. I might target two or three dozen libraries with information about my latest book. Or I may contact several writing website hosts and ask to be interviewed.

Barbara Florio Graham is the author of three books. She says that she tends to promote her books all the time. In other words, she's always in promotion mode. She shares one of her promotional ploys, "I include brochures and bookmarks in every mailing, even bill payments and letters not related to my work. It's surprising how many book orders have come from that simple effort."

I know another author who uses those pre-stamped envelopes that come with a variety of junk mail as a means to promote her book. She simply tucks her brochure or a flyer into the envelope and mails it off at no cost to her.

Give Customers More Than They Expect

Think about how you feel when you go to the store to buy an avocado and discover that you can get two for the price of one. Delight your customers by giving them something extra. Package your dog grooming book with a good comb or brush. Wrap your novel with a small box of chocolates or a book light. Combine your book of cat stories with a stuffed kitty or a packet of cat stationery.

Provide occasional perks. Send out press releases, mail notices, and post announcements stating that during the month of June, you'll provide tickets to an upcoming play for customers who purchase your novel or that you'll give away calendars featuring photographs of dogs to everyone who buys your book on pet photography.

Some authors gift wrap their books for special occasions. When customers order your book, give them a place to check if it is a gift. Wrap the book accordingly. Or do as Linda McGinnis does when she gets an order for her book, *The Art of Hairdressing Success*: wrap it in pretty paper for every customer.

As authors, we stay so busy trying to make a living, keeping up with our contacts, processing the enormous volume of materials we receive each day, coming up with new marketing ideas for our books, and trying to maintain some order in our personal lives, that we sometimes miss promotional opportunities. This is why I urge authors to be in promotion mode all the time. If you're constantly thinking about your book, you'll be aware of opportunities when they come up.

Gloria is a marketing hound. She is always promoting and she sells a lot of books. She carries a copy of her historical novel in her purse and a box of books in her car. She keeps appropriate denominations of change in her wallet and, of course, she's never without a stack of business cards and brochures.

She shows her book to everyone she meets. When someone expresses an interest, but doesn't buy it on the spot, she takes their business card and follows up with an email, letter, or phone call. She's the only author I know who actually sold fifty copies of her book at her class reunion. She is also the only person I've ever met who can sell a novel to people who claim they never read the stuff. Gloria's mantra is, "There's a potential sale in every encounter."

Sell Books through Articles and Excerpts

One of my favorite methods of promoting my books is through articles. Not only do I get to tout my book (usually in the bio at the end of the piece), I am positioning myself as an expert. And I even get paid.

Magazines will generally pay anywhere from $50 to $1,000 for a good article. Of course, there are also a lot of nonpaying magazines. While I discourage freelancers and authors from writing anything for free, I wonder—isn't the opportunity to promote your book a form of payment? In some cases it is.

Keep in mind, however, that an article is not an advertisement for your book and should not come across as such. In fact, most editors will reject anything that looks like an ad. Editors want articles that are timely, informative, and/or entertaining.

Many magazines use excerpts. A chapter from your book on butterfly migration would surely be of interest to the editor of a children's magazine or a teachers' journal. You could probably sell excerpts from your book on depression to women's, men's, health, regional, religious/spiritual, association, ethnic, and even teen publications. An excerpt is a good way to generate sales.

What about fiction? Hey, you can write articles related to your fiction book, too. Write a short story on any topic and include in your bio that you're the author of *My Way, By the Way*, a novel set around the movie industry in the 1930s. Offer excerpts for this book to entertainment, history, regional, nostalgia, senior/retirement, and women's magazines.

Don't forget about the opportunities for articles and excerpts on the Internet. I have to tell you that the pay isn't much, but the exposure is pretty grand in many cases.

Think ahead! This should be the mantra for all freelance writers and authors who wish to promote his/her book through articles. You can't look at your calendar and say, "Hey, it's October. I think I'll write something about my most memorable Thanksgiving for *Vermont Life Magazine*." Oh no!

While some magazines need only a few months editorial lead time, other editors such as, Thomas Slayton at *Vermont Life*, outlined his Fall/Winter edition nearly a year earlier. You could possibly send him your idea in October of this year for next year's issue.

Most article writers live in the fast-lane—always planning for the future. We think Christmas in May and Easter in September. We must be aware of the trends and fads before they occur. This is the nature of writing for magazines. The editorial lead time for *Reunions Magazine* is six months. Send queries to *Robb Report* five months in advance. *Woman's World* has just a four month editorial lead and *Wired* will accept material three months in advance. *Florida Review* needs ideas nine months ahead and *AARP The Magazine*, six months. The editors at *Woman's Life* plan their editorial line-up a year in advance.

So what should we be thinking about in October? Forget thoughts of pumpkin pie and Christmas trees. Focus, instead, on summer vacation, travel, barbecues, litters of kittens, hot weather, water safety, and class reunions.

It's especially important to consider the seasons when you have a book to promote. If your book would make a good Christmas gift item, you'll want to submit your articles for the November/December issues. This means that you will start sending out queries in the spring/summer or earlier.

Before submitting an article to a magazine, study a couple of issues. Note the style, focus, scope, and tone of the magazine and pay attention to the topics they typically publish. Find out if they've run a piece on your subject within the last several months. If so, perhaps you can offer a new twist. Using the pet photography theme, maybe you notice that *Dog Fancy* published an article just last year on studio photography for pets. You might suggest an article teaching dog fanciers how to photograph their pets in unique natural settings or how to get that action shot.

Study the submission guidelines for each magazine as they will differ from magazine to magazine. What is their preferred word count? Do they publish essays? Do they use pieces with expert quotes and lots of statistics? Do they seem to like bulleted articles? Do they prefer being contacted via email or regular mail? And specifically who do you contact? You may also be interested in their pay scale.

Most editors prefer receiving a query letter first. Once the article is requested, write it to that magazine's specifications. Learn more about submitting articles to magazines in my book, *A Writer's Guide to Magazine Articles for Book Promotion and Profit* (http://www.matilijapress.com) and in *Writer's Market* (available at most bookstores).

Let's Go Sell Books at a Book Festival

If you have a book to promote, sooner or later you'll probably participate in a book festival. There are hundreds of book and author festivals held throughout the world each year where you (or your publisher) can rent a booth and sell books. Organizations such as SPAWN often purchase booth space at book festivals in order to provide members with the opportunity to participate at a reduced rate.

What Does It Cost to Participate?

The organizers of major book festivals, such as the prestigious Los Angeles Times Festival of Books, charge $950 per booth. But there are plenty of smaller book festivals, and probably some right in your own neighborhood, that charge anywhere from $50 to $200 for booth space.

How Many Books Can You Sell at a Book Festival?

We'd all like a guarantee before getting involved in a book festival. The truth is that you could walk away $1,000 richer or it might cost you money to participate. Your success depends on several factors. While no one can second-guess the public's book-buying habits, there are steps you can take to ensure greater success. For example, it's important that you choose the right venue. In other words, bring the right books to the right place.

If I'm doing a book festival or craft fair close to home, I always bring my local history books. If I'm out of town, these books won't be of much interest to festival goers. When I'm participating in the SPAWN booth, I always sell my writing/publishing-related books. Because we are a publishing organization, many of the folks coming to our booth are interested in writing and publishing.

I may sell anywhere from six to forty copies of my books at a book festival. There was one time, however, when I sold nothing. And it was because I chose the wrong venue. I joined a fellow author in his booth at a large book festival in Los Angeles. I had a metaphysical memoir and books on writing. A large banner above this booth advertised that we were selling mysteries and children's books. And people came to our booth to purchase mysteries and children's books, not books on writing and spiritual matters.

A booth displaying a large variety of books attracts more attention than one with just a few titles. If your book has a dull, uninteresting cover, however, chances are that it won't be noticed. People are drawn first to books with colorful, eye-catching, appealing covers. Next, they seem to gravitate toward a book on a subject of their interest: horses, writing, history, poetry, or a period novel, for example. Some people are attracted by catchy titles.

Focus on Exposure, Not Sales

Naturally, you hope for sales when you participate in a book festival. But what if you don't sell as many books as you expected or you don't sell any? Sure, it's disappointing, but this doesn't mean that the festival (or you) failed.

A sale isn't the only way to measure success. Exposure has value, too. And a book festival is a good way to get exposure for your book—to make people aware of it. Anytime you display your book or talk about it, you're getting exposure. There are those sales you make on the spot—spontaneous sales. And there are those that come only after exposure. The point is to view each person you talk to as a potential customer. If he doesn't buy your book now, if you're doing your job as promoter, there's every possibility that he will in the future.

It's important that you hold to this belief. It will help you maintain a good attitude, and a good attitude will go a long way toward making friends and making sales.

Here are a few examples of how this type of exposure has benefitted some SPAWN members who had space in the SPAWN booth at various times over the years. One author got a consignment agreement with a large independent bookstore. Another member met a radio show host and got a gig on her show. A new author hooked up with a columnist who was interested in interviewing him on the topic of his book. Several of our self-published authors captured the attention of traditional royalty publishers—some of these connections resulted in contracts. I remember one new author who received an agent recommendation for her next book project. And an author of a military memoir captured the interest of a documentary film-maker. His documentary airs on the military channel occasionally.

Here's What to Bring to a Book Festival

For one book, you may want to bring a single book display stand, perhaps a fourteen by twenty (or smaller) poster showing off your book cover, twenty to fifty books, promotional material, and maybe even some candy or stickers to hand out. Give people a reason to come to your area and something to remember you by.

Bring plenty of change in appropriate denominations. And, if you have a merchant account, bring credit card forms. When setting up your merchant account, make sure that you can charge customers' cards by hand—without having to use an electronic connection on the spot.

I generally round off the prices of my books for festivals. Rather than charge $15.95 plus tax, I'll ask $15. I might advertise that I'm selling my $12.95 book for the special festival rate of $10.

Invest in a handcart or a luggage carrier with wheels to transport boxes of books. You can also transport your books in a piece of luggage with wheels.

Book festival organizers generally provide one six or eight-foot table per booth, one or two chairs and an identifying banner. Some supply canvas booth enclosures and table covers. You can sometimes get electricity for an additional fee.

Make sure that your booth is appropriately categorized. You might want the title of your book on the banner they provide or the genre/subject matter, instead of your publishing company name. Additionally, at some book fairs, the booth banners are tacked to the front of the tables. People can't see your banner when others are standing in front of your booth. I suggest making a large banner that you can post above your booth or at the back of it just in case you need the extra signage. Save banners from book festivals to reuse.

A small sign that says "autographed copies" will attract and impress some shoppers.

Bring extra pens (at least five of mine walk away during every event), felt markers, tape, bookstands, scissors, paperweights (we use painted rocks), name tags, and any advertising posters you might have. Don't forget your professional quality promotional pieces and business cards.

Display With Pizzazz

Presentation is everything. If you have a sweet little book of poems, for example, wrap some of them in pretty paper and tie them with ribbon. This can make a most appealing display.

Plant seeds about gift-giving. Wrap a few books in appropriate gift paper. Put up signs that state, "Perfect Gift for Dad," "Easter Gift Idea," or "Do Your Holiday Shopping, Now."

Maybe your book cover is particularly lovely. Create some note cards featuring the cover. Offer them for sale separately or together with the book. Have gift bags made with the cover of your book on the front.

Wear a tee shirt with the cover of your book in color on the front.

Bring a vase of flowers for your table or sprinkle the table cloth around your book display with confetti hearts or candy kisses.

If the booth is covered, hang posters and make sun catchers or streamers from your promotional material to hang here and there. If there's room, place an easel at the back of the booth (or, if allowed, in the front) and display your poster.

Get people to participate. Ask visitors to color in a section of a large paint-by-number picture. Give away promotional pencils or bookmarks to folks who answer a question correctly. Or have a drawing. This is a good way to add to your mailing list.

If you produce a free monthly or weekly newsletter, provide a sign-up sheet.

Sell More Books at a Book Festival

A key to selling books at festivals is to connect with the potential buyer. When someone looks at my books on writing/publishing, I ask, "Are you a writer?" Invariably, we become engaged in conversation which affords me the opportunity to give my sales pitch.

I once watched a man with a children's book ask everyone who walked past his booth, "Do you know a child who likes to read?" Most people stopped and he was able to engage them in conversation. Many of them bought his book. In fact, he sold out before the day was half over.

If someone expresses an interest in your book, but doesn't buy it, make sure they walk away with one of your professional quality promo pieces and, if at all possible, get his or her card.

A book festival can be a worthwhile endeavor, but you have to be well prepared and willing to stretch and grow.

Seek Out Special Venues

Special venues might also be considered niche markets for your particular book. There are oh so many ways to make sales. Here are some that have been successful for other authors.

One author I know wrote a book featuring dessert recipes for diabetics—sweets without the sugar. She and her husband went on a cruise and were surprised to learn that there were no dessert choices on the menu for diabetics. This author requested a meeting with the head chef. She showed him her book and he actually prepared one of her recipes the next evening. The diabetic dessert option was so well received that he added the dish to the permanent menu. This author also negotiated to have the title of her book printed on the menu for travelers who were interested in purchasing it.

Another author I know went door to door with his novel. He told me, "I thought people would think it was cool to have a local author going around selling his book and it worked. I met new people and made some friends." Did anyone buy the book? According to this author, they sure did. He said, "Some people bought four or five copies."

There's a program called Character Counts in many schools throughout the U.S. This multi-faceted program includes reading requirements—books related to character issues such as honesty, trustworthiness, and responsibility. If you have a children's book that fits into this niche, you might be able to sell numbers of copies through this organization. http:/// www.charactercounts.org/members.htm.

Get your book listed in a Directory of Authors who do school visits. Learn more at http://www.authorsillustrators.com or call 360-560-7766.

Consider piggyback marketing. This means partner with another author who has a similar or complementary book and do a combined mailing or a seminar together.

Do a book signing at an unusual venue: StarBucks, a local military installation, Sam's Club, at a dog show, a dog park, during a county-wide historical celebration, or at an appropriate sporting event, perhaps.

Seasonal Promotion

Take advantage of the seasons to promote your book. Pitch your mystery novel or a barbecue how-to book for Dad or Grandpa on Father's Day. Promote a book of poetry for Mother's Day, Grandparents Day, or Easter.

Of course, December provides the biggest holiday promotion opportunity of all. Here are some ideas for making Christmas sales that you may not have thought of:

1. Remind your family and friends about your book and suggest how they might use it as a gift. They could include a book on gardening in a gift basket with gardening tools, bulbs, and packages of flower or vegetable seeds. They might give a local history book to a new neighbor. A book of delightful stories or poems is always a good gift idea for several people on anyone's Christmas list. This goes for a novel, too.
2. Mention your books at work and club meetings—bring them in, pass them around, and take orders.
3. Send Thanksgiving cards this year with a discount coupon for copies of your books that are purchased during the month of December.
4. Sell something with your book. Include a mug, a package of hot cocoa mix, and a cinnamon stick with your novel or package your book, *Doggie Dress Up*, each with a dog cape. Of course, you may have to charge more to cover costs.
5. Ask appropriate specialty store proprietors if they would display and sell your book for the holidays. Provide your own point-of-purchase display. If your book does well, the proprietor may carry it year round.
6. Take your children's book to school. Offer to read from your book or create a play from your book with the children taking on the character roles. Send order forms home with each child. Diana Zimmerman does school programs related to her young adult fantasy, *Kandide*. She sends kids home with discount coupons for the purchase of her book that evening at a local bookstore during one of her scheduled signings.
7. Invite neighbors in for a poetry or novel reading. Create an atmosphere related to the theme of your book and find a way to have plenty of audience participation.
8. Arrange to speak before various civic organization meetings this month. Rather than pitch your book, share the story around your publishing experience, talk about why you wrote the book, or teach from the book. Of course, plan to sell books in the back of the room after the meeting.

Use Interesting Seasonal Prompts

There are hundreds of wacky, bizarre, and fun seasonal prompts you could use in the promotion of your book. Have you heard of audio book appreciation month, corn and cucumber month, hot air balloon day, Raggedy Ann and Andy day, say something nice day, women's golf month, and read a book in the bathtub day? Find prompts related to the topic/genre of your book and carry it into your book promotion. Here are links to some interesting seasonal prompts:

http://www.gone-ta-pott.com
http://www.holidayinsights.com
http://www.brownielocks.com

Boost Sales—Produce Spin-offs

What's a spin-off? It's a by-product or a follow-up to the original. Within the context of a book, it might be a sequel or any number of other writings related to the theme of your book.

The point of a spin-off is to generate more sales. Not only will you have additional items to sell, but each book, pamphlet, guide, or list that you produce is a marketing tool for the original book.

Let's say that you've written a book on raising healthy children. You might follow up with pamphlets featuring how to develop the habit of exercise in youngsters, good-for-kids snacks, recipes for healthy families, or an activity workbook for kids featuring healthy life choices.

Follow a book on growing a kitchen herb garden with one on selling herbs at local farmers markets or how to make herb teas or simple herbal remedies.

Spin-off books or pamphlets can boost sales for fiction books as well. If your novel depicts life in a small town in Oregon, follow up with a book featuring bed and breakfast inns in that state or create a mystery for readers to solve based on some of the characters in your original book.

Maybe you've compiled a book of poetry. Next, produce a pocket calendar or greeting cards highlighting some of the lines from your best poems.

Plan carefully before launching your spin-off. Ask yourself:

- Who is my audience?
- What have my readers asked for?

- Is there something I should have included in my original book?
- How will I distribute the spin-off item?
- Is it cost effective to produce another book/pamphlet or other items?

How to Deal with Promotion Burnout

There may come a time when you are sick of talking about your book. You'll get doggone irritated with having to work for every sale—you sometimes feel as though you are begging. It's humiliating and it's tiring. What happened to all of the enthusiasm that you entered into this field with? It's temporarily gone. In its place is a sad case of burnout.

Don't fret. This isn't fatal, nor is it permanent. But it does come with the territory. What to do? When you feel yourself bordering on burnout—if you get to the point where you don't even want to look at your book—take a break.

Take a time-out. Do something else for a few days. Go on a trip. Meet friends for lunch and shopping. Put your energies into something that you enjoy—preferably something creative. Start your next book or shift gears and do some gardening, painting, or carpentry. When you return to the task of promoting your book, you'll feel renewed and refreshed. Really, you will.

Recommended Reading:

The Complete Guide to Book Marketing, by David Cole (Allworth Press, 2004).

Bookkeeping Tips for Authors

There's no getting around it, if you're the author of a book, you're in business. If you're selling books, you must keep records. Whether you're collecting royalties or working with retailers, wholesalers, and distributors, it's important that you account for every expense and earning. Keep accurate and complete records for your own sanity and to appease Uncle Sam.

Do You Know Where Your Manuscripts Are?

It's not difficult to keep track of one manuscript. Most likely, you can recall the exact date that you sent it to X publisher. Do you remember when you approached Y and Z publishers? Shouldn't you have heard back from them by now? By the way, was it a book proposal or just the query letter that you sent? Uh oh. It's starting to get complicated.

You wouldn't operate a retail business without documentation. Can you imagine having to recall each business transaction occurring in a supermarket at the end of every month? Neither should you leave the details of your writing/publishing business to memory. Log each submission as you make it. Note publisher comments or instructions when you receive them. Maintain an accurate record of every transaction related to each manuscript. When a publisher calls to remind you that he requested three sample chapters, you should be able to tell him the exact date that you sent them. If you wonder whether or not it's time to follow up on a submission, you can check your records to find out.

If yours is a pay-to-publish book or you have a traditional royalty publisher, you'll still want to document expenses. Log costs related to editing, publishing, and promotion. Promotion costs might include brochures, a large mailing, booth space at a local flea market, invitations for a book signing, ads in a couple of appropriate newsletters, and the cost of having a website built. By keeping track of major expenses related to your book, you can more realistically evaluate the success of this project. Comparing expenses against earnings creates a pretty accurate measuring stick.

In each book ledger, reserve several pages for logging sales. Note those sales to resalers separately from those to individuals. Keep a tally on sales tax you collect. You'll need this information when filling out your annual State Board of Equalization paperwork.

Reserve several pages in the accounting book for logging promotional books. That is, books that you give away for promotional purposes—review copies, donated books, and those given to friends and key players in the production of the book.

Create an inventory page where you log the number of books distributed whether sold, donated, or given away for promotional purposes. This way, you can keep a running tally of books in stock.

Record-Keeping for Uncle Sam

As I mentioned earlier and as I'm sure you've been advised, keep receipts. I simply toss my receipts in a file folder marked "Receipts" and the current year date. Keep receipts for all of the expenses incurred while you are working on a book. This might include research materials, cassette tapes used for recording interviews, your page layout and cover designer, editor, mileage for trips related to your book, and telephone expenses.

Also log expenses involving writers/publishers conferences, supplies and equipment (paper, ink cartridges, and a new FAX machine), and organizations you joined that are related to either writing/publishing or the topic of your book. Keep receipts even though you log some of these things in your ledger book. Save receipts even when you're unsure as to whether it is a legitimate deduction. Your accountant will let you know what is and what isn't acceptable.

I strongly urge you to stay on top of things. Do not deposit or even file a check until you have accurately logged it. Update your log books either daily, as information comes in, or weekly. I ship almost daily and

I log relevant information at the same time. I toss correspondence from publishers and receipts in a basket and log/file this information at least weekly.

Donating Books Is Good Business

Don't be afraid to give books away. This is a legitimate business expense. It's also a good way to generate sales. In order to get your book reviewed, you must send free copies to appropriate reviewers. To get publicity for your book, donate copies. While not every copy given results in sales, many do.

You and the IRS

When do you begin to claim your earnings and expenses? When is yours considered a viable business? According to the IRS, a business must have a clear business purpose and profit motive before the owner can claim business expenses.

I claimed my expenses and earnings for several years before I actually made any money with my writing. I considered myself a writer—this was my profession, but, while I was still raising kids, I really wasn't making any money. My expenses were minimal and my earnings were even less. But I was taking in a little money, so I felt it was honorable to claim it. I really didn't like that the expenses over-powered my earnings, but that was the reality of the situation. When I established my publishing company, in 1983, that changed.

I have hired a tax preparer ever since. And I recommend that you do, too. It's almost impossible to keep up with the changing laws for the ordinary tax return. Throw in the complications of operating a business, and things can get pretty complex. If, of course, you are comfortable with things financial, do it yourself. As with production tasks, when contemplating your business tasks, I suggest that you do the things you do well and hire out the rest.

From what I understand, you should keep receipts for seven years. For more information about taxes and your small business visit http://www.irs.gov/smallbiz or call 800-829-3676. Ask for a free copy of publication number 3207. *The Small Business Resource Guide* CD-Rom 2004.

Welcome to the Shipping Room

I generally send books media rate (or book rate) when I'm paying for shipping. This would include review, donated, and gift copies. When I charge a customer for shipping, I always send the book first class or flat-rate Priority Mail.

When I ship just one book, I use a bubble mailer. They weigh less, thus cost less to mail than the fiber-filled mailers. When I send more than one book, I use recycled boxes for as long as I have them.

The post office also offers Priority Mail Flat Rate Envelopes and Boxes.

Pack books so they are tight in the box. You don't want them doing the boot scootin' boogie while in route. Books packed too loosely will scrape against one another and become marred. Use plenty of newspaper, bubble wrap, or Styrofoam peanuts when packing books to prevent them from sliding. My preference, when it comes to shipping, is to wrap sheets of bubble wrap around a stack of books which are then placed in an appropriate-size box. Fill in any leftover space using wads of the bubble wrap or Styrofoam peanuts.

If you have an accurate postage scale at home, you can calculate postage by weighing your shipment and going to http://www.usps.gov.

If you do a lot of shipping, it might be worth your while to rent a postage meter.

Copyright Law and Contracts

You can't become a published author without some exposure to copyright issues and contracts. If you have absolutely no tolerance for things legal, run, don't walk, to the nearest attorney.

Copyright Briefly Explained

One thing that most people fail to understand is that one cannot copyright an idea or words. It's the way the words are strung together that makes them unique, thus copyrightable.

Another thing that's hard to comprehend is that your writing is automatically copyrighted as soon as it is created. You don't have to register a copyright, but there are advantages of protection if you do. It is recommended that an independent publisher go through proper channels to file for a copyright. If you are working with a traditional royalty publisher, he or she will generally copyright the work in your name. If you're publishing through a pay-to-publish company, be sure to ask how the copyright will be handled.

How to Keep from Crossing the Libel Line

Hopeful authors often ask us here at SPAWN if they can get away with publishing a book featuring real people if they change the names. Some authors wonder if they can write a story that's derogatory to people who are still living as long as it is truthful. These are the sort of questions you want to discuss with an intellectual properties or literary law/publishing attorney.

I always advise erring on the side of caution. Anyone can sue for almost any reason. If someone feels that you have written something that is damaging to them personally or financially, they can take you to court—even if what you wrote is the truth and even if you have attempted to conceal that person's identity. And you can't hide behind a publisher, either. Most publishing contracts include clauses holding the author responsible in case of any libel suits.

Understanding Publishing Contracts

Publishing contracts come in all types and styles. Some comprise a page and a half and are fairly straightforward, while others run on for pages and pages and seem filled with a lot of double-talk. I am not an attorney, but I recommend that you contact one anytime you receive a contract that you do not understand. Don't sign any contract that conjures up questions or that you cannot completely agree with. Often, we are so eager to be published and we work so long and hard to land a contract that, when one comes, we blindly sign. Contracts are negotiable, folks. And if you don't have an agent to help you navigate the deep crevices of a publishing contract, please hire a good attorney. This could well be the best $200 to $800 you spend in the process of becoming a published author.

For clarity on contract terms, visit http://textbookpublisher.com/contracts.html. This author has defined just about every term you will find in a contract including publication rights, royalties, ancillaries, subsidiary rights, and so forth.

Lloyd J. Jassin is a book publishing and entertainment attorney. He also handles issues of copyright, trademark, and Internet law. Read his articles at his website, http://www.copylaw.com. I particularly like his article on contracts at http://www.copylaw.com/new_articles/final.three.html. Herein, he coaches hopeful authors in how to negotiate a book publishing contract. Jassin is also coauthor of *The Copyright, Permission and Libel Handbook* (Wiley & Sons, 2010).

Also read Tad Crawford's book, *Business and Legal Forms for Authors and Self-publishers* as well as The *Writer's Legal Guide* by Tad Crawford and Kay Murray.

Recommended Reading:

Kirsch's Handbook of Publishing Law by Jonathan Kirsch (2nd edition/ revised, Silman-James Press, 2005).

Literary Law Guide for Authors; Copyright, Trademark and Contracts in Plain Language, second edition, by Tonya Marie Evans-Walls (Legal Write Publications, 2005).

Index

Books from Allworth Press

Allworth Press is an imprint of Skyhorse Publishing, Inc. Selected titles are listed below.

Promote Your Book: Over 250 Proven, Low-Cost Tips and Techniques for the Enterprising Author
by Patricia Fry (5½ × 8 ¼, 224 pages, paperback, $19.95)

The Profitable Artist: A Handbook for All Artists in the Performing, Literary, and Visual Arts
by Artspire; copublished with the New York Foundation for the Arts
(6 × 9, 256 pages, paperback, $24.95)

Starting Your Career as a Freelance Writer, Second Edition
by Moira Anderson Allen (6 × 9, 304 pages, paperback, $24.95)

The Writer's Guide to Queries, Pitches and Proposals, Second Edition
by Moira Anderson Allen (6 × 9, 288 pages, paperback, $19.95)

Starting Your Career as a Freelance Editor: A Guide to Working with Authors, Books, Newsletters, Magazines, Web Sites, and More
by Mary Embree (6 × 9, 256 pages, paperback, $19.95)

The Author's Toolkit: A Step-by-Step Guide to Writing and Publishing Your Own Book, Third Edition
by Mary Embree (5 ½ × 8 ½, 224 pages, paperback, $19.95)

The Writer's Legal Guide: An Author's Guild Desk Reference
by Tad Crawford and Kay Murray (6 × 9, 320 pages, paperback, $19.95)

Business and Legal Forms for Authors and Self-Publishers, Third Edition
by Tad Crawford (8 ⅜ × 10 ⅞, 160 pages, paperback, $29.95)

The Complete Guide to Book Marketing, Revised Edition
by David Cole (6 × 9, 256 pages, paperback, $19.95)

The Complete Guide to Book Publicity, Second Edition
by Jodee Blanco (6 × 9, 304 pages, paperback, $19.95)

Marketing Strategies for Writers
by Michael Sedge (6 × 9, 224 pages, paperback, $24.95)

Writing the Great American Romance Novel
by Catherine Lanigan (6 × 9, 224 pages, paperback, $19.95)

To see our complete catalog or to order online, please visit *www.allworth.com*.